HELL

IN THE PACIFIC

FROM PEARL HARBOR TO
HIROSHIMA AND BEYOND

HELL
IN THE PACIFIC

JONATHAN LEWIS
BEN STEELE

BOOKS

First published in 2001 by Channel 4 Books,
an imprint of Macmillan Publishers Ltd,
25 Eccleston Place, London SW1W 9NF, Basingstoke and Oxford.

Associated companies throughout the world.

www.macmillan.com

ISBN 0 7522 1949 9

Text © Jonathan Lewis and Ben Steele, 2001

The right of Jonathan Lewis and Ben Steele to be identified as the
authors of this work has been asserted by them in accordance
with the Copyright, Designs and Patents Act 1988.

1 3 5 7 9 8 6 4 2

A CIP catalogue record for this book is available from the British Library.

Design, typesetting and reproduction by Production Line
Printed and bound in Great Britain by Mackays of Chatham plc
Maps © ML Design, London

This book accompanies the television series *Hell in the Pacific*
made by Carlton Television for Channel 4.
Written, produced and directed by Jonathan Lewis

CONTENTS

Pacific War Theatre

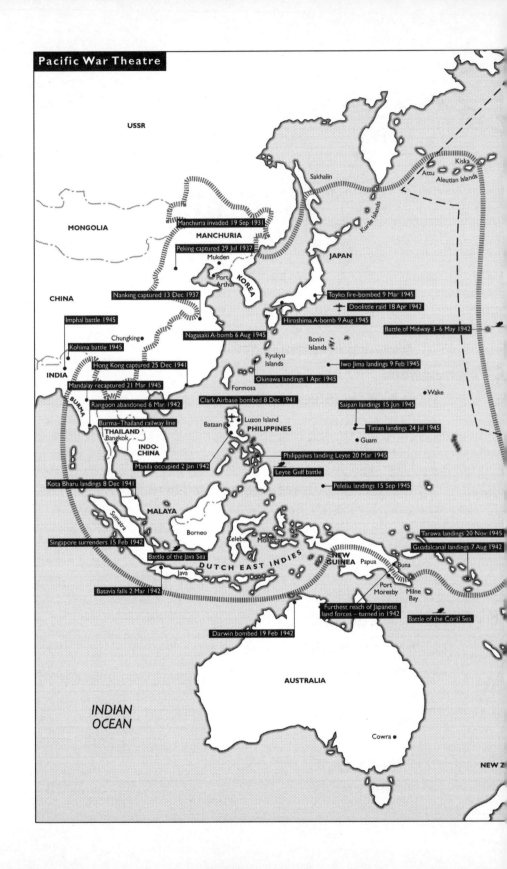

USSR

MONGOLIA

MANCHURIA

Manchuria invaded 19 Sep 1931

Peking captured 29 Jul 1937

Mukden

KOREA

Port Arthur

JAPAN

Sakhalin

Kurile Islands

Kiska

Attu   Aleutian Islands

CHINA

Nanking captured 13 Dec 1937

Toyko fire-bombed 9 Mar 1945

Doolittle raid 18 Apr 1942

Hiroshima A-bomb 9 Aug 1945

Battle of Midway 3–6 May 1942

Imphal battle 1945

Chungking

Nagasaki A-bomb 6 Aug 1945

Bonin Islands

Kohima battle 1945

Ryukyu Islands

Iwo Jima landings 9 Feb 1945

INDIA

Hong Kong captured 25 Dec 1941

Okinawa landings 1 Apr 1945

Wake

Mandalay recaptured 21 Mar 1945

Formosa

Clark Airbase bombed 8 Dec 1941

Saipan landings 15 Jun 1945

BURMA

Rangoon abandoned 6 Mar 1942

Bataan

Luzon Island

Tinian landings 24 Jul 1945

Burma–Thailand railway line

PHILIPPINES

Guam

THAILAND

Bangkok

INDO-CHINA

Manila occupied 2 Jan 1942

Philippines landing Leyte 20 Mar 1945

Leyte Gulf battle

Kota Bharu landings 8 Dec 1941

Peleliu landings 15 Sep 1945

MALAYA

Sumatra

Borneo

Celebes

Moluccas

Tarawa landings 20 Nov 1945

Singapore surrenders 15 Feb 1942

NEW GUINEA

Guadalcanal landings 7 Aug 1942

Battle of the Java Sea

DUTCH EAST INDIES

Papua

Buna

Java

Port Moresby

Milne Bay

Batavia falls 2 Mar 1942

Furthest reach of Japanese land forces – turned in 1942

Battle of the Coral Sea

Darwin bombed 19 Feb 1942

AUSTRALIA

INDIAN OCEAN

Cowra

NEW Z

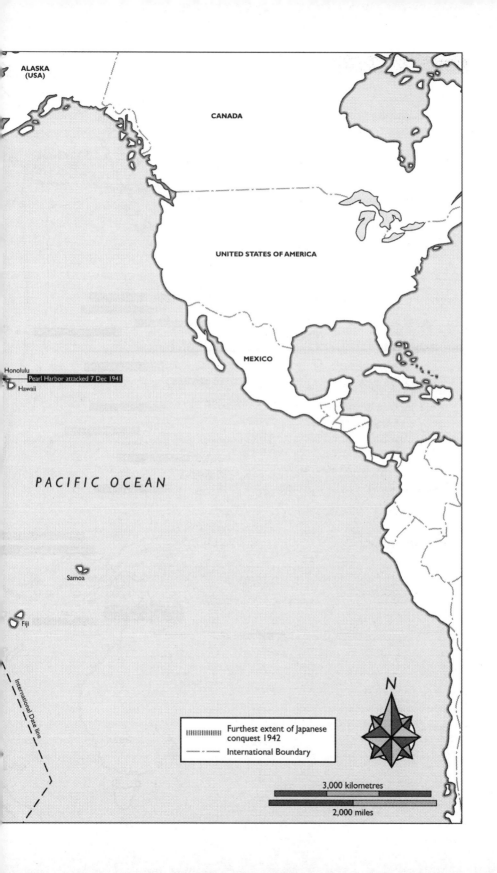

ALASKA
(USA)

CANADA

UNITED STATES OF AMERICA

MEXICO

Honolulu
Pearl Harbor attacked 7 Dec 1941
Hawaii

PACIFIC OCEAN

Samoa

Fiji

International Date line

N

|||||||||||||||| Furthest extent of Japanese
conquest 1942

International Boundary

3,000 kilometres

2,000 miles

To those who were there

ACKNOWLEDGEMENTS

FIRST AND FOREMOST OUR DEEPEST THANKS must go to Isobel Hinshelwood, whose hard work and accurate criticisms have both supported and improved our efforts at every turn. Her name properly belongs alongside ours on the cover.

Tim Gardam and Janice Hadlow at Channel 4 have unstintingly supported this long, arduous and costly project since its inception; Janice has been the model of all one could hope for in a commissioning editor. Steve Hewlett and Polly Bide at Carlton Television have given wise advice and rock-solid backing throughout. Charlie Carman and Emma Tait at Channel 4 Books have mixed a heady cocktail of wild enthusiasm and tough love. Our patient and diligent book editor, Christine King, has spotted all the dog-legs and non-sequiturs we hoped no one would notice – and more than a few we hadn't noticed ourselves.

Our gratitude to the ninety men and women we had the honour to interview on film is heartfelt. Their preparedness to speak frankly and movingly, without trying to justify or excuse their actions or experiences, has made the book and television series possible. Thanks are also due to the hundreds of other survivors, eyewitnesses and veterans we spoke with.

The production team behind the book and television project has been truly dedicated. Our thanks to:

Claire Beaumont, Debashis Bose, Elly Bradburn, Akai Chairuddin, Peter Eason, Justine Espina, Oliver Greene, Jim Howlett, Cliff Jones, Mary Kane, Martin Lubikowski, Alison McAllan, Nadia Mcleod, Jane Manning, Kalyan Mukherjee, Fuyuko Nishisato, Liz O'Brien, Diarmid O'Sullivan, Susanna Posnett, Chris Rodmell, Akiko Sakamoto, Mike Sanders, Inky Santiago, Chris Smith, Julie Stoner.

Thanks also go to: American Defenders of Bataan and Corregidor, Bob Arons, Australian War Memorial, Battle of Midway Roundtable, Battling Bastards of Bataan, Terry Beaton, Rod Beattie, Sheila Brass, the British Library staff, John Bullen, Burma Star Association, Children of Families of Far East, Britain Burma Society, Chindits Old Comrades Association, Rev Donald Crosby, Don Dencker, John DeVirgilio, Lori DeWaal, Dorothy Dowlen, Rebecca Farrell, Ed Fox, Carroll Glines, Ian Lyall Grant, Walter Haan, Gilbert Hair, Jim Halsema, Lamont Harvey, Ann Hassinger, Jan Herman, Major (Retd) N. Hogan, Keiko Holmes, Foong Choon Hon, Bob Jackson, Don Keliinoi, Vickie Kim-Sobe, Violet Lai, Lucius Legg, Lila-Pilipina, Jeremy Lillies, Jim Litton, Robert Mcauslan, Audrey McCormick, 1st Marine Division Association, 2nd Marine Division Association, Lorraine Marks-Haislip, Arifin Marpaung, Tom Matlosz, Alan Matthews, Professor Nakahara Michiko, Joe Milner, Jonathan Moffatt, Tom Nastick, National Federation of Far East POW clubs and associations, Gerry Newhouse, Charles Peall, Pearl Harbor Survivors Association, David Perrin, Rev. Robert Phillips, Bill Price, Ambassador Juan Jose P. Rocha, Larry Rodriggs, Doug Rollo, Royal British Legion, Penny Russel-Smith, Trudy Schwarz, Thian Boon Seng, Brig Gen Edwin Simmons, Alex Simpson, Melissa Tanji, Agnes Tauyan, University of Houston, USS *Arizona* Memorial staff, USS *Houston* Survivors and Next Generation, USS *Missouri* (BB-63) Association, Vincent Vlach, Linda Wood, Peter Wygle, Suhaimi Zen.

Several eminent academics have been kind enough to comment on some or all of the chapters: Professor Richard Aldrich at the School of Politics, University of Nottingham; James McMullen at the Oriental Institute, University of Oxford; Dr Anthony Best at the International History Department, London School of Economics; and Dr John Pritchard. The book has also indirectly benefited from the advice given in the making of the television series: Professor Joan Beaumont at Deakin University, Victoria; Dr Tim Moreman at the Department of War Studies, King's College, University of London; Professor Akira Yamada at the Japanese Modern History Department, Meiji University, Tokyo; Dr Ann Waswo at St Antony's College, University of Oxford; Associate Professor Ricardo Trota Jose at the History Department, University of the Philippines; and Gavan Daws. Any errors are, of course, our own – except for the ones they made.

We would also like to thank 'The Authentic History Center: Primary Sources from American Popular Culture', our source for the last message from Corregidor quoted in Chapter 4. The website for this rich collection of information is *www.authentichistory.com*. The Australian War Memorial in Canberra holds a copy of the newsreel referred to in Chapter 5, the commentary of which describes the attacks on Japanese troop transports heading for New Guinea. The accession number is F01442. While every effort has been made to provide accurate text credits and secure permission for use of copyright material, we apologize for any omissions, and would be happy to make any amendment in a reprint of the book.

INTRODUCTION

YOU CAN READ ABOUT a war, tour the battlefield, study all the photographs and film of the fighting, and still not have the faintest idea of what it was like to be there. Only the soldier knows that. Much of a war's legacy lies in the memory, rather than the archive. Perhaps more so in a conflict fought on remote islands, in dense jungles. How many official historians or guardians of the Geneva Conventions staggered up the beaches of the Pacific, noting the hardships, recording the violations in the rules of war? As one soldier said, the Pacific War was easy – there weren't any rules to observe.

Oral testimony is regarded warily by some historians; it does not measure up against the authority of documents in archives, it is inherently untrustworthy as memory fades, and it rarely helps with the 'big' questions that most historians want to answer. But stray from the comparatively brightly lit realm of strategy, policy and official orders into the grim shadows of close combat and atrocity, and the archive paper trail often runs out. The history books tell us that Admiral Halsey argued against invading the island of Peleliu. The fight there, which led to the loss of well over 12,000 Japanese and American lives, was avoidable and almost certainly unnecessary. We can look up when the Marines landed, where they fought, how many casualties they suffered. But for what it was like to endure appalling horrors in the coral fastness of Bloody Nose Ridge, we must listen to men like Eugene Sledge and Kiyokazu Tsuchida. War is hell, runs the cliché; only they can explain why.

It is not only combat that is illuminated by personal testimony. The experience of the war's victims cannot be gleaned from statistics about the number of prisoners taken, or the date Singapore was occupied, or the location of military brothels serving the Japanese Imperial Army. The perpetrator is unlikely to document his misdeeds. Listen, though, to the American POW forced to dig coal in Fukuoka, the woman tortured by the Kempeitai, the Filipino 'comfort woman' raped daily by thirty soldiers. This book attempts to meld the eyewitness account with the conventional narrative, to record and value the lives lived and lost within the history of the Pacific War.

A distinguishing characteristic of the Pacific War was the sense that so many soldiers on both sides had of the inevitability of their own deaths. Sy Kahn had it summed up for him by his friend Pap after an appalling day: 'He said something that has rung in my head ever since... he said, "Do you know, Sy," he said, "we came here to die, we came here to die."' The Allies in their landing craft knew they could expect no mercy if they fell into Japanese hands: few tiny Pacific islands contained prison camps – let alone decently run ones. They expected, and got, ferocious fighting, booby traps, and Japanese who surrendered with hand-grenades hidden in their loincloths. The Japanese in their bunkers knew they were not going to be evacuated, reinforced or resupplied, knew they were expected to 'die for the Emperor', and held out no hope that the Americans would show them any pity. Kiyokazu Tsuchida on Peleliu was certain what the future held for him: 'We were determined to eliminate as many Americans as we could, and in the end face an honourable death.'

The impression of the war as a history of Japanese savagery alone has been eroded by the growing body of evidence of Allied brutality. The issue here is less whether the two sides were as bad as each other, but whether they had more in common than was ever thought at the time: the peculiar conditions of fighting and surviving in the Pacific and the Burma campaigns, the no-holds-barred mentality necessary in combat; an intense devotion to comrades; the effect of an unending flow of grim experiences on young men just starting out in life; the ubiquity of death and ugliness; the evermore distant sense of home. The ease with which some veterans have closed the gap and befriended their old enemies has more than a little to do with this. In a modern world that cannot conceive what both endured, a Marine from Pearl

Harbor may see more that he recognizes in the Japanese Zero pilot who strafed him than in the neighbours on his own street. There are reunions between those who fought in Burma in the British 14th and Japanese 15th armies, in which men – who have told their wives little – never run out of things to say. There are also Allied ex-POWs who, whatever their hatred for their old captors, have gone out of their way to meet and talk to the younger generations of Japanese, and have come away emphatic in their endorsement of the argument that 'it is not genetic'.

Wartime Allied propaganda was obsessed with the idea that there was 'something about the Japanese' – that being brutal was in their blood. What makes the Pacific War so gripping is precisely the opportunity it affords to see how war makes savages of all young men regardless of nature or nurture. This war muddled easy distinctions between protagonist and victim; between 'good guys' and 'bad guys'. An American medical orderly would supply quinine to fellow Americans dying from malaria only if they could pay for it at $5 a tablet. Was he any better than the Korean guard who slapped them for not bowing low enough? It is, perhaps above all else, a war of acute moral complexities with an undimmed capacity to trigger controversy, law-suits and protest. The victims still call for apology, or recognition, or compensation. The Filipino 'comfort women' still picket the Japanese embassy in Manila. The survivors of Hiroshima and Nagasaki campaign for peace in a world that has renounced neither war nor nuclear weapons.

What are the lessons of the Pacific War? How should it be remembered? How and when will it end? If the answer is: only with the deaths of those who were there – then let us listen to them while we can. They have been to hell and back.

1

OUT OF THE BLUE

Heaven permits not two suns to shine;
Seize the flag of the stars and stripes:
At His Majesty's command we rise
And traverse across the stormy sea
Of the Pacific to Pearl Harbor.

'Hawai daikaisen' – The Great Sea Battle of Hawaii,
by KITAHARA HAKUSHU, 1942

We were young, we thought we were tough, invincible.
We weren't.

EVERETT HYLAND, US Navy survivor, Pearl Harbor

THE OUTBREAK OF WAR in the Pacific took the world by surprise. The shock was not so much war itself; it was the way it began. Japan's opening strike, like America's closing use of nuclear bombs, is still argued over today. Both events, opposites in scale and purpose, triggered seismic change and formed lasting national self-images. In America's eyes, Pearl Harbor placed her on the highest moral ground as the victim of outrage; in Japan and beyond, Hiroshima and Nagasaki turned America into transgressor and the Japanese into unique victims of the most terrible weapon ever. The bitterest years of war in world history were bracketed by two shocking, pre-emptive, brutal acts.

The Japanese leadership saw the attack on the US fleet and air force in Hawaii as a way of resolving, not escalating, their problems in Asia. Japan needed resources to continue the war of expansion she had been fighting in China for a decade. The

Asia–Pacific region had all the oil, rubber and minerals she coveted. The fact that these were in the hands of western colonial powers buttressed Japan's propaganda argument that Asia should be for Asians. Western trade embargoes felt to Japan like a noose around her neck. In late 1941, economic need and political rhetoric combined with military opportunity: Britain, Australia and New Zealand were absorbed in the desperate fight against Nazi Germany in North Africa. The Netherlands had been overrun and her government had fled to exile in London, leaving the oil-rich Dutch East Indies isolated and vulnerable. Russia was fighting for her life against Hitler. America seemed so determined to keep out of war that she might perhaps take her punishment in Pearl Harbor and the Philippines, be forced to the negotiating table and sink back into insularity. That, anyway, was the Japanese gamble. A briefing document for an Imperial Conference on 6 September 1941 summed up Japanese hopes:

> *Although America's total defeat is judged utterly impossible, it is not inconceivable that a shift in American public opinion due to our victories in South-east Asia or to England's surrender might bring the war to an end. At any rate, our occupation of vital areas to the south will ensure a superior strategic position... By co-operating with Germany and Italy, we will shatter Anglo–American unity, link Asia and Europe, and we should be able to create an invincible military alignment.*

Japan's answer to years of shadow boxing was synchronized strikes across the vast waters of the Pacific: hitting the Allies with the force to roll back centuries of white colonial rule. Carrier-based air attacks on Hawaii blunted America's capacity to retaliate in a war in which sea power would be crucial. Successful invasions on the north-eastern coast of Malaya and southern Thailand would enable Singapore, the key to the region's shipping lanes, to be breached from the rear. Heavy bomber and fighter raids on the Philippines won control of the skies, the prelude to a massive invasion. Relentlessly pursuing their objectives, Japan's armed forces attacked Hong Kong, bombarded the American island outposts of Wake, Guam and Midway, and commandeered Allied gunboats off Shanghai. In just twenty-four hours Japan had ignited the north Pacific region in war and laid the groundwork for military dominance across a vast swathe of Asia and the Pacific.

The Allies knew Japan was preparing for war. Prime Minister Winston Churchill had personally insisted that HMS *Prince of Wales*, one of Britain's newest and finest battleships, be sent as part of a naval squadron to Singapore in late October. The hope was that a display of strength would deter the Japanese. But if it came to war, as Churchill cabled US President Franklin D. Roosevelt, 'There is nothing like having something that can catch and kill anything.' Roosevelt announced to his War Cabinet on 25 November: 'We are likely to be attacked as soon as next Monday December 1, for the Japanese are notorious for making an attack without warning.' The Commander-in-Chief of all UK land and air forces in the Far East, Sir Robert Brooke-Popham, announced in his official communiqué on the outbreak of war:

We are ready. We have had plenty of warning and our preparations are made and tested. We do not forget at this moment the years of patience and forbearance in which we have borne with dignity and discipline, the petty insults and insolences inflicted upon us by the Japanese in the Far East... We are confident. Our defences are strong and our weapons efficient.

So what went wrong? Why were the defences of both Britain and America so impotent? Before we answer this, we must first examine the attacks themselves.

THE FIRST CASUALTIES OF THE PACIFIC WAR were Japanese sailors washed overboard in the struggle to connect pipelines between the oil tankers and the Japanese armada on its 4,000-mile journey to Pearl Harbor. December is a month of storms in the north Pacific and tankers need quiet waters to allow refuelling. 'A high pressure front from heaven' is what the architect of the plan, Admiral Isoroku Yamamoto, called the calm seas accompanying the task force. The sea at the refuelling point – 43° north, 170° east – on 3 December was not calm enough, but the main risk on the journey was of detection. A commercial liner had scouted a northerly route away from regular shipping lanes; the Japanese task-force had been ordered to keep radio silence, and its crews threw no telltale refuse overboard. The biggest aid to the Japanese ambush was, as we will see, the West's failure to read Japanese intentions accurately.

In the early hours of 7 December 1941, six Japanese aircraft carriers and their accompanying ships arrived unnoticed 220 miles north of Oahu, the main island of the Hawaiian group. There was still time to abort the attack. The Japanese consul had reported that none of the American aircraft carriers was in Pearl Harbor, but the decision was taken to proceed.

At six o'clock the lead Japanese aircraft carrier, the *Akagi*, turned into the wind. The five carriers behind followed in unison. The pilots knew they were about to make history. One man had chalked 'First bomb in the war on America' on his payload. Nor were they blind to the danger of their task: they were about to attack the Pacific naval headquarters of the world's greatest power. Not all expected to live to tell the tale, as Zero fighter pilot Iyozo Fujita recalls: 'I couldn't sleep the night before the attack. I had a few beers – I tend to fall asleep when I get drunk. So I had six large bottles but I still didn't get at all drunk. I had to take off the next day without having had a wink of sleep... I think we all left with the feeling, "This is the end of my life."'

In the pre-dawn light, crews of the first attack wave began their take-off. Mechanics, ordnance men and superiors stood by to salute and cheer them on. Dive-bomber pilot Zenji Abe, who went off in the second wave, watched the planes gather in formation: 'As they glided into the air, the lights trailing behind the planes resembled a school of fireflies... I was taken by the sight, thinking how beautiful it all looked.' Just ninety minutes later, the first wave reached their targets.

In Pearl Harbor, all was quiet. Anti-aircraft defences had been stood down for the weekend and many of the ships' crews had taken shore leave. Admiral Husband E. Kimmel, the Commander-in-Chief of the US Pacific Fleet, was at home and looking forward to a Sunday morning game of golf. Dick Fiske, Marine bugler on the battleship USS *West Virginia*, was on watch with his shipmate Stanley. They idly observed a group of torpedo planes skimming the waves towards their ship: obviously US planes on a practice run. It was a strange irony that recent training exercises had dulled rather than honed their sense of alarm:

We thought it was going to be a Sunday drill... We went to the port side of the ship. We said, 'Let's watch them drop the dummy torpedoes on us.'... We were looking at the track of the torpedoes, and then all of a sudden – three of them exploded, and blew Stanley and me to the starboard side of the ship. We're 118 feet wide! We picked ourselves up, and Stanley said, 'They're not supposed to use live torpedoes!' I said, 'What the hell's going on?'

No one could believe what was happening that morning, either on or off the base. Al Fernandez was a nine-year-old schoolboy on his way to church with his father when the first wave of planes came in, guns blazing. But they did not think to take cover: 'We were waving at the pilot. He didn't wave back... This person came running in the church and said, "Get out of here, get out of here, we're at war with Japan, we're at war with Japan."' In Washington the signal picked up was the same as that being relayed around the port: 'Air raid Pearl Harbor this is no drill'. Frank Knox, Secretary of the Navy, demanded confirmation that the target was really Pearl Harbor, and not the Philippines, before telephoning the White House. Presidential aide Harry Hopkins saw the stunned expression on Roosevelt's face.

On Battleship Row in Pearl Harbor there was now no doubt that this was the real thing. Dick Fiske watched in horror as the battleship USS *Oklahoma* rolled over in flames on the next berth, the USS *Tennessee* alongside the *West Virginia* received a direct hit, and his own captain, Mervyn Bennion, was virtually torn in half by shrapnel. Minutes later Fiske witnessed the greatest tragedy to occur that day: 'We were looking aft towards the *Arizona* when all of a sudden she burst into one of the loudest noises I've ever heard in my life. And the forward part of the ship was just a tremendous ball of fire. I would say it would be like 400 feet in diameter. It was awesome.' The battleship sank in less than three minutes. More than a thousand men were killed; some died outright, others were trapped on board alive and then suffocated or drowned.

The Japanese inflicted the heaviest casualties in their first attack. An hour later, when the second wave flew in, the defence was better organized. A few army fighters had managed to get airborne and all available anti-aircraft guns were manned. Pilot

Iyozo Fujita testifies to their spirited resistance: 'I remember being impressed how good the US anti-aircraft guns were... We started strafing, and oh, how terrifying the anti-aircraft fire was! Shells like lollipops buzzed up towards me and split right before my eyes – just missing me. That happened several times... I seriously feared I would get hit.'

Iyozo's plane in the centre of the formation was hit, but not critically damaged. His colleague leading the attack, Lieutenant Iida, was less fortunate: his plane was badly shot up. The two men had discussed that very scenario on the voyage out. The *kamikaze* phenomenon is associated with the last, desperate phases of the Pacific War. In fact the underlying ideal, that you should sacrifice your life honourably to cause maximum damage to the enemy, was in evidence on the very first day of the war:

Lieutenant Iida said that if he decided he could no longer return to base, he would choose a target nearby and crash into it, and that was exactly what he did... He signalled us... that he had no fuel left. He waved to me and gestured downwards, meaning, 'I'm going down'. I followed him but he did a quick turn and crashed... I must have cried because my vision was blurred for a while.'

The task of navigating back to the carrier task force now fell on Iyozo Fujita's shoulders, as second in command. Back on board, he found a tremendous feeling of satisfaction. The ambush had worked. It had taken less than two hours of combat to kill some 2,400 American servicemen, strike all eight battleships in the harbour, wreck almost twenty warships and destroy nearly 200 planes. At a cost of just twenty-nine aircraft, Japan had removed the immediate threat of American counter-attack to their sweeping invasions across the Pacific and the Far East.

But the hammer blow Japan delivered that Sunday morning still left intact the biggest prizes of the US Pacific Fleet: its aircraft carriers. They had been Japanese dive-bomber pilot Zenji Abe's primary target: 'I was a bit disappointed when I heard there were no carrier ships in Pearl Harbor... I remember momentarily losing motivation... From the navy's strategic viewpoint, the outcome of the event was extremely negative. Within a month's time, the

Americans were attacking the Marshall Islands using one of the aircraft carriers which had survived our strike...'

Black as everything seemed, this was not America's only lucky break: the huge fuel tanks on Oahu were unscathed, and the shallowness of Pearl Harbor made salvage easier: six of the eight battleships were eventually raised and returned to service. Perhaps no less damaging to the Japanese was the attack's legacy of hatred, as Marine Dick Fiske remembers:

We were so darn mad. And I never felt hate like that in my life. I said those lousy... why did they do it? Why – why wasn't there a declaration of war? And the language was... I mean, you try to control yourself, but we called them everything in the book, and we were so damn mad. Well, because our captain was killed, and he was one of the nicest guys you'll ever want to meet. And I'm ashamed to say this, but I carried that hate all the way to Iwo Jima, when we landed on Iwo Jima in 1945. It's horrible to hate like that.

It was a hate that would have devastating effects on the war. Admiral William F. Halsey observed the next day: 'Before we're through with 'em, the Japanese language will be spoken only in hell.' It was a prophetic warning of the apocalyptic slaughter to come.

SEVEN THOUSAND MILES AWAY on the other side of the International Date Line, Japan had already begun her campaign to invade Singapore, positioned at the very heart of a strategic junction of seaways. Two and a half hours before the Pearl Harbor attack, 5,000 shock troops began their assault on the north-east coast of Malaya at Kota Bharu. With nothing more than sand for protection against the defenders' triple line of pillboxes, wire traps and mines, the fighting was bloody. In securing the beachhead, the Japanese lost almost a thousand men, and many defending British and Indian soldiers died in their positions. Yet stubborn Allied defence on the beach was frustrated by panic at the nearby airfield that afternoon. A false alarm led the base's only squadron to fly south and the RAF ground staff to flee their positions. Their departure triggered a spate of withdrawals at other aerodromes in the north of the country and left the army unprotected. Kota Bharu aerodrome was just one of six abandoned on the first day. The Japanese found them conveniently well stocked with fuel, ammunition and food.

The bulk of Japan's invasion force landed a short distance north, in southern Thailand. The British army had predicted this, knowing the beaches of the Kra peninsula offered a tempting landing site. Furthermore, from about noon on 6 December (local time) they found and began plotting the position of Japan's convoys as they crossed the Gulf of Thailand. All British forces in Malaya were brought to the highest degree of readiness but Operation Matador, the plan to secure airfields and easily defensible positions in Thailand, was not implemented. The fear was it might appear Britain was invading a neutral state and that could legitimize Japan's own invasion. While Britain's senior commanders procrastinated, the main part of Japan's fleet arrived unchecked. Even as Pearl Harbor came under attack, vast quantities of men and equipment were being disgorged. By daybreak advance parties had reached the capital, Bangkok.

Perhaps the most extraordinary defence failure on the first day of the Pacific War was in the Philippines, a US colony since 1898. Much closer to Japan than Hawaii, it was here that America had long predicted a possible strike. Richard Gordon was a professional American soldier serving in Manila: 'We knew that Japan would be the enemy if it came to war, and we knew that because we were trained to believe that... As early as July and August of 1941 while we were training we were told we will be at war with Japan in a relatively short period of time...'

Despite all warnings and preparations, despite immediate notice of the attack on Pearl Harbor and despite orders from Washington, US commanders in the Philippines failed to avert the calamity bearing down on them. Heavy fog over Formosa (now Taiwan) delayed the 400 planes of the Japanese strike force on the ground, giving Generals Douglas MacArthur, Richard Sutherland and Lewis Brereton precious time to ready their defence forces. Between them, the hours were squandered in still unexplained paralysis and indecision.

The Japanese bombers found the recently expanded US Air Force in the Philippines lined up like sitting ducks on Clark Field, wing-tip to wing-tip. When a radar operator in the north of the country detected a massive formation closing in five and a half hours after the Pearl Harbor attack, he was unable to get a message through because the signals man was at lunch. Lester Tenney was in a tank battalion guarding the airbase, with a ringside view of what happened next: 'The planes came over, and within a matter of ten or fifteen minutes, we had no aeroplanes left. Our B-17s [bombers] were destroyed, our P-40s [fighters] were destroyed. The few P-40s that tried to take off were damaged immediately, they never did take off. And so we lost almost all of our aeroplanes, on that first day.'

Subsequent raids on docks and aerodromes across the Philippines in the next two days ensured Japan's complete mastery of the skies. MacArthur committed a litany of errors during the defence of the Philippines – only America's fervent hunger for heroes saved him from the consequences.

THIS SNAPSHOT OF JAPAN'S PROWESS in the opening hours of the war allows us to return to the question of the Allies' pathetic defence. Why was their guard so low when they knew war was likely? The simple explanation is that the West grossly under-estimated their potential foe. They never credited the Japanese with the resources, skills and sheer guts to attack Pearl Harbor on the scale they did, let alone launch simultaneous strikes across the vast Asia–Pacific region. Furthermore, the intelligence pointers to this scenario were never taken together as a whole; most were ignored or not passed on to the commanders who could have acted on them.

Underpinning these decisive errors in western thinking was racial prejudice, epitomized by the comment of Sir Shelton Thomas, the Governor of Singapore, when he was woken up by General Percival and told that the Japanese had landed in Malaya: 'I trust you'll chase the little men off.' Many decades of unbroken western rule over much of Asia and the Pacific proved – to white men – that they were superior to yellow men, that white men will always win. In 1940 Sir Robert Brooke-Popham had observed Japanese troops across the Hong Kong border in mainland China: 'I had a good close-up, across the barbed wire, of various subhuman species dressed in dirty grey uniform, which

I was informed were Japanese soldiers.' A year later these sub-humans would be subjecting the great British Empire to its greatest ever military defeat.

But not everyone was blind to the threat the Japanese posed. In April 1941 Colonel G. T. Wards, the British military attaché in Tokyo, visited Singapore and delivered a lecture to the officers of the garrison. Colonel Wards told his audience that he considered the Japanese army a first-class fighting machine and detailed the reasons why: the excellent physical fitness of their enlisted men, their extreme patriotism and the intelligence and skill of their high command. He went on to say that he had observed in Singapore a widely held conviction that the Japanese were poor soldiers; they had little technical competence; could not perform night operations; and had failed even to subdue the grossly ineffi-cient Chinese armies. Such an erroneous view of the Japanese military was, Colonel Wards underlined, totally false and highly dangerous. He concluded by saying that while the British in Malaya and Singapore were largely ignorant of Japanese capabili-ties, the Japanese were bound to have an accurate knowledge of British strength and dispositions. A novelist could not have invented a more accurate warning, but the lecture was not over yet. Responding to the disquiet in the room, the General Officer Commanding, General Bond, got to his feet and announced:

> What the lecturer has told you is his own opinion and is no way a correct appreciation of the situation. I will tell you that every morning the telegrams which the Japanese Consul-General sends to his government are placed on my office table and from these I know exactly what the Japanese are up to and just how much or how little they know about us... I do not think much of them and you can take it from me that we have nothing to fear from them.

Although his remarks contained an obvious breach in security, they met with a murmur of approval and the meeting broke up. The lecturer's attempt to rouse Singapore from its stupor had failed.

Not surprisingly, when Japanese bombers from southern Indo-China appeared over Singapore in the first hours of the war, they found the city ablaze with light. The Air Raid Precautions authority had been told the Japanese could not fly at night so did not bother manning their offices in the hours of darkness. Eighteen-year-old student Lee Kuan Yew, later Singapore's first Prime Minister and pre-eminent statesman, remembers the shock as Japanese bombs shattered parts of Singapore – and its inhabitants' long-held faith in the inviolability of this vital outpost of the mighty British Empire: 'Nobody really believed that the British had so depleted their forces in the Far East that in fact we were defenceless, and when the bombs dropped on 8th December, early in the morning – about four or five o'clock – it was a great shock. We didn't think that the Japanese would take on the British, let alone the Americans, but they did.'

Nothing forced revision of Japanese capabilities as resoundingly as the fate of Churchill's beloved battleship HMS *Prince of Wales* and the battlecruiser HMS *Repulse*. These two ships, together with four destroyers, comprised Force Z, which left Singapore on the first night of the war to intercept the Japanese navy supporting the landings up the coast of Malaya. Although their accompanying aircraft carrier had earlier run aground, they were allowed to proceed without air cover – a decision that tragically defied the trends of modern warfare.

Cecil Brown, an American CBS journalist on board the *Repulse*, was at first much impressed by British officers' nonchalant demeanour. It was some hours before he became disturbed by their bravado, noting a sequence of remarks in his diary exemplifying their attitude. One officer remarked: 'Oh, but they are Japanese. There is nothing to worry about.' Another declared: 'Those Japs are bloody fools... All these pinpricks at widely separated points is stupid strategy,' and yet another stated baldly: 'Those Japs can't fly.'

Unable to locate the enemy, Force Z steamed first one way, then the other. Two days later it came under skilled air attack. The astonished crew could hardly believe their eyes. Cecil Brown heard a gunner say, 'Bloody good bombing for those blokes.' Another observed, 'Plucky blokes, those Japs. That was as beautiful an attack as ever I expect to see.' It was – he was dead before the day was out.

The loss of these two precious ships and the death of almost a thousand men was Britain's first taste of the bitter humiliation

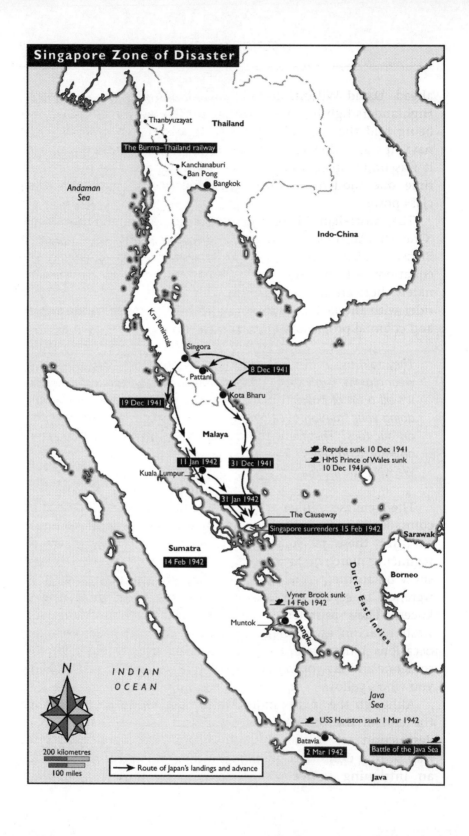

Singapore Zone of Disaster

Thanbyuzayat

Thailand

The Burma–Thailand railway

Kanchanaburi
Ban Pong
Bangkok

*Andaman
Sea*

Indo-China

Kra Peninsula

Singora

8 Dec 1941

Pattani

Kota Bharu

19 Dec 1941

Malaya

Repulse sunk 10 Dec 1941
HMS Prince of Wales sunk
10 Dec 1941

11 Jan 1942   31 Dec 1941

Kuala Lumpur

31 Jan 1942

The Causeway

Singapore surrenders 15 Feb 1942

Sarawak

Dutch East Indies

Borneo

Sumatra
14 Feb 1942

Vyner Brook sunk
14 Feb 1942

Muntok

Bangka

*Java
Sea*

N

*INDIAN
OCEAN*

USS Houston sunk 1 Mar 1942

Batavia
2 Mar 1942

Battle of the Java Sea

Java

200 kilometres

100 miles

→ Route of Japan's landings and advance

ahead. David Wilson, an officer in the Argyll and Sutherland Highlanders fighting the Japanese in Malaya, can still remember being told the devastating news: 'It wasn't just a blow to the navy, it was a blow to everyone. I mean we just didn't believe it, it was impossible to believe, but there it was. And for the first time one suddenly realized that one was up against a first-class power.'

The Australian Major General Gordon Bennett announced, 'One AIF [Australian Imperial Force] man is equal to ten Japs.' A British soldier retreating down Malaya ruefully amended the equation: 'A British soldier is equal to ten Japanese, but unfortunately there are eleven Japanese.' Dick Lee, a motorbike despatch rider with the Royal Artillery, is still livid at the misinformation and colonial propaganda the men were fed:

They told us, in the early days, the Japanese can't see, they all wear glasses, can't shoot straight, and crap equipment. You know, it's all a lot of bullshit, but this is what you get fed while you're doing your training out there. We are the people, who dare tread on our toes? These are only inferiors. They showed us different, anyway, didn't they? They had us on the hop from start to finish. We were the inferior ones.

The Japanese soldiers who fought to dislodge Dick Lee and his comrades from Malaya and Singapore had the underdog's urge to overturn these racist preconceptions. Masao Maeda saw his regiment's march on Singapore in historic terms: 'We were keen to show off to the people of Japan what we were doing. There we were, off to invade the fortress of the Orient and bring it to its knees.' Their prisoners would later catch the backlash from western racism, as American sailor Otto Schwarz recalls: 'On many occasions I have heard the Japanese go into a frenzy beating someone and say you call us the yellow race – we're going to show you who's yellow.'

Although the invasions in Malaya and Hong Kong hastened the end of the British Empire and the Japanese left a trail of destruction across the Philippines, it was the attack on Pearl Harbor that dominated public attention then, and has remained an intriguing source of controversy ever since. Conspiracy theorists have had a field day. Why was the armada not detected? Did Roosevelt or Churchill have foreknowledge of the operation? If so, did they purposely mislead their generals in the hope that the destruction of most of the US fleet and air force in Hawaii would achieve exactly what it did achieve – total American commitment for a global war?

Hard though conspiracy-mongers have worked to conjure up evidence for their claims, the evidence to date shows that America's failure to anticipate the attack on Pearl Harbor belongs under the heading of 'cock-ups', not 'conspiracies'. The most important element of decision-making is not the information available but the climate of opinion. Warnings of Japan's sneak attack were made, but ignored not because of some fantastical all-embracing plot, but because they did not fit with the firm matrix of preconceptions in both Britain and America that Japan would strike in South-east Asia, not mid-Pacific.

The best illustration of this is the signal of 27 November 1941 sent to the Pacific Fleet Commander-in-Chief, Admiral Kimmel, in Hawaii. The signal read: 'This despatch is to be considered a war warning... aggressive action expected by Japan in the next few days.' Admiral Kimmel discounted the warning because an attached intelligence summary stated Japan's assault would be on the 'Philippines, Thai or Kra peninsula or Borneo'. Not Pearl Harbor.

Code-breakers and signals intelligence experts in Britain and America had made some notable achievements before the war. They could read the majority of Japanese signals sent in the standard diplomatic cipher known as 'Purple', and had begun to understand a small fraction of the tens of thousands of code groups in the two Japanese high-security ciphers JN-25-A and JN-25-B used for naval operations signals. Using a combination of direction finding and radio 'fingerprinting' techniques, they could also track fleet bearings. The bulk of this data suggested, as anticipated, an imminent Japanese invasion somewhere in South-east Asia. But deep within the mass of material were a few prophetic warnings that did indicate Japan's intention to attack Hawaii. These overlooked signals acquired significance only after the strike.

On 24 September 1941 the Honolulu consulate received an instruction in code to gather precise details of the Pearl Harbor berthing facilities. These were to be reported to Tokyo on a grid system along with other very detailed information on the port. Since dubbed the 'bomb plot' signal, this message received no special attention; Admiral Kimmel was never told the Japanese wanted to map the location of his ships in Pearl Harbor. In the month before Pearl Harbor, a series of further intercepts indicated that war was increasingly likely. A few days before the attack, the Japanese embassies in London and Washington were known to have destroyed their cipher machines. More specifically, there is some evidence to show that British intelligence knew that a Japanese fleet was steaming towards Hawaii, maintaining radio silence. Intelligence expert Richard Aldrich has uncovered strong hints that London might have passed on this information to its American counterparts. He quotes Victor Cavendish-Bentinck, chairman of the Joint Intelligence Committee in London: 'We knew that they [the Japanese] had changed course. I remember presiding over a JIC meeting and, being told that a Japanese fleet was sailing in the direction of Hawaii, asking, "Have we informed our transatlantic brethren?" and receiving an affirmative reply.' Corroboration from the American end came in 1988, from ex-Director of the CIA William Casey, who was an intelligence officer in the Second World War: 'The British had sent word that a Japanese fleet was steaming east towards Hawaii.'

Scholars who have studied Allied signals intelligence relating to the outbreak of the Pacific War remain divided on what the United States and her Allies really 'knew' or 'ought to have known' with the sources at their command. The problem was that the snippets of disparate intelligence which, taken together in hindsight, seem to point so clearly to what actually happened, in 1941 fluttered haphazardly into a vast, uncoordinated military system cherishing beliefs that ran counter to the intelligence. Aldrich quotes tellingly from an official long experienced in intelligence matters: 'Intelligence is like cheese: you buy the sort you like, or the sort you bought last week.'

America's failure to make full use of their code-breakers' potentially rich clandestine harvest is matched by a sequence of defence failures on the spot. The Hawaiian archipelago was not comprehensively patrolled by regular spotter flights – despite US fleet exercises in 1928, 1932 and 1938 that all incorporated successful carrier-based surprise air strikes on the port – so the vast Japanese fleet was never seen. There were no anti-torpedo nets in Pearl Harbor. The water was held to be too shallow for torpedoes to be used, even though the British had successfully attacked the Italian navy in somewhat similar conditions in Taranto harbour on 11 November 1940. Indeed, this operation was closely studied by the Japanese in their planning of the Pearl Harbor assault.

Just before four o'clock on the very morning of the attack, crewmen on the minesweeper USS *Condor* sighted a periscope and submarine conning tower within the harbour's strictly enforced no-submersion zone. Shortly before seven o'clock, the destroyer USS *Ward* also glimpsed a submarine, this time actually heading through the harbour entrance. The *Ward* opened fire and rammed the sub, dropping depth charges for good measure. Then, just after seven o'clock, two radar operators in a mobile unit at the north of the island picked up the largest group of planes they had ever seen heading direct for Oahu. According to Private George E. Elliot, it was 'something completely out of the ordinary on the radar screen'. Their attempts to get a response from the information centre resulted in a duty officer with no experience in the new radar technologies telling them not to worry about it. He had assumed the incoming aircraft must be B-17s from the mainland (in fact these were coming in from a bearing only 5 degrees away from the approaching Japanese air squadrons).

Had any of these incidents been recognized for what they were – the prelude to a massive assault – there would still have been time to scramble planes, man battle-stations and wake commanders. But confidence and cock-ups overruled caution: no action was taken.

Japanese successes can only partly be attributed to the prejudices of the Allies. The courage, skill and conviction of their men undoubtedly played an important role, as did their superior technology and tactics. In the mind of the Emperor, the crucial factor was Japan's thorough preparation for war. When he received news of Singapore's capitulation, Emperor Hirohito told one of his leading courtiers, the Lord Keeper of the Privy Seal: 'My dear Kido, I know I harp on this all the time, but as I've said before and will say again it all shows the importance of advance planning. None of this would have been possible without careful preparation.'

Across South-east Asia a network of informers, including undercover officers posing as barbers and gardeners, reported to Tokyo. In Singapore, the naval base's official photographer was actually a Japanese agent. In Hawaii, Tadashi Morimura collected information on the Pacific Fleet by disguising himself as a Filipino and getting a job washing dishes at an officers' club. He snooped on the harbour and took a 'lovers' sightseeing flight over the island with a geisha girl. His information helped the Japanese pilots who were practising low-level bombing runs over the city of Kagoshima and its bay.

Credit for masterminding the invasion of South-east Asia was claimed by Colonel Masanobu Tsuji. With just six months' research, he provided Tokyo with a detailed blueprint drawn up for the conquest in Malaya, Singapore, Burma, Java and the Philippines. The ground was prepared, and so were the men. Every Japanese soldier and officer embarking for the south was given the booklet 'Just Read This and the War Is Won'. It became their jungle warfare bible. Written in plain language 'so that anyone could read it lying on his back, on a hot, crowded and uncomfortable ship', it contained instructions on how to prevent seasickness and get into a landing craft in high seas; warned of the dangers of sunstroke; detailed what fruits could be eaten; outlined what local plants make good firewood; and even stipulated shoes should be removed when entering a mosque. As for the 'weak-spirited westerners', the Japanese soldier was advised to 'regard yourself as an avenger come at last face to face with your father's murderer'.

Japan's strategy was thorough and based on hard facts. The Allies' defence was patchy and governed by prejudice. The discrepancy, coupled with the surprise factor and determined, well-equipped troops, gave Japan the victories she hankered after. Success had been elusive in China. The war there had become a stalemate. Now the Japanese public had a string of triumphs to celebrate. Zenji Abe, one of the Pearl Harbor pilots, remembers the exhilaration: 'It felt like a breakthrough, a victory from the frustrating ambiguous path we had been pursuing for ten years since the onset of war.' It was an emotion many people shared and was encapsulated in Mokichi Saito's hit song: 'More victory news on the radio! I can't sit still, the excitement, the joy. Aren't our men superb, divine heroes in action.'

2

CITY OF CORPSES

When I got home, my old auntie said how pitiful I looked: 'Child,'
she said, 'I did all I could to find you – I turned over piles of dead
bodies but you weren't there – where did you go?' I said, 'My God!
I've been to the City of Corpses. I've been to hell and back.'
PAN KAI-MING, survivor of the Nanking massacre

FOR A DECADE BEFORE HER WARPLANES flew over Pearl Harbor,
Japan had been locked in a bloody and undeclared war against
China. Japanese diplomats preferred to call it an 'incident'. Their
excuses for it ranged from the need to safeguard Japan's trading
interests, to the obligation to defend Japan against unwarranted
Chinese aggression. The truth was, China had what Japan wanted:
vast territory, markets, natural resources and a huge, tappable
labour force. China would not hand them over, so they would
have to be grabbed. That was, after all, what imperial powers did,
and for over sixty years Japan had been re-inventing herself as just
that. A popular Japanese song of the 1880s went:

There is a Law of Nations, it is true,
But when the moment comes, remember,
The strong eat up the weak.

Japan came late to the game of empires. While the great
European states were jockeying to extend their power in Africa,
Asia, the Caribbean and South America, Japan was living in self-
imposed isolation under the Tokugawa Shogunate, with the
Emperor as impotent figurehead. For 250 years from 1600, she had

turned in on herself, with few links to the outside world – among them some favoured Dutch merchants and, latterly, the Emperor's subscription to the *Illustrated London News*. But since 1720, when the Shogun, the military dictator, lifted his ban on foreign books, there had in fact been some influx of new ideas into Japan.

There is a conventional picture of US Commodore Matthew Perry sweeping into Tokyo Bay in 1853 with his shockingly modern steamships, to waken Japan like Sleeping Beauty, bringing her gently back into the world. In fact, both the waker and the sleeper had been thinking – or dreaming – about the same thing: China. Perry, representing his American paymasters, had stopped in Japan in part to open up her re-coaling facilities on the crucial US–China trade route, coal being one of Japan's few natural resources. Meanwhile, Japan had been trading with China throughout her long, apparent seclusion, while quietly considering how to displace her giant neighbour and reposition herself at the centre of the Asian world. As historian Walter LaFeber has argued:

> Scholars now see the Tokugawa era as the base of post-1890s, and especially 1930s, Japanese expansion over Asia. As the less civilized Manchus swept over China in the seventeenth century, Japan saw itself as the old China, that is, as Japan-as-central-kingdom. The Tokugawas gave refuge to Chinese scholars, and even set up a form of tribute system in which Korean, Ryukyu and Dutch envoys paid homage to the Shogun. Japanese self-isolation before the 1850s thus ironically led to a self-definition and identity in the handling of foreign relations that helped propel Japanese expansion over Asia after the 1890s.

Following the restoration of the Emperor in 1868, the country set about establishing the modern army and industrial base needed to succeed in a competitive world. The slogan was *fukoku kyohei* – 'enrich the country, strengthen the armed forces'. The Japanese unashamedly copied western institutions and methods as needed: borrowing a penal code here, a national education system there. The big lesson to be learned was: how to be an empire. For that, Japan turned to Britain, also a small island monarchy but with invaluable experience of bossing and exploiting lesser mortals.

The Union Jack flapped lazily from flagstaffs across Asia: in India, Burma, the nominally independent Malay States, Singapore and at treaty ports in China. Britain was the undisputed master of parasitic colonial growth, living off an empire on which the sun famously never set and encompassing a fifth of the world's land mass and 400 million people. Britain's example taught Japan a number of sharp lessons: the strong beat the weak; democracy is not as important as monarchy and class; political parties are not the route to power in an imperialist world; run your empire with an iron fist. First, though, find your empire. Japan had some catching up to do.

By the late nineteenth century, the Dutch controlled most of what today is the Indonesian archipelago in their East Indies; the French governed most of Indo-China and, along with Britain, had obtained treaty rights and territorial outposts in China. Portugal, Italy, Germany and Russia all had territorial concessions from the Chinese. Spurred on by the global scramble in Asia and the Pacific, America was also on the move, gaining Alaska and the Midway Islands in 1867; the Aleutian Islands and Samoa in 1889; the Hawaiian Islands and Guam in 1898; and Wake Island in 1899. But it was America's acquisition of the Philippines in 1898 that propelled her into the big colonial league.

Buying out Spain's interests for $20 million did not ensure America an easy time in the Philippines. She was now plunged into war against Filipino freedom fighters. The President of the day, the Republican William McKinley, ordered the military to put down 'the insurrection', while declaring that the US came not as 'invaders or conquerors, but as friends'. Others within the government were less obtuse about their intentions; the permanent chairman of the Republican Convention, Henry Cabot Lodge, wrote in the *New York Times*: 'We make no hypocritical pretence of being interested in the Philippines solely on account of others... We believe in trade expansion... [and the] greatest of all markets is China. Our trade there is growing by leaps and bounds. Manila, the prize of war, gives us inestimable advantages in developing that trade.'

The man in charge of crushing all Philippine resistance was Major General Arthur MacArthur, whose counter-insurgency skills had been honed in America's war against her native population.

Many of his men also made the jump from killing 'redskins' on the frontier to killing 'brownskins' in the Philippines. His son Douglas continued the family connection with the Philippines in the Second World War, memorably pledging 'I shall return', and then devastating Manila when he eventually did so. The fighting in the Philippines under his father was brutal, with large sections of the American press and public horrified at the violence exemplified in the order given by Field Commander Jacob Smith to his troops: 'I wish you to kill and burn; the more you kill and burn the better it will please me. I want all persons killed who are capable of bearing arms in actual hostilities against the United States.' In the process over 20,000 Filipino soldiers died, some 200,000 civilians perished from disease and mistreatment and over a thousand Americans were killed in action.

It took until the summer of 1902 for America to crush the uprising. We can only guess at the signals her widely reported use of brutality in the Philippines sent out to Japan, plotting her own colonial expansion. Significantly, after acquiring the Kurile Islands in 1875, Japan had looked to China for the initial building blocks of her empire. In 1879 she annexed the Ryukyu Islands as the Okinawa Prefecture. By 1891, she had also annexed the Bonin Islands, south of Japan. The Sino-Japanese war of 1894–5 was Japan's first overseas war since the sixteenth century, and her victory spoils included the island of Formosa (now Taiwan) and its off-shore Pescadores Islands. Triumph over a vast enemy whetted Japan's appetite, and she returned for more in the 1904–5 Russo–Japanese war. Russia had moved 100,000 troops into Manchuria and was extending her power into northern China and northern Korea. Japan went to war to curb Russian ambitions in the East, which inevitably were in conflict with her own ambitions and security interests.

Japan's victory over Russia made the world sit up. There was approval rather than condemnation for the method: a sneak attack on Russia's navy at Port Arthur – a far cry from Britain and America's response thirty-seven years later when the same trick was played at Pearl Harbor. Western observers in 1904 marvelled at the daring of the Japanese army and navy. There was approval too, for Japan's decent treatment of her Russian prisoners of war. The eyes of the world were on her, and she carefully curbed the brutality she had shown Chinese prisoners and civilians in the war of 1894–5.

Japan won both international respect and control of the southern half of Sakhalin, a leased territory on the Liaodong Peninsula and parts of Manchuria. In 1910 Japan annexed Korea. Honouring the Anglo–Japanese alliance, she joined in the First World War within three weeks. She rolled up German forces, territorial acquisitions and commercial interests in China and in German-held islands in the Pacific (north of the equator). She also took part in anti-submarine warfare operations against German U-boats in the Mediterranean. By the time the victors sat down at Versailles in 1919 to divide the spoils of the Great War, Japan had a seat at the top table: she scooped up Germany's Pacific colonies as her share of the booty. Yet what seemed like triumph bred disaster. Shiro Azuma was brought up in a Japan luxuriating in the dangerously confident afterglow of these successes: 'War was about winning or losing... We didn't think about humanity at all. We believed we could do anything to win. When we won the war against China, because we'd won all our previous battles, we were very arrogant.'

Colonial enslavement of the vanquished has a long history. In Japan's case, the Chinese and Koreans were despised even as their resources were plundered, their labour abused and their markets dominated. Popular songs of the day both reflect the pervasive sentiment of racial superiority and helped to instil it, with lines such as 'Evil Chinamen drop like flies, swatted by our Murata rifles and stuck by our swords. Our troops advance everywhere' and 'As always our troops are victorious, victorious. Chinks lose because they're afraid'.

Schoolchildren of the time, such as Naka Kansuke, have written how these attitudes were fostered and promulgated. In *Gin No Saji* (The Silver Spoon) he describes the excitement during the 1894–5 Sino–Japanese war and their incessant classroom chanting: 'The teachers urged us on like a pack of puppies yelping after a Chinese bone. We repeated it at every chance: "Brave Japanese, cowardly Chinks, brave Japanese, cowardly Chinks."' Kansuke also records a war report written by his teachers and posted on the school notice board: '22 September 1894. Battle Report. Japanese troops defeat Chinese at P'yongyang and win a great victory. Chinese corpses were piled up as high as a mountain. Oh, what a grand triumph. Chinka, Chinka, Chinka, Chinka, so stupid and they stinka.'

In later years such attitudes hardened, as Shiro Azuma remembers: 'When we were taught the Chinese were inferior and the Japanese were a superior race, the result was we believed they should be killed off.' The youth of Japan were taught to despise their neighbours, and to believe that it was their destiny to control them, as Shiro Azuma again recalls: 'When we were small, we were often taught this song, which went, "We are tired of living in this small country Japan. Across the sea lies China with its 400 million people".' Another schoolboy, Kiyoshi Sakakura, was instructed: '"Japan is the leader in Asia. Therefore, Japan's destiny is to rescue China, Korea, the Asian race." That's what we were taught. And that in order to do that, Japan has to go to China and South-east Asia to give direct leadership.'

Japanese anti-Chinese education had its effect on Shiro Azuma and Kiyoshi Sakakura, both of whom later served in China and committed terrible crimes against the local population.

Lee Haku Rae is a Korean born in 1925, fifteen years after his country's annexation. He recalls life as a second-class citizen, with racial prejudice and discrimination the foundations of society. The systematic Japanese attack on Korean culture would extend to the banning of the Korean language in public life, while all other national manners and customs were to be eradicated:

Everything had to be done the Japanese way. Koreans had traditionally worn white clothes, but we were forced to wear colourful clothes... They also issued the Short Hair Order. Koreans used to have their hair tied in a top-knot, but they made us cut it. Everything was enforced in a high-handed way. So, talking about my own race, because I was brought up since my early years in the Japanese way, I didn't actually understand what my own race or customs were like.

The precedent was well established: similar practices had been adopted by the Americans in Native American schools, by the Australians in aboriginal schools and by the French in Indo-China. The aim was to force indigenous populations into an acceptance of the 'civilized' man's world and governance.

WAR WITH THE WEST became inevitable when Japan extended her colonial ambition in 1931. Indeed, the first shots of the Pacific War were fired in northern China ten years before Pearl Harbor. A group of Japanese officers acting on their own initiative blew up a section of railway line near Mukden in Manchuria, blamed it on Chinese soldiers and used it as an excuse to swallow up the whole of the province. The Japanese government had not been asked about the operation, let alone approved it, but knew a good thing when they saw it. They renamed Manchuria as Manchukuo and installed their own puppet ruler.

The military in Japan operated independent of civilian control, requiring only the Emperor's authority to act. Yet the plotters had not received permission from Emperor Hirohito and had acted outside the chain of command. To rectify this, he belatedly approved the movement of forces from Korea into Manchuria. The Imperial Army and Navy not only enjoyed freedom from civilian authority; they also wielded considerable power over it. By withdrawing their ministers and refusing to co-operate with the rest of the Cabinet, they could force a stalemate in which the frequent outcome was the fall of the government. Uninformed of military actions, excluded from the decision-making process and powerless to influence the outcome, the government often discovered what the military was up to only after the event. One prime minister, Prince Konoye Fumimaro, specifically asked the Emperor to keep him informed of any big decisions about Japan's future taken, inevitably, in the prime minister's absence.

Whatever the major powers thought about Japan's move into Manchuria, none was prepared to act. It was left to the League of Nations in Geneva to deal with the problem. Its response was toothless – the League agreed that Japan had forcibly seized Manchuria yet required her to do little more than negotiate a settlement with China. Nevertheless, Japan responded by walking out of the assembly hall and later withdrawing altogether from the League. She was now powerful and confident enough not to need the good opinion of others, least of all countries such as Britain, France, the Netherlands and the USA. They had all, Japan perhaps felt, pulled off 'Manchurian Incidents' in their time, and were now driven less by morality than by hypocrisy and the need to protect their own interests in China.

For the next four years, fighting and unrest continued in Manchuria and sporadically flared up elsewhere in China. The nationalists under Chiang Kai-shek, the communists under the leadership of Mao Tse-tung and the Japanese all fought with each other. On 7 July 1937, a minor shoot-out initiated by Chinese troops at the Marco Polo Bridge on Peking city outskirts led to a renewed escalation of the bloodshed. Although some senior Japanese figures urged caution, the troops on the ground had early successes and pushed south. In the winter of 1937 the Japanese closed in on the nationalist capital, Nanking.

Brought up to hate the 'Chinks', the soldiers were ordered to live off the land. It was a fatal combination, as Shiro Azuma recalls: 'When we went searching for food, we found women hiding. We thought, "Oh, they look tasty." So we raped them. But every single time a woman was raped, the soldiers would kill her.' Any villagers who had not run off by nightfall would be murdered – to ensure no one could report where the invaders slept. The Japanese took particular revenge on Chinese men who they believed had shed their uniforms and were passing themselves off as civilians. With remorse, Shiro Azuma remembers being ordered to kill three farmers suspected of being Chinese soldiers:

> One of them somehow reminded me of my father, and so I wasn't all that willing... I kept cutting into his head, into his skull, instead of his neck. The blood squirted out. My pal Majima shouted, 'You're too high,' and I tried again and chopped his head off. Anyway, what's stuck in my mind ever since then is the second man who insisted he was not a soldier – he was a farmer. He told us he had a wife, two children and his parents waiting at home for him. 'I am just a farmer,' he said. 'I'm no soldier.' He begged us not to kill him. I killed him. This incident has stayed with me to this day.

Jiang Xiu Ying's village was in the path of the Japanese. Although she frantically hid from their soldiers, it soon became clear they were conducting a thorough search. Jiang had a desperate choice: face the soldiers and certain rape or continue hiding in the knowledge they would kill her and others if discovered.

[We] were asleep in the house. That's when they caught me. My relative said: 'You should go with those people [the Japanese].' I said I wouldn't go with them. What advantage was there in that? 'But if you don't go with them, then they'll use their guns, they'll kill you.' So when my time came... I was raped by them. And after being raped, I came home crying.

At least Jiang's life was spared after her ordeal; instead of being murdered she and the other women raped in the village were allowed to flee, albeit in circumstances of wanton humiliation:

After this they caught thirty of us women, and they escorted us to a big field and made us take all our clothes off, in that November weather! They told us to run. And if we didn't run, then they'd stab us to death like this with their bayonets... Who wouldn't run? We ran! We were running and crying and crying – running and running while the Japanese, holding their bayonets, laughed and clapped.

Nanking was breached on 13 December 1937 and the rape of the city began in earnest. Shiro Azuma wrote in his diary that day: 'All types of bombs were dancing the dance of hell and the gunfire sang the songs of death, and the conductor was death.' For the civilian population it was the start of six weeks' living nightmare. The Japanese race hatred of the Chinese was often combined with vicarious sexual sadism, as Li Xiu Ying witnessed:

There was one person, an older woman of fifty or so, and her son who was just twenty. The Japanese wanted her son to pick out his mother from a crowd of people to rape her, but he wouldn't listen, and when they beat him, he still wouldn't listen; the mother was fifty-odd, the son was just twenty-odd – of course he didn't listen. And when he didn't listen, the Japanese killed him with a single shot.

Li Xiu Ying took refuge with other Chinese in a deserted primary school for the children of foreign diplomats. She was nineteen years old and pregnant. On 18 December, Japanese troops came and dragged away the men. Li, hiding in the cellar with the women and children, heard their horrific end. The next day the Japanese returned for the women. Unable to take the strain, Li decided to end it all herself: 'I started banging my head against the wall. I thought: if I'm going to die, I want to die with my honour intact. I was bashing my head against the wall, and I fainted.' She came round hours later, her attitude changed: 'I thought, they've got mothers and fathers too, they're human too, so they're afraid of death, aren't they? When they come I'm going to fight them.' When the Japanese entered some hours later she resisted, wrestling a bayonet out of one man's hands before being turned upon by the others. They immediately set about her, slashing her all over with bayonets, and leaving her for dead. Li regained consciousness only as her father was taking her to be buried. She was rushed to Nanking University Hospital inside the Safety Zone set up by Nanking's foreign community.

Ten days after her arrival in the hospital she was filmed by the Reverend John Magee, Chairman of the Nanking International Red Cross Council. He smuggled a 16mm camera into the hospital to secure a unique record of Nanking's victims which stands as an indisputable rebuttal to all subsequent right-wing Japanese attempts to deny the Rape of Nanking ever happened. There, on the film, is Li Xiu Ying: 'I had eighteen cuts on my face, and another eighteen cuts on my legs... and one here on my stomach. If it hadn't been for that cut, my child wouldn't have died. At that time, I had a seven-month-old little boy in my belly. That night I had a miscarriage. The doctor listened, and the baby wasn't breathing.'

The fate of the city's men was equally awful. Pan Kai-Ming, a rickshaw puller, was taken away and locked up as a suspected soldier. He was incarcerated, without food or water, together with a group of some 300 or so others. Two days later they were led out of the building, trussed up and marched down to the banks of the Yangtze and shot by machine-gun. Some hours later in the freezing cold he regained consciousness: 'When I came to, I thought, my God! Am I human or a ghost? I mean, the Japanese had shot me dead with a machine-gun. I lay there thinking, I must be a ghost. Then I felt the bodies pressing down on me – by now, after five hours or so, they were going stiff. Uugh! But my body was still soft! My breath was still warm. My mouth was telling my head: maybe I'm not dead.'

Wriggling free from his bonds, Pan escaped that night, explaining to his worried aunt that he had 'been to the City of Corpses. I've been to hell and back.' He had been doubly lucky, for the Japanese later went round bayoneting the bodies to make sure no one survived. Elsewhere they poured petrol over bodies and set fire to them. When the soldier Shiro Azuma left the city in late January, the bodies of the dead still blocked the Yangtze: 'There was one soldier working there – he told me what his job consisted of. First he had to push the prisoners into the Yangtze. Then he had to shoot them. He sounded proud of what he was doing. Our ship couldn't get close in to the bank because of all the floating bodies. The only way to get out to it was to use the bodies like a pontoon. We had to step across dead bodies to reach the ship.'

Shiro Azuma, now repentant of his crimes, has returned to China on seven pilgrimages to beg for forgiveness. The testimony of such outspokenly honest Japanese soldiers casts light on the burden of guilt carried silently by other perpetrators. He describes visiting a dying colleague from Nanking days – Rokusuke Matsuda, one of five machine-gunners who slaughtered 600 Chinese at the Genbu Gate:

When I went to see him in hospital, he cried out, 'When I die, I'm going to hell.' I comforted him by telling him that he'd just followed orders. I told him, 'It's the officers who have to go to hell.' I said he wouldn't go to hell because all he'd done was to obey a command. Nevertheless, this shows that even though we carried out things under orders, what we actually did remains in our minds for ever.

The sheer scale, as well as the nature, of the carnage unleashed upon the city is truly revolting – western and Chinese estimates place the number of Chinese killed at over 200,000, figures denied by many Japanese. But these crimes were not restricted to Nanking. The Japanese expeditionary forces in China inflicted violence across the land, as one of its members, Kiyoshi Sakakura, testifies. He recalls a peaceful village he entered with his unit on the eve of the spring festival, the biggest celebration of the calendar that marks the coming of the Chinese New Year. Ordered to search for weapons, the soldiers tried to prise information from the peasants. Kiyoshi and another soldier first crucified a peasant, then tortured him. Their commanding officer chopped the village elder's head off, tossing it and the body into the communal well.

Brutality governed their interaction with the local people: 'Regardless of whether they were the communist army or farmers, anyone who tried to escape or showed the slightest signs of defiance was killed... every possible crime was done.' Encouraging the officers and their men in their vicious cycle of killing was the skewed yardstick used by the Imperial Army to evaluate the effectiveness of any particular unit. Rather than measuring their achievements by recording the area covered, numbers of prisoners captured, or any indicator of stability, the sole measurement was damage caused: how many killed and how many weapons seized.

The people in Japan followed the fighting in China as closely as propaganda would allow. The fall of Nanking was a grand triumph, as Hiroshima schoolgirl Suzuko Numata remembers: 'We didn't know what horrible experiences local people had to go through in the battle of Nanking because of the Japanese army. We were all lost in happy emotion because of Japan's victory. We celebrated Japan's capturing the town, shouting "Banzai!" We all raised our hands in the air and rejoiced together.'

The Japanese media sanitized news from China. Some stories that slipped through might not have been seen as atrocities by Japanese brought up to regard the Chinese as subhuman. On 13 December 1937 *Nichi Nichi Shimbun* ran a report on a contest between two officers as to who could first kill a hundred Chinese. Beside the photograph of the two men ran the banner caption: 'Contest to kill first 100 Chinese with sword extended when both fighters exceed mark – Mukai scores 106 and Noda 105'.

The atrocities did not help the Japanese towards victory. Tokyo soon became bogged down by the task of subduing an increasingly defiant populace in an unmanageably huge country. The Japanese military, imbued with the idea of the Chinese as miserable dogs, had never suspected they might put up a stiff fight. The Army Minister remarked soon after the escalation of the war in 1937: 'We'll send large forces, smash them [the Chinese] in a hurry and get the whole thing over with quickly.' The Army

General Staff were similarly confident: 'We thought China would soon throw up its hands and quit.' From the very beginning, however, the immensity of the country and its population awed the Japanese. By 1941 over 185,000 Japanese soldiers are known to have died in the war. As Mao Tse-tung stated, 'Since China is a vast country, even if Japan has occupied enormous stretches of territory where 120 million people live, we are still not defeated.'

THE OUTBREAK OF WAR IN EUROPE in 1939 was less significant to the Japanese than the German Blitzkrieg advance into, and occupation of, the Netherlands and France. By the summer of 1940 a power vacuum had developed in the Far East; Paris and the Hague no longer ran France and the Netherlands, let alone Indo-China and the Dutch East Indies. Even Britain's possessions were vulnerable: under pressure of invasion, her beleaguered military could hardly be expected to spare the resources necessary for the adequate protection of its 'glittering prizes'. The policy that evolved in London and Washington was a combination of aggressive posturing and sanctions.

Yet it was by no means a cut-and-dried decision in Tokyo that military expansion should be pursued, and that if it were, it should be taken south into the Pacific, rather than north into Asia. Indeed, attempts were made by both the military and the government to try to broker a peace settlement with China. They failed because although Japan was willing to limit its control to the province of Manchukuo, it still wanted to garrison troops on the mainland to protect its economic interests.

Others were keen to take the fighting north against the communist enemy. In the summers of 1937 and 1938 Japanese forces stationed along the frontier with the Soviet Union launched border clashes. In 1939, however, the now annual skirmish went disastrously wrong. Russian motorized forces under Lieutenant General Georgi Zhukov (who would later distinguish himself in the war on the Eastern Front) counter-attacked against the largest incursion yet, encircling and killing some 20,000 Japanese in just ten days. It was the first major defeat the Japanese army had ever sustained.

This misadventure put an end to army plans to strike north, although proponents of the strategy continued to advocate it.

The president of the Privy Council, Hara Yoshimichi, sought to avert war with Britain and the United States, telling the Emperor at the Imperial Conference on 2 July 1941: 'The Soviet Union is spreading communism throughout the world, so it must be attacked sooner or later... The public is all in favour of an attack on the USSR.' An officer who fought in the Burma campaign, Hiroshi Yamagami, remembers his surprise that Japan ignored its most hated enemy, the communists, to thrust south instead: 'I'd never in my life thought of the Japanese army fighting the British and Americans. People of our generation were taught that the arch-enemy was the Soviets. Manchuria was the limit of our aspirations. We had never dreamed of taking on the mighty British or American armies with their tens of thousands of soldiers!'

Japan's collision course with the West set in motion by the Manchurian Incident seemed inevitable, as America backed Chinese nationalist forces and, with Britain, threatened trade embargoes against Tokyo. At the Imperial Conference of 2 July 1941 the fateful decision was taken to strike south, not north. Japan and the western democracies were locked into an escalating war of troop movements and sanctions.

The Japanese army moved into the northern part of French Indo-China in September 1940, with the unsurprising acquiescence of the Nazis' puppet government in Vichy; the US retaliated with a total embargo on the sale of scrap iron and steel. Japan signed the tripartite agreement with Germany and Italy and started new offensives in southern China; the US increased its military supplies to Chiang Kai-shek. In July 1941 the Japanese repeated their diplomatic charade and marched into southern Indo-China; the British, Americans and Dutch responded by freezing Japanese assets and cutting off the oil supplies upon which the Japanese depended for their very existence as a modern state. Japan regarded herself as a country in mortal peril. Both she and the western democracies had good reason to believe the other side understood only the logic of force, not reason.

Okazaki Ayakoto, who worked in the navy's ordinance bureau, recalls the impact made by the sanctions on their thinking: 'The problem was oil. If our reserves were dribbled away, Japan would grow weaker and weaker, like a TB patient gasping along, till he dropped dead on the road. A grim and humiliating end. However, if we could strike boldly and get the oil in the south...' Without fresh supplies, the war in China would have to be abandoned. Imperial Army officer Hiroshi Yamagami reconciled the unexpected direction of the strike with the imperatives of military logistics: 'Japan was not strongly equipped to fight a war. I believe that gaining resources was a major objective of Japan's fight in the Southern Pacific. Rather than being about acquiring territory, it was to be able to continue fighting.'

In essence the military hierarchy in Tokyo faced a grim choice: extend the war to grab the vulnerable oil-producing regions controlled by the Allies, or pull out of China. Public opinion in Japan was bellicose and unwilling, after years of censorship and skewed education, to accept a total withdrawal from China. But America would consider nothing less; it remained distrustful of Japanese diplomatic efforts to find a compromise solution and preferred to maintain its bold stance until Japan caved in. This tough view was shared across the water by Churchill, who cabled Roosevelt in early November: 'The firmer your attitude and ours, the less chance of their taking the plunge.' Diplomats on both sides who counselled caution were ignored.

Caught between a rock and a hard place, the autonomy of Japan's military and its concomitant lack of accountability enabled it to make a wantonly reckless decision. It pursued war, well aware that victory was by no means guaranteed. As Prime Minister General Hideki Tojo said: 'You have to plunge into war if there is some chance, however slight, of winning.' No one could give the Emperor the assurances he sought, that Japan would definitely win. The scenario they presented to him was implicitly based on the certainty that America – twenty-five times the size of Japan – would win a long war. The logic was that Japan would therefore have to fight a short war, and that meant a surprise, deadly attack to force a shell-shocked America to the negotiating table. In short, the military were presenting the Emperor with an almighty gamble – using his own people as principal. He wrote a secret account of his actions and thoughts during the war, including his memories of the momentous Imperial Conference of 1 December 1941 that took the final decision to pursue war:

The oil embargo really drove Japan up against the wall. The prevailing opinion, that it would be better to try and win even if it meant we had to count on some unexpected good luck, was natural in that situation. If I had gone against the advocates of war, the public would no doubt have thought that we were meekly surrendering to America when our army and navy had superior forces, and a coup d'état *would have been staged. It was truly a trying time.*

Ignorance of their enemy's character played its part in Japanese miscalculations. As Colonel Masanobu Tsuji wrote: 'Our candid ideas at the time were that the Americans, being merchants, would not continue for long with an unprofitable war.' Some war planners knew what they were up against. The architect of Pearl Harbor, Admiral Isoroku Yamamoto, had studied at Harvard and served as Japan's naval attaché in Washington. No pacifist, he nevertheless had a very realistic sense of America's almost limitless industrial capacity, and that they would not be frightened of a long war: 'I shall run considerably wild for the first six months or a year, but I have utterly no confidence for the second and third years.'

The Foreign Office mandarin Toshikazu Kase, who drafted Japan's final note to the United States, knew that Japan had little hope of winning the war as soon as he received word that hostilities had begun: 'I knew we were going to lose. So, my mind was always on what Japan was going to do after her defeat. Someone at my level in the Foreign Ministry wouldn't be much good if he couldn't foresee the outcome of the war. Of course, we were going to lose, but by then it was too late to turn back.'

Others, more senior, also realized the attacks were reckless and raised objections. Admiral Mitsumasa Yonai, a former prime minister known for his anti-war stance, questioned Prime Minister General Tojo on the shrewdness of the gamble: 'In attempting to prevent Japan from gradually being weakened and reduced to a minor power by embargoes, pressure to withdraw from China and so on, the government should be very careful that the result is not instead our rapid defeat and destruction.' A week before the attack on Pearl Harbor, the Emperor had a meeting with nine former prime ministers, not one of whom urged war. One of the nine,

Fumimaro Konoe, had awful presentiments: 'It is a terrible thing...
I know that a tragic defeat awaits us at the end.'

PEARL HARBOR was only a limited success for Japan. She secured
the temporary naval dominance needed to pursue her expansion,
but America was in no mood to beg for peace, then gratefully
return to isolation. Instead, the country screamed for nothing less
than the total destruction of Japan.

The long war in China had warned the world of the way Japan
was prepared to fight on foreign soil. In the Pacific she would have
to battle for her very existence. Her military had already shown an
absolute disregard for the sanctity of Chinese life. Now other
nations and even her own troops and people would not be spared.

It is to this that we now turn – to examine the Japanese way in
war and to ask why it observed no rules and brooked no pity.

3

NO PRISONERS, NO SURRENDER

I said I didn't want him to become a prisoner of war. He didn't say anything. Deep in my mind I'd rather he died than became a prisoner of war.

MIHO YOSHIOKA, saying goodbye to her fiancé in Japan

Cruel bastards. They were – it's the only way to describe them.

DUNCAN FERGUSON, British prisoner of war
on the Burma–Thailand Railway

THE ORIGINS OF JAPAN'S WAY IN WAR are one of the least understood aspects of the conflict. Why was surrender such a taboo? Why were many of her soldiers so heartless? How could they butcher entire cities, raping and killing non-combatants by the thousand? Why did they treat their prisoners with such cruel contempt? And how could they sacrifice their own lives with such apparent ease?

A number of different groups have wrestled with these questions: wartime psychologists in America trying to 'know the enemy'; a succession of lawyers and military judges in war crimes trials; Allied prisoners of war still puzzled as to why they were starved and had their bones broken when the Burma–Thailand Railway would have been built faster and better by fit men; repentant Japanese veterans facing up to their pasts. Surprisingly few academics have explored the subject deeply, although its Nazi equivalent has received the attention of some of the smartest historians of their generation. Some of those who have examined Japanese behaviour in wartime have been fixated on finding a purely Showa-era explanation: that is, since 1926 when Hirohito became Emperor. Japan's decent treatment of prisoners in the Russo–Japanese war of 1904–5 and in the First World War has so dazzled them that they cannot see the dark past stretching behind. It is as if historians of the Holocaust had decided to work from the false premise that there was no anti-semitism in Germany and Austria before 1933.

One of the reasons for this may be the reluctance of historians to come up with explanations that suggest that 'the Japanese were brutal because they've always been brutal. It's in their blood.' Better to attribute Japanese brutality to the effect of totalitarian thinking in the 1920s and 1930s, neatly completing an Axis/communist hat-trick. The shift towards democracy that preceded Hirohito's reign, like the liberality of pre-Hitler Weimar, just makes this argument tougher to sustain. In Japan's case, only five years elapsed between the death of the previous Emperor and the invasion of Manchuria in 1931. Not long to inculcate, from scratch, an entire army and nation with brutal racism, without a messianic orator to whip up the people.

Hirohito was no demagogue, no Stalin or Mussolini. His people heard his surprisingly squeaky voice only in 1945, when he announced the end of the war in almost incomprehensibly archaic court Japanese. Japan's pre-war governments changed so often that no single voice became intimately familiar to the Japanese public. General Hideki Tojo – the bogeyman of Allied propaganda – in fact became prime minister only seven weeks before Pearl Harbor (and was thrown out of office a year before the end of the war). The lack of a single leader preaching unifying national goals makes tracking Japan's progressively totalitarian shift more difficult than in Germany or Russia. This does not mean there were no extremist political ideas in the period between 1926 and 1941 – there were, but they were planted in minds prepared over many decades.

The people who have perhaps thought hardest and longest on this subject are the Japanese veterans themselves. Many had years in Chinese and Soviet prison camps to reflect on what they had done. Now in their old age, they are having to come to terms with the actions and beliefs of their youth. The veterans have diverse opinions but there is a marked recurring theme: the origins of the Japanese way in war can be traced long before the twentieth century. One such veteran, Takeo Yamauchi, believes the widespread indoctrination and dissemination of militaristic values began when the Emperor Meiji was restored to the throne:

> Unlike the Nazi style of brainwashing, it was a much longer-term project that would take several decades, having begun in 1868 at the onset of the Meiji restoration. It aimed to foster loyalty towards the Emperor, and furthermore to establish militarism as the prized ideal. These principles were gradually imprinted into society and, as a result of the Russo–Japanese War, Japan took on a rather arrogant view of herself as a major power in the world. The people were imbued with this propaganda every day from childhood.

Another veteran, Hiraoka Hisashi, believes the common soldier obeyed commands, no matter how cruel and no matter what the consequences, 'because we were brainwashed. And also because we Japanese have always been rice farmers who lived by obeying the orders of the person who had power over the water source. As a result, the Japanese lost the ability to think and make decisions for themselves.' According to Hiraoka Hisashi, the majority of Japanese did not encounter independent thought until after 1945. Before then, they simply did what they were told.

The roots of Japanese psyche in the Pacific War are, like the origins of anti-semitism in Germany and the Terror in Russia, buried deep in the country's history and culture, and yet are in no way 'in the blood'. Certainly, both America and Japan proclaimed the Japanese as a race apart, the former to proscribe it, the latter to promote it above all other races. But this was propaganda. Some who suffered at the hands of the Japanese say such things as, 'There's something about the Japanese...' and refer to their taste for humiliating and painful television game-shows. Yet a run of inconvenient facts utterly undermines the genetic argument: the significant numbers of Japanese who daubed anti-war slogans on walls, refusing to succumb to the ruling ethos; persistent stories of the kindness of individual Japanese even in places of pressure-cooker violence such as the Burma–Thailand Railway; the surrender

of Japanese, sometimes en masse, on certain islands; national acceptance of the final surrender and subsequent docility, with suicide
very much the extremist exception.

There are examples of Japanese revulsion at excesses. General
Iwane Matsui was responsible for the Japanese forces in Nanking.
He arrived in December 1937 just after the massacre, realized
something terrible had happened and publicly criticized 300 of
his officers. He even confided in the press: 'I offer my sympathy,
with deep emotion, to a million innocent people... the Japanese
army is probably the most undisciplined army in the world today.'
At home, he erected a shrine to the memory of those who suffered
at Nanking, but remorse did not save him from the hangman's
noose in 1948.

Dick Lee was an eyewitness to the massacre of staff and
wounded patients at the Alexandra Hospital in Singapore. He
recalls a visit soon after by the commander of the victorious
Japanese forces himself: 'His interpreter says, General Yamashita
is apologizing for the behaviour of the front line troops, but
they were over-excited, and he apologizes for the over-excite-
ment of his front line troops, but there will be no more Japanese
in the hospital; he's going to put the guard round the hospital
now and everything will get back to normal. That's the little
speech he gave.'

Yamashita too was executed after the war, for the appalling
behaviour of troops during the 'Rape of Manila' in 1945. There is
good evidence to suggest that he was made a scapegoat for the
crimes of others.

Kiyoshi Sakakura was a Japanese soldier in Manchuria in 1943,
when someone at headquarters had a pang of conscience:
'Instructions for men and officers were issued, saying, "Do not
burn. Do not steal. Do not kill"... I'm sure everyone in the unit
knew about it. I saw it pinned up on the wall of the company
barracks and remember thinking, "What is this about?" I thought
these were things we'd been ordered to do.'

Occasionally, a soldier shrank from atrocity. Kiyoshi was
present when a Chinese peasant was used for bayonet practice:

Forty to fifty soldiers took turns poking him. His body was torn to
pieces. But of course, some people couldn't do it. On the other

hand, there were some of us watching who willingly tried it. I didn't feel like doing it, though. I would have got my rifle messy. It's really hard to clean a dirty rifle and I thought even if I didn't do it, somebody else would and indeed, some people did. All second-years were usually forced to have a poke. If anyone didn't or hesitated, people thought him a useless coward and that had an effect on your promotion. If you had the nerves to do it first, then you were sure to be promoted rather quickly because it showed you were courageous.

Convenience here mingles with moral qualms and brutality. Also notable is the way Kiyoshi Sakakura paints a picture of the Japanese Imperial Army in Manchuria having the banal social interactions of a modern corporation, with its patchy group motivation: some anxious for promotion, others skulking at the back.

The behaviour of the Japanese who lived outside their culture also casts a fascinating light on the nature/nurture argument. As we will see in Chapter 5, the Japanese-American response to Pearl Harbor was largely one of intense patriotism – to the USA. Ted Tsukiyama's parents were both born in Japan, but he himself was born and brought up in Hawaii. He found the behaviour of Japanese soldiers in war utterly alien:

The Japanese military ethic and mindset is totally, totally foreign to a Japanese American. For instance, when the battle seems to be lost, we would never think of taking a grenade to our gut and demolish ourselves, rather than be captured. The Japanese had been taught that to be captured is a great shame, it's a disgrace, you can't come back to your country, it's better to blow yourself up... We might be the same race, but that's a totally foreign idea which we do not subscribe to at all.

There are important distinctions to make between the responsibilities of individuals, combat units and the military establishment. Some atrocious behaviour was centrally ordered and organized, such as the germ warfare experiments on live humans, torture to obtain information and the 'comfort women' system of forced prostitution. Some was unofficial but silently condoned, the inevitable result of both a moral and logistical vacuum from the top down. This category includes plunder by soldiers ordered to live off the land, and by extension the violence that accompanied it. Cannibalism in places such as New Guinea and the Philippines was the end-product of the refusal or failure to resupply troops ordered to advance beyond sensible limits.

Then there is a complex, blurred range of acts half-known, assumed or turned from with a blind eye, such as rape and the slaughter of prisoners, medical staff and non-combatants. The Japanese had a repertoire of vicious battlefield practices: playing dead and then leaping up and killing; mutilation of the dead; targeting stretcher parties and corpsmen – the battlefield medical aides. A favourite trick was coming in to surrender but concealing grenades, knives or even a machine-gun strapped to the back of one man, who suddenly dropped on all fours while a second soldier fired the gun. Stories about such conduct sometimes grew in the retelling and became a justification for extreme countermeasures.

Japanese behaviour is also, as we shall see later, a function of the kind of war both sides fought in the Pacific. And both sides, under certain circumstances, killed civilians, desecrated bodies and slaughtered captives. Eugene Sledge, a Marine on Peleliu and Okinawa, describes how they would kill Japanese prisoners 'unless some officer stopped us'. This is not an argument about genes.

JAPAN'S SOLDIERS WENT INTO WAR in Manchuria and the Pacific with a ragbag of ideas, some centuries old, some recent, some common to all soldiers, others peculiar to the Japanese: Our master deserves absolute loyalty to death. You can do anything to win. Do not let the side down. Surrender equals unbearable shame. Other races are lesser races. Women are inferior to men. Enemies who surrender have no rights and are beneath contempt. An order from an officer is an order from the Emperor himself. Death is easy and holds no horrors. Death in battle is honourable and glorious. We can do horrible things because no one is going to stop us. We can do horrible things because we are all doing horrible things. We can do horrible things because that is what they would do to us. We can do horrible things because they are not humans, but vermin.

Some of these notions combine lethally: defeated foreign enemy's womenfolk were intensely vulnerable to the Japanese Imperial Army in 1941, as they had been to their predecessors 400 years before. In the late sixteenth and early seventeenth centuries, the warlord Hideyoshi fought a succession of wars which were depicted by near-contemporary artists in minute detail. The *Summer War in Osaka* shows women hiding from marauding warriors, being carried off, begging for their lives, distraught and weeping, drowned. Families are torn apart, their homes plundered.

Makoto Atobe, the Osaka Museum curator and specialist in Japanese medieval history, has studied the contemporary literature. His conclusion is that 'these sorts of things – death, plunder, rape, civilian horrors – happened very often according to the late fifteenth- to seventeenth-century written records, although they are very rarely depicted except in the *Summer War in Osaka*.' What makes this significant – after all, soldiers do commit brutalities, and those were doubtless cruel times – is that twentieth-century Japanese soldiers felt themselves to be the linear descendants of those 'honourable' medieval warriors. Officers such as Masao Maeda carried the symbol of that legacy of values: 'In those days we naturally accepted the tradition that Japanese samurai in olden times fought with a sword. I believe that by carrying swords we ourselves became samurai.'

As far back as medieval times, Japanese warlords are known to have attempted to codify the behaviour and virtues of their fighting men (or samurai). The word 'bushido' literally means 'the way of the warrior' and was first used in the sixteenth century. Up until the restoration of the Emperor it was a fairly rare term and implied a series of values, of which loyalty was the most highly prized. The word fell from use until the book *Bushido: The Soul of Japan*, published in 1900, popularized it for the first time. Nationalists and militarists were quick to enlist what they perceived as a venerable tradition in the struggle to legitimize their recent invention of the cult of the Emperor. As a result of their manipulation, bushido in the early twentieth century became synonymous with slave-like obedience, while retaining its authenticizing link to an 'honourable' past.

In fact, as always with soldiers of any country, the existence of an ethical warrior code is no guide to how soldiers were really expected to act or did actually act in battle, as the appalling behaviour of 'gentlemanly' British regiments in the Boer War reminds us. They looted and burned farms, occasionally murdering menfolk they found hiding, and incarcerated their non-combatant families in grim concentration camps where tens of thousands died of malnutrition and disease. It is therefore meaningless to quote old texts that require soldiers to treat their captives well. After all, the 1941 Field Service Code required the Japanese soldier to 'show kindness to those who surrender'.

The evidence, from the *Summer War in Osaka* to the war in the Pacific, is that doing whatever your masters expect of you overrides everything else. Japanese army veteran Takeo Yamauchi has no illusions about 'the way of the warrior': 'Bushido taught that you could sacrifice everything in order to show loyalty to your master. That is my understanding of it. Bushido is not about universal human morality.' Another veteran, Shiro Azuma, reminds us that it is not up to soldiers to do much thinking about ethics or motives – or, indeed, anything: 'We didn't think we would lose. Neither did we think it was a war of aggression. We simply followed orders and fought; there was no ideology behind it.'

The wars that preceded the restoration of the Emperor in 1868 were characterized by their relentless violence, culminating in further proof of the lethality of loyalty, as the families and households of defeated warlords committed suicide, right down to the girls and small children. But other seemingly bona fide links between the behaviour of Japanese in their ancient past and in the period after the restoration of the Emperor are more questionable. This is because the ruling elite from 1868 onwards used history to legitimize their cult of the Emperor. Historical icons were converted into tokens of legitimacy. Japan's rising sun flag, the banzai cheer and the Imperial Palace had all existed in earlier times – but they acquired a new national significance only after the restoration of the Emperor. The past was similarly manipulated to promulgate the myth that the Emperor was divine and had ruled the land in an unbroken reign for 2,600 years. Notices across the country proclaimed these 'facts'. One in Nagasaki declared: 'In this land called Japan there is one called the Emperor, who is descended from the Sun Deity. This has not changed a bit from long ago and just like the Sun being up in the heavens He is the Master.'

From 1868, political and social necessity saw the grafting of new ideas on to old roots. The young samurai warriors who precipitated the re-emergence of direct imperial rule wanted to encourage the modernization and westernization of the country. They feared and envied the power commanded by the old colonizing nations. As a result they were determined to create a modern state that could resist outsiders and pursue its own policy of expansion. To achieve this, they set about reorganizing both the economy and the military along European lines. The speed of change was rapid. In 1872 the first rail track was laid; in 1880 all major cities were linked by telegraph; and by 1890 over 1,400 miles of railway were in use. Japan's feudal peasants suddenly found themselves transformed into subjects of a centralized state. A shared set of loyalties and a sense of national identity were needed to bind together disparate communities and allegiances. The emperor system would provide this social cohesion.

The Emperor's success at unifying the nation in part derived from his universal appeal. Initially, at least, he was all things to all people. He managed to embody the spiritual authority of a Shinto deity, the transcendent moral authority of a Confucian sage, and the national sovereignty of a western-style constitutional monarch. Then, as his position became ever more elevated, he started to legitimize what he had formerly just supported: the nation state. The Emperor became the father that the people, his children, must serve. The men behind his restoration stamped on competing views. Historian Saburo Ienaga elegantly summarizes the absence of free thought: 'The Meiji political system gagged and blindfolded the populace. Denied the basic facts and a free exchange of opinion on the major issues of state and society, the public could hardly participate in Japan's future.' Within this intellectual vacuum, Japan's elite built the edifice of the emperor system with the twin supports of universal public education and military conscription. Both these institutions were perfect for mass indoctrination.

The principle of universal education was established in 1872, when primary school was made compulsory between the ages of six and fourteen. By the turn of the century, 90 per cent of children of both sexes attended, and soon the figure touched 99 per cent – far more than in many other advanced countries. In 1880 certain books advocating democracy were banned from the classroom, and from 1886 only texts certified by the Ministry of Education could be used (as in many countries to the present day). But by far the most significant amendment was the 1890 Imperial Rescript on Education. From then until the end of the Second World War, schools clearly defined service to the state in terms of loyalty to the Emperor. Patriotic ceremonies, group events and national occasions were used to reinforce pupils' sense of obligation to him. Japan's youth, the country's future, were taught to focus their nationalist spirit on the Emperor.

The textbooks published in the years following the Imperial Rescript on Education provide an insight into the way patriotism and militarism were encouraged. A 1904 elementary school reader contains the following exchange from the lesson 'Takeo Joins the Service':

Takeo: 'Father, the idea of "joining the service of my country" makes me so proud and happy. I'll be trained and when war comes, I will not be afraid to die. I'll give everything I have to show what a good Japanese fighting man is made of.'
Father: 'That's the spirit! You must be determined. Don't be afraid to die. Don't worry about us here. And you must always be faithful to the Imperial Precepts to Soldiers and Sailors.'

Another school reader issued in the mid 1920s contains a similar theme in the story called 'A Sailor's Mother':

A sailor receives a letter from his mother: 'You wrote that you did not participate in the battle of Toshima Island. You were in the August 10 attack on Weihaiwei but you didn't distinguish yourself with an individual exploit. To me this is deplorable. Why have you gone to war? Your life is to be offered up to fulfil your obligations to our benevolent Emperor.' An officer, seeing him reading the letter and crying, comforted the sailor: 'Son, there'll surely be another glorious war before long. Let's accomplish great feats of *bravery then and bring honour to our ship* Takachiho. *Explain that to your mother and put her mind at ease.'*

A veteran of the Pacific War, Yoshio Shinozuka, explains the impact of his education:

From birth, from primary school, we were taught the Emperor was god and we were his children. We couldn't even enter the school without bowing to the picture of the Emperor. Whenever the national anthem was sung, we had to stand to attention. Whenever we saw the rising sun flag we had to bow. Everything was done under the command of god.

Universal male conscription was established in 1873, two years after the national army was founded. Young men called up into the armed services found that the abstract sense of loyalty to the Emperor inculcated at school was now given a clear practical application. Memorized by officers and recited by the rank and file, the Imperial Rescript to Soldiers and Sailors of 1882 demanded: 'With a single heart fulfil your essential duty of loyalty, and bear in mind that duty is weightier than a mountain, while death is lighter than a feather. Never by failing in moral principle fall into disgrace and bring dishonour upon your name.' Superseding all these core values was the injunction of absolute loyalty to the Emperor. The ethos of loyalty to death went back to the twelfth century; surrender was unthinkable.

The Field Service Code (known as *senjinkun*) issued in January 1941 to all soldiers was in essence an updated and more explicit version of the 1882 Imperial Rescript. Veteran Kiyoshi Sakakura recalls its exhortation: '"Do not live to be shamed." Do you understand? Shame meant becoming a prisoner of war.' Nothing was left to chance; nearly half a century before the Pacific War, General Aritomo Yamagata, the father of Japan's army, had issued the specific order that all soldiers must commit suicide rather than surrender. The appalling by-product was that the Japanese came to regard the lives of those who surrendered to them as worthless. Scenes depicted in the *Summer War in Osaka* suggest this was an attitude with a history. Its future was to lie in the brutal treatment of prisoners in the Pacific War.

Soldiers had value only as long as they could fight for the Emperor. Their unquestioning obedience was reinforced by brutality. The peasants who had always made up the bulk of the army were treated to an incessant stream of humiliation and beatings. There were even special words to denote different types of violent blow: *tekken seisai* (or 'iron fist'), *ai-no-muchi* (the 'whip of love') and, even more euphemistically, *bentatsu* (an 'act of love'). Oppression gathered momentum as it rolled through the ranks, each tier heaping physical abuse and mental anguish on the men beneath them, until it reached the first-year recruits. These were the lowest of the low: men without rights. Only when they became second-years or were sent overseas did they have a chance to vent their frustrations on someone lower in the pecking order. Yet, as Saburo Ienaga has noted, the army was an easier option for many: 'The "toughness" of the Japanese military, which produced an endless supply of good fighting men by these brutal methods, actually came from the poverty of rural Japan, where the struggle for survival was more demanding than even army life.'

We can see the effect of the dangerous mix of tradition, teaching, official orders and barrack-room practices in Japan's first modern war: with China in 1894–5. In July 1894, the Japanese intercepted and sank a Chinese transport ship off the Korean Peninsula, and then machine-gunned several hundred Chinese soldiers in the water. Four months later, the Japanese attacked the Chinese town of Port Arthur (today known as Lushun) and then massacred both their enemies and non-combatants. American war correspondent James Creelman secured a worldwide scoop. His New York-based paper *The World* printed his report on 20 December 1894 under the following sequence of headlines and by-lines:

THE MASSACRE AT PORT ARTHUR
At Least Two Thousand Helpless People
Butchered by Japanese Soldiers

THE TOWN SACKED FROM END TO END
Streets Cloaked with Mutilated Bodies of Men,
Women and Children While the Soldiers Laughed

STOREKEEPERS SHOT AND SABERED
Complete Details of the Startling Story Originally Cabled
to The World by Its War Correspondent with the Japanese
Army – Several Europeans and Americans Were
Present and Some Were in Danger.

The article contextualizes the massacre as a response to Chinese mutilation of Japanese dead:

When the Japanese troops poured into Port Arthur they saw the heads of their slain comrades hanging by cords, with the noses and ears gone... A great slaughter followed. The infuriated soldiers killed everyone they saw. I can say as an eyewitness that the wretched people of Port Arthur made no attempt to resist the invaders. The Japanese now claim some shots were fired from the windows and doorways, but the statements are utterly false. No attempts to take prisoners were made. I saw a man who was kneeling to the troops and begging for mercy pinned to the ground with a bayonet while his head was hacked off with a sword... An old man on his knees in the street was cut almost in two...

The London *Times* special correspondent was also present:

I saw the Japanese march in... killing every live thing that crossed their path... Many went down on their hands and knees... and in that attitude were butchered mercilessly by the conquering army... All [the Japanese] were overflowing with enthusiastic patriotism and the delight of a day's work done, a splendid triumph after a hard-fought fight: none of the Japanese dreamed that their guests from the West were filled with horror, indignation and disgust...

A few days after witnessing the massacre, Creelman rushed to Tokyo where 400,000 attended a national victory celebration. He saw grisly mock heads of Chinese swinging from poles and heard the crowds incessantly chanting a new poem vowing their readiness to die for their Emperor and country.

In Japan's next war of expansion, the Russo–Japanese war of 1904–5, we can find clear evidence of the attitudes that underpin the *kamikaze* ideology some forty years later in the Pacific War. A contemporary account of the siege to capture the fort above the town of Port Arthur, this time held by the Russians, is entitled *Human Bullets: A Soldier's Story of Port Arthur*. Written by a young lieutenant, Tadayoshi Sakurai, the book was a runaway success, selling over 40,000 copies in its first year: 'Yes, we were all ready for death when leaving Japan. Men going to battle cannot expect to come back alive. But in this particular battle to be ready for death was not enough; what was required of us was a determination not to fail to die. Indeed, we were "sure-death" men, and this new appellation gave us great stimulus.'

As befitting his desire to die in battle, Tadayoshi Sakurai outlines the shame and fear he experiences at the prospect of being taken captive: 'If I did not expire then, it was certain that I should soon be in the enemy's hands, which meant a misfortune far more intolerable than death. My heart yearned to commit suicide before such a disgrace should befall me, but I had no weapon with me, no hand that could help me in the act. Tears of regret choked me.'

Although the Japanese were taught that capture was worse than death, Russian prisoners of war were apparently treated well. Keen to impress the colonial powers who governed the world, according to Russian figures just 500 of the 70,000 Russians in Japanese care died from their wounds. Treatment included the provision of artificial limbs, a recent invention, paid from imperial funds. The British journalist Ernest Brindle wrote in the *Illustrated London News*: 'The chivalry displayed by the Japanese soldier to a fallen foe has been demonstrated on innumerable occasions since the momentous crossing of the Yalu. I have witnessed the considerate treatment accorded to Russian prisoners which could not be excelled in point of consideration by any army in the world.'

In the First World War, the few thousand Germans captured by the Japanese in German colonies in the Pacific were also looked after well. But the sad truth is that the decent treatment received by Russian and German POWs was more the product of Japan's political desires than the result of humanitarian concern. Although the Japanese Red Cross society was the largest in the world (with roughly one in ten of the population members), it was no different in its aspirations to other super-patriotic societies flourishing at the time. The volunteerist spirit at the heart of the movement was missing: all its members had been drafted in. The military used the Japanese Red Cross to further their aim of gaining international respectability. It was a trick that worked; the war had achieved far more than territorial concessions. The military victory and selfless behaviour of her troops led the western powers dominating international politics to pronounce the country 'civilized'. The fact that both the Russian and German prisoners were white Europeans no doubt played its part. The rabid racism aimed at the Chinese had not yet been directed westwards.

While examining Japan's past, it would be wrong to claim that all Japanese were swept up and indoctrinated. For despite the best efforts of militarists and nationalists, dissent persisted up until the end of the Second World War. One of the most beautiful examples of this is a poem written by Akiko Yosano: 'My Brother, You Must Not Die'. It was published in a small arts magazine a month after the start of the 1905 siege and resulted in the poet's vilification in the national press:

My brother, you must not die.
Whether the fortress at Port Arthur falls or not – what does it matter?
Should it concern you? War is not the tradition of a merchant
    family...
Let the Emperor himself go off to war.
'Die like a beast, leaving pools of human blood.
In death is your glory.'
If that majestic heart is truly wise,
He cannot have such thoughts.

Japan's most tolerant period was in the 1920s. For a moment liberalism flowered: the electorate was increased to universal male suffrage; jazz music and dance halls flourished; baseball, Hollywood movies and western hair styles became popular. But this social relaxation coincided with a contest for political ascendancy in Japan. The men who had restored the Emperor and guided Japan into modern statehood – with the power to win wars against bigger nations – were all dead. There was no longer a clear power structure, no place where the buck stopped. Then a succession of events changed the climate: the world slid into depression; Chinese nationalists threatened to reclaim Japanese territory and renegotiate old treaties; America took an increasingly protectionist stance. The Japanese army and navy grew restive about the impasse in domestic and foreign policy. Military officers started taking initiative on the streets with uprisings and assassinations, while civilian leaders became increasingly militarized.

By the early 1930s, Japan had turned away from liberalization. The Communist Party was made illegal and its leaders rounded up. In the space of a few years around 30,000 people were arrested for allegedly subversive activities. As the nation became swept up in widening military conflicts in Manchuria, China and on the frontiers of the Soviet empire, Japanese civilian leaders, too, became increasingly militaristic and hard. The liberal 1920s were displaced by a grim determination to prepare the country for survival in a world racked by economic depression, upheaval and opportunism.

The power vacuum became filled with ever more repressive governments who would call in the debt owed by the people to their Emperor and country. Reworked ancient traditions, harsh training, uncompromising ideological education and the satisfying experience of previous victories over 'lesser races' had taught the nation what was expected of it. Lieutenant General Mikio Uemura, the first director of the POW Information Bureau, made it clear that Japan now felt free of all restraint in the handling of prisoners: 'In the war with Russia, we gave them excellent treatment in order to gain recognition as a civilized country. Today such need no longer applies.' The stage was set for the boundless brutalities of the Pacific War.

4

LIKE RATS IN A TRAP

The Japanese were invading the northern part of Malaya... four hours from Singapore, and there were tea dances at the Raffles... That to me represents the attitude of the imperialism at the time, the invincibility of it. They just could not understand that they were in fact beatable... The entire imperial system just collapsed overnight.

FRED SEIKER, pre-war marine engineer in the Far East

THE CAPITALS OF WESTERN COLONIAL rule in Asia fell in quick succession, but in very different ways. After bitter fighting, Hong Kong capitulated on 25 December 1941. The next day Manila in the Philippines was declared an 'open city' – simply abandoned as the troops withdrew. Singapore and all its defending troops capitulated on 15 February 1942, sending shock waves around the world. Dutch troops yielded Batavia (now Jakarta), the capital of the Netherlands East Indies, on 2 March. Five days later, the last British troops in Rangoon quit the city, as the Japanese entered the suburbs. By mid-1942, the Japanese had the power of life and death over half a million British, Commonwealth, European and American men, women and children, and a quarter of a billion Asians.

The Japanese had neither the time nor the inclination to treat their captives with care and humanity. They were on a tight timetable: subdue the country, seize control of the lines of communication, and start resupplying their war-machine and homeland. As we will see in Chapter 7, a range of models evolved for the relationship between the Japanese and the indigenous populations of Asia and the Pacific: exploitation, collaboration, re-education, partnership and total subjugation. The last was the most common, but there were examples of the others. The white peoples caught in the Japanese net experienced only total subjugation.

Some jumped from frying pan into fire, like the American forces that evacuated Manila only to be caught in the hell of the Bataan peninsula. An estimated 13,000 British and Indian troops died in a desperate overland retreat from Burma to India. Brigadier David Wilson was hurried out of Singapore on a cruiser with a handful of others so they could pass on painful lessons about Japanese fighting methods. Some individuals daringly fled from under the noses of the Japanese, sailing leaky yachts 1,000 miles from Ambon in the Dutch East Indies to Australia, or continuing resistance from dense mountain ranges in the Philippines. Anthropologist Ursula Graham-Bower ran a network of native spies in the hills around Imphal in India.

These were the exceptions. Captivity was the rule, often leading to death. The transition from freedom to prison camp entailed some of the most traumatic experiences of the war, as people who believed they were masters of both Asia's destiny and their own learned they were powerless chattels.

The war correspondent for the *Daily Express*, O'Dowd Gallagher, had arrived in Raffles' City of Lions in September 1941. He found the British civilian population of Singapore had scant concern for the Japanese threat, and only a passing curiosity for the war back home: 'With a few exceptions the white civilian population evinced no interest in the war whatsoever, except at the breakfast-table when their papers, reporting news from the battlefronts of Russia and North Africa, gave them something to chatter about.' They foolishly believed that Singapore 'was that non-existent quantity, an uncrackable nut'.

Pat Darling, Vivian Bullwinkel, Kath Neuss and Florence Syer were in a group of 140 Australian military nurses sent to Singapore in February 1941. Pat Darling fondly recalls their taste of colonial lifestyle: 'We entrained to... a charming little town on the west coast of Malaya, and we led a very pleasant life. We met many of the colonial service people, we met the planters and people like that, and naturally they entertained us... I mean it was almost like a pleasant feudal system.'

In Manila, the pearl of the Orient, American army nurse Madeline Ullom recalls the extravagance of life in the tropics: 'We had about three changes of clothes a day... and the shops were beautiful, and oh, the Filipinos did beautiful handiwork, and then at night we often dressed up and wore long dresses for dinner, or went to the Manila Hotel or Army and Navy Club. It was a beautiful existence.'

It was a world that gloomy prophecies of war seemed unable to penetrate. But Japan's armies would have less difficulty breaking through, as some wiser soldiers knew. Pat Darling heard their warnings: 'There were British and Australians, and there were Gurkhas, there were Indians, there were Sikhs all in uniform, and you would just naturally assume that the country and the cities were well defended. But occasionally one of the older patients might say to you, oh Sister, you know, if war does break out we'll be caught like rats in a trap.'

By 1 February 1942, war had not only broken out – it was about to engulf them. The surviving British and Commonwealth forces in Malaya had retreated across the narrow causeway to Singapore. Argyll and Sutherland Highlander Duncan Ferguson was one of the very last men over. The regimental bagpipers set the pace as usual with 'A Hundred Pipers' and 'Heilan' Laddie', but it wasn't fast enough for Ferguson and his comrades: '"Can ye no play a quicker tune?" the lads were muttering under their breath.' He was still on the causeway at quarter past eight in the morning when the sappers blew the charges.

Lee Kuan Yew heard the bang at Raffles College: 'One morning I was doing my medical auxiliary services duties... and there was a big BOOF, and we knew that the causeway had been blown up, and we were a fortress under siege... I said to my squad chief, I said, "That's the end of the British Empire." I think it was.'

The trap that Pat Darling had been warned about was snapping shut. Colonel Masanobu Tsuji, the architect of Japan's successful invasion, wrote: 'The enemy, exhausted and demoralized after their retreat from the mainland, had sought shelter in the fortress. We had to begin our attack without giving them even a day's respite to rest and reorganize and recover their morale.' The causeway was easily patched up; boats and rafts were also used to cross the shallow waters to Singapore island. To their delight they encountered little resistance. It would take just one more week for the island's 30,000 invaders to force the surrender of Britain's garrison of 120,000 men.

This is not as reprehensible as it might appear: many of the British and their allies were support, not combat, troops. Furthermore, thousands of reinforcements had arrived far too recently to be organized into a fighting force, whereas the Japanese attackers were highly trained, motivated and co-ordinated.

WHY DID BRITAIN'S GATEWAY to the East collapse so readily? Singapore's poor landward defences, lack of air cover and the shortage of first-rate equipment all contributed to its eventual defeat. But there was another factor: desertion.

The men defending Malaya and Singapore were a mixed bunch. British 'Tommies', Indian 'Jawans', Australian 'Diggers' and local volunteer troops did not integrate smoothly. With the exception of the Argylls, they had not been properly trained in jungle fighting. The speed and ease with which these disparate uncoordinated units had been routed by the Japanese inspired a belief that their foe was superhuman. Field Marshal Viscount Slim wrote after the war: 'We began by despising our Japanese enemy; the pendulum then swung wildly to the other extreme. We... frightened ourselves with the bogey of the superman of the jungle.'

General Gordon Bennett, commander of the Australian 8th Division, accused British troops of having a 'retreat complex'. Arrival in Singapore did little to cure the condition. The defences there inspired no confidence, as Duncan Ferguson recalls: 'I used to say to the sergeant, "Where are the defences here?" and he says, "Bloody don't ask me," he says, "I've never seen any defences..."' The reason was not hard to find: in December 1941 Britain's Army Commander, General Percival, argued that 'defences are bad for morale – for both troops and civilians'. With the Japanese snapping at their heels, many of the men who had fallen back on Singapore turned and fled – even when there was nowhere left to run. Duncan Ferguson was in the reserve line behind the forward beach defences in the north-west of the island. Australian troops were just ahead of him, supposedly holding the front, when the main Japanese assault landed on the night of 8 February 1942:

I was in the slit trench with this little bloke – 'Wham' Hughes his name was – and the Aussies were streaming through, and wee 'Wham' says: 'Where are you going, Digger?' He says: 'It's OK, Jock, we're being relieved.' And 'Wham' says: 'Who the hell has relieved you? – there was nobody went down here.' He says: 'It's OK, Jock, we've been relieved.' They hadn't. The lot got off their mark and left us.

Some drunken British and Australian troops wandered the streets, looting liquor to pass the time. Civilians hid or desperately tried to get aboard the last ships in the harbour. The chaos and panic were so complete that women and children selected for evacuation needed armed guards to ensure their safe passage. Duncan Ferguson was one of those who escorted them to the docks; his anger towards the deserters grew with what he saw: 'We took the first load down, and you should have seen the Aussies streaming up the gangway... they were pushing the women off so as they could get up... We saw an Aussie shooting a naval officer, a merchant naval officer, shooting him so he could get up the gangway.'

Challenging as this is to the national self-image of the fearless Digger, it fits into a pattern of corroborative testimony. Australian historian Joan Beaumont believes that there is 'persuasive evidence that the discipline of some Australian troops cracked in the last stages of the defence of Singapore. Too many credible accounts of Australian deserters fighting their way on to ships evacuating civilians exist for this charge to be dismissed.' Indeed, the allegations of widespread Australian desertions were acknowledged in Australia itself in August 1942 after months of rumours. The Director-General of the Australian Department of Information wrote an article headlined 'New Light on the Last Days of Singapore' in which he stated: 'We were overwhelmed in our forward positions... our reserves failed to make effective counter-attacks, or even effective stands; and a good many of our men appeared far behind our lines, unnerved and not knowing where to go... The only landing for the first two days was against the Australians. Singapore was lost in the first day's fighting.'

Australians counter-accuse the British of betraying Australia by failing to defend Singapore adequately, and of sacrificing Australian troops, when their proper use should have been in the defence of their homeland against expected Japanese attack. Certainly one cannot generalize; some Australians units did fight valiantly in Malaya, and others abandoned their posts. Many Indian soldiers in Malaya defected to the enemy, causing General Percival to write on 12 January 1942: 'Am NOT repeat NOT happy about state of morale of some Indian units. Believe Garhwalis and Dogras [regiments] will continue to fight but some others doubtful.' As we will see in Chapter 7, Malaya and Singapore were rich recruiting grounds for the Indian National Army, which sided with the Japanese against their old colonial masters to fight for Indian independence. British desertions on Singapore are confirmed by Colonel Ian Stewart, who stated, 'It is true that a number [of Australians] straggled down into town and did make an early getaway but that equally applies to British troops.'

With the Japanese firmly moving towards Singapore's centre, all Australian nurses were ordered to evacuate. Ominous rumours had been filtering out of beleaguered Hong Kong – rumours of Japanese soldiers rampaging through a field hospital, shooting and bayoneting wounded and unarmed men, and gang-raping British nurses on the bodies of their murdered patients. Two days before she left Singapore, Pat Darling was called in to the dispensary: 'The pharmacist wanted to see me. So I went across and presented him with a couple of treatment sheets that he had to fill in. And he gave me a phial of morphia and said Sister, you know what to do with that, and I said yes...' After the war, she found out that the orderlies in her own hospital had been given rifles 'and they were going to shoot us... they weren't going to let the Japs touch us'.

The first group of Australian nurses left Singapore on 11 February. They stopped at Batavia (where about a hundred deserters were removed from their boat) and then on to Australia. Pat Darling, Vivian Bullwinkel, Kath Neuss and Florence Syer were in the final group of sixty-five nurses who escaped the next night aboard the *Vyner Brooke*. As they sailed towards an uncertain fate, Florence 'looked back on Singapore – it was just a mass of smoke and flames. It was a terrible sight, you'd never forget it... the oil refineries burning, and Singapore burning itself.'

The nurses were at sea for just two days before Japanese planes bombed and sank their boat, leaving around 300 survivors in the water. Amid the confusion and panic Vivian and Kath got into a lifeboat, Florence latched on to a floating rail, and Pat held tight to a wooden spur. All around them floated the bodies of the dead, many of whom had been strangled by their life-vests when they jumped into the water.

The Bangka Straits, where the *Vyner Brooke* went down, separate the oil-rich island of Sumatra from Bangka Island, then the source of much of the world's tin. On the night of 14 February the Straits were unusually busy. Over fifty vessels had been sunk that day and the Japanese were about to seize the islands – before the Dutch could destroy their mining and drilling equipment. Hundreds of survivors were pulled by the Straits' dangerous currents towards Bangka Island's northern tip, where the lighthouse stands and even today the hulks of wrecks still litter the shoreline. Twelve of the Australian nurses – and many civilians – drowned trying to reach the shore.

All that day and night, the *Vyner Brooke*'s shipwrecked passengers were washed up on Bangka Island. Some, including Vivian and Kath, landed on Rajik Beach and lit a fire to guide the rest in. The currents were too strong, and Pat, Florence and others were carried around the headland to another beach. They were picked up by the Japanese on their way into Muntok town the next day and imprisoned. On 16 February the 100 people on Rajik Beach decided to surrender. Some set off into the nearest town; the twenty-two nurses stayed to tend the wounded. But by cruel irony, they were on the one island in the Pacific now garrisoned by Captain Masaru Orita's unit, believed responsible for the Hong Kong atrocities. The fate they had left Singapore to avoid now stared them in the face. Only one nurse – twenty-six-year-old Vivian Bullwinkel – would survive the encounter. She recalled what happened when the Japanese soldiers appeared on the beach: 'All the men who were there, which would have been about fifty or sixty – still there – were rounded up... and taken around the bluff. And when they came back, some little time later, they were all wiping their bayonets. So we looked at each other and said, "They're not taking prisoners."'

The nurses were ordered into the sea, almost up to their waists. Vivian recalls Kath Neuss turning to her with a last, bitter comment:

'The two things I hate most – the Japs and the sea. And I've got them both.' They then machine-gunned us from behind. I was hit just in the back there, and it came out here. And being very young and naive I suppose I always thought that once you were shot, you know, you'd had it. That was it. And really to my utter amazement I found that I was still alive, and then of course I became fright-ened. I had taken in a lot of salt water therefore I was being horribly seasick, and I thought, 'Oh, they'll see my shoulders moving,' so then I tried to stop being seasick, but – and I just lay there, because, well, I was too frightened to do anything else, and then gradually the waves brought me in back to the beach. And I finally plucked up enough courage to sit up and look around and there was no sign of my colleagues, the Japanese party had gone, and there was just, you know, the usual travel brochure of blue sea, blue sky, palms and golden sand.

Vivian crawled into the jungle and hid. Some days later, with a friend's water bottle hiding the bullet hole in her dress, she gave herself up to the Japanese and was reunited in captivity with the nurses who had been captured earlier. They agreed to keep the massacre a secret for all their sakes; as historian Hank Nelson has observed: 'Bullwinkel, the lone survivor and the one link with so many dead colleagues, was both precious and dangerous to the other nurses.'

Survival in Japanese captivity was an arbitrary, random experi-ence. Florence Syer recalls her brush with death after drifting past her friends' fire signal on Rajik Beach and being picked up by the Japanese. She still does not understand why her group was spared: 'We got up to where they wanted us to go and it just looked like a sort of mosque... and they made us... turn our backs to them, and they were going to shoot us. So we just all said, "Goodbye and may they be quick." But suddenly they decided they weren't going to shoot us; we don't know why or whether they suddenly got a message from somebody...'

The suffering and anguish of life in Japanese captivity would in time lead many, like Pat Darling, to consider the dead better off than the living: 'We actually did envy the girls who had been lost at sea... Even the girls who were massacred we thought were luckier than we because it was all over so quickly.'

After the war, the *Australian Women's Weekly* held the massacre up as a commanding argument against clemency: 'If ever, anywhere in the world, a plea for mercy or leniency for the Japanese race is heard, there will rise before Australian eyes the accusing picture of twenty-two gallant women walking, with heads held high, into the sea as the Japanese machine-guns opened their murderous fire.' The Australian authorities tried to bring those responsible to justice. Captain Orita was arrested, but committed suicide in his cell. The 229th Infantry's Regimental History makes veiled references to a war crime cloud hanging over its time in Hong Kong and Bangka, but gives no details. The surviving veterans regard Captain Orita as a hero and refuse to discuss what happened under his command on that beach in 1942.

While the nurses were being machine-gunned on the beach, British forces in Singapore withdrew past Alexandra Hospital. Dick Lee, wounded by a bomb blast, lay on a stretcher bed in a corridor. He was one of 900 men crammed into a building clearly marked with red crosses. But the Japanese took no notice, angered perhaps by machine-gun fire coming from the hospital grounds (in violation of the Red Cross Convention). Dick could hear the battle closing in. Mindful of the atrocities in Hong Kong, orderlies gave out instructions: if the Japanese enter the building, raise your hands, let them see you are offering no resistance, keep silent, and do not move about.

It was not long before his first sight of the enemy. It was a one-sided encounter: 'He grinned. And he had a gold filling. I can see it now... And, course, I don't know whether I smiled back, maybe I fucking did, because I was shitting myself anyway... you're not brave in these circumstances. You can't run anywhere, you can't defend yourself... you get that butterfly feeling: what's going to happen here?'

But Dick Lee was lucky; the Japanese's attention was drawn to an Australian who had wandered down the stairs into the corridor: 'As he's got to the foot of the stairs, he's leaned against the concrete pillar, and the other Nip that was standing there, you know – your eyes are just watching everything – he just went straight over to him, right into the guts with a bayonet.'

Dick could not see much beyond his stretcher but he heard shouting and screams of agony. The Japanese passed through, demanding watches, rings and cigarettes, slaughtering patients and hospital staff. Even a patient in the operating theatre was bayoneted; the surgeons working to save his life were shot and stabbed. For Dick Lee the killings cannot be explained: 'They could see people were lying there defenceless. I couldn't imagine, in my wildest dreams, our blokes ever going in and doing what they done.'

The massacre in Alexandra Hospital continued into the next day; meanwhile, a few miles away, the British began surrender negotiations with the Japanese. For General Yamashita, the commander of Japan's army in Malaya, the surrender was an occasion for relief as well as triumph. He dreaded the British finding out how low his forces were on ammunition and supplies, and bluffed the British into capitulation. Churchill had called for an outcome more typical of the Japanese facing defeat: a fight to the death 'among the ruins of Singapore City'. General Percival on the spot took a more humanitarian and realistic approach: with his water supply cut off, his communications down and thousands of deserters roaming the streets, he surrendered Singapore and around 130,000 men. Like Pat Darling, some of them later wondered if it would have been better to have died quickly in a battle for Singapore, than slowly in the wretched labour camps of Thailand and Burma.

Control of Singapore helped the Japanese achieve their main goal in the region: capture of the oil fields of the Dutch East Indies. The Allies' defence was organized through a complicated command structure that pooled US, British, Dutch and Australian resources. Otto Schwarz was an American sailor on the cruiser USS *Houston*, which was sunk in the Sunda Strait after a series of battles against overwhelming Japanese naval forces. He had a narrow escape on his long swim through the night to land:

I heard screaming in the distance and I heard machine-gun fire, and I thought oh my God, you know, they're killing the men in the water. And sure enough, a little while later, a torpedo boat approached me... I took the collar of my life jacket and I formed a pocket, and I put my face in it, and I bobbed up and down. The boat came up to me. I could hear them speaking Japanese on the deck, I could see the searchlight coming through the water, and I fully expected the bullets to follow but instead, for some reason or other, they poked me with some sort of a pole and then the light went out, the engines revved up and they took off and I got away with it.

Otto's relief was temporary. The Allied defeat in the battle of the Java Sea sealed the fate of the Dutch East Indies. On 8 March 1942, approximately 25,000 Dutch troops, some 7,000 British and Australian, and several hundred Americans were ordered to surrender. Fred Seiker, a Dutch merchant navy volunteer trapped on Java, soon realized that life in captivity was going to be a living hell. Three men were executed for attempting to escape:

These lads took over a day to die... They were bayoneted in such a way to prolong life as much as possible so they could be viewed as long as possible by us, and the image of this is – I am eighty-five this year – still a part of nightmares I still have, this scene. And then you realized for the very, very first time, for the very first time, this is something that we've never heard of, seen, don't under-stand and we had better get used to it.

American attempts to defend their empire in the East were ultimately, like the efforts of the British and the Dutch, a failure. Guam fell after a brief skirmish on 10 December 1941, but Wake Island's Marine Corps gun batteries and planes put up a remark-able fight, sinking two Japanese destroyers and hitting three cruisers, a third destroyer and a transport ship. 'Send us more Japs' was the mythical message from the garrison dreamed up for an American public desperate for heroes. Wake Island could have been reinforced and held, but was not.

Then on 22 December 1941, Japan landed its main assault force in the Philippines at Lingayen Gulf. General Douglas MacArthur's plan to confront the invaders on the beach met with instant disaster. The bulk of his force were poorly trained and ill equipped: no match for Japanese veterans from the war with China. After just four days MacArthur was forced to change strategy. He declared Manila an open city and implemented Washington's long-held plan – a retreat into the Bataan peninsula whose terrain heavily favoured defence. At its tip, in the mouth of the bay, lies tiny Corregidor Island whose huge guns guarded the harbour's entrance.

'I hope you will tell the people outside what we have done and protect my reputation as a fighter,' was MacArthur's request before General Brereton boarded the last transport plane out of Manila. Unfortunately, it was what MacArthur had not done that would hasten disaster and reinforce belief that he was obsessed with reputation at the cost of responsibility. He utterly failed to ensure that his army in Bataan had adequate food and medicine. Warehouses across Luzon were left full of supplies. The Japanese were bequeathed 3 million gallons of fuel, half a million artillery rounds and invaluable reserves of quinine, essential anti-malaria protection for one of the most infested areas in the world. According to historian Harry Gailey, one depot alone contained enough rice to feed the soldiers and civilians on the peninsula for five months.

In America General MacArthur was awarded the Congressional Medal of Honor, and the President praised his 'heroic conduct of defensive and offensive operations on the Bataan peninsula'. On Bataan he was derided as 'Dugout Doug'. His men composed a song that included the verse:

Dugout Doug's not timid, he's just cautious, not afraid;
He's protecting carefully the stars that Franklin made.
Four-star generals are as rare as good food on Bataan;
And his troops go starving on.

Holed up on Corregidor Island, MacArthur made just one trip to the beleaguered peninsula throughout the entire siege. But although the men on Bataan rarely saw him, MacArthur made sure he was prominent in his press communiqués. Of the 142 press releases issued by his headquarters between December 1941 and March 1942, 109 mentioned only one individual: General MacArthur. Then, midway through March, he and his family were ordered by Roosevelt to leave the underground tunnels of Corregidor for the safety of Australia. It was there he made his famous pledge: 'I shall return.' What he chose not to declare was the $500,000 that the Philippine President had given him shortly before his departure, as recompense for his 'magnificent defence' of the archipelago.

In his absence, Bataan's defenders fought on for six weeks, but the lack of supplies and reinforcements sealed their fate. By the end, the men were so ill that the test for fitness simply consisted of being able to walk 100 yards carrying their weapons. On 9 April 1942, around 75,000 survivors – over 60,000 of them Filipinos – were surrendered to the Japanese. The Japanese commanders in the Philippines never expected to have so many prisoners on their hands and treated them without consideration. Sick, starving and dehydrated, they were ordered to march 65 miles in sweltering heat to the railhead of San Fernando. Lester Tenney quickly realized that a new fight had begun – for survival:

If you fell out of line, you were dead. Well, this fellow fell out of line, and the Japanese officer came over, started talking to him, and hollering, and telling him to get up and go, and he didn't do it. And the Japanese officer just picked up his samurai sword… and went like this, wham. And hit the fellow on the back of the neck, and went right straight through it, and the head fell off. And that's the part that's horrible, and will live with you for ever, never forget it. You never forget seeing the head on the floor… with his arms still moving, his legs still moving, but the head is off. Never forget it, no, never.

If a man stopped to defecate, if he stopped to lap at a stagnant pool of water, if he collapsed from the heat, or if he was just walking too slowly, then he was liable to be beaten, bayoneted, beheaded or shot. The Japanese made particular hell for the Americans along the Bataan road, by forcing them to do terrible things to one another, as Lester Tenney explains: 'The Japanese called four men out of line, and had them dig a ditch. When they dug the ditch, they told them to bury this man. One of the fellows said I can't bury him, he's still alive, so the Japanese shot this one man, called four more men out, and said now dig two ditches.'

To live you had to make harsh choices: 'You don't want to bury your friend, you don't want to bury a live person, but you know that if you say no, you're going to be buried.' Lester's life was saved by two friends who carried him part of the way. Richard

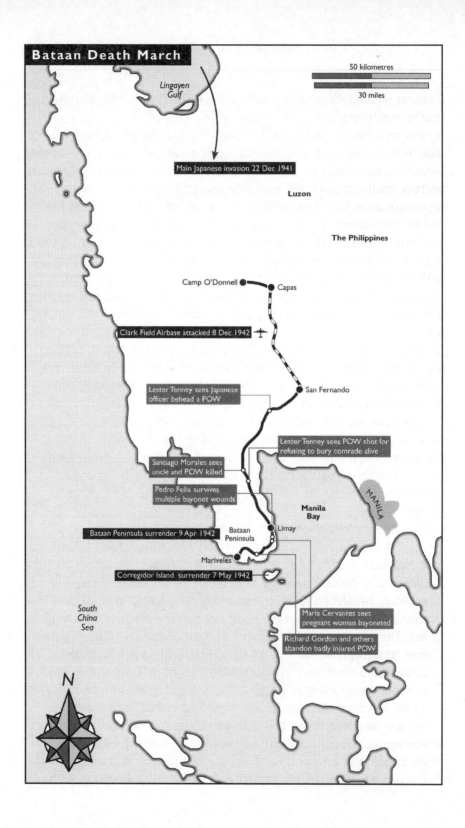

Bataan Death March

Lingayen Gulf

50 kilometres
30 miles

Main Japanese invasion 22 Dec 1941

Luzon

The Philippines

Camp O'Donnell ● ━━━ ● Capas

Clark Field Airbase attacked 8 Dec 1942

San Fernando

Lester Tenney sees Japanese officer behead a POW

Lester Tenney sees POW shot for refusing to bury comrade alive

Santiago Morales sees uncle and POW killed

MANILA

Pedro Felix survives multiple bayonet wounds

Manila Bay

Bataan Peninsula surrender 9 Apr 1942

Bataan Peninsula

Limay

Mariveles

Corregidor Island surrender 7 May 1942

South China Sea

Maria Cervantes sees pregnant woman bayoneted

Richard Gordon and others abandon badly injured POW

N

Gordon walked the Bataan road among strangers. He discovered that it was 'every man for himself' after a day carrying a wounded soldier with three others: 'Not one soul ever stepped forward to relieve us, so we carried that man all day long in a condition that I could barely carry myself... The next day the original four bearers, including myself, had gone in different directions because to continue to do that without getting any relief all four of us would have been dead... and that's not a very pleasant memory.'

Despite grave risk of reprisals, many Filipino villagers offered whatever food or water they could, particularly near the march's end. Ten-year-old Santiago Morales was with his uncle handing out food to passing Filipino and American soldiers: 'When the Japanese saw my uncle trying to help an American, they stabbed him in the armpit and [the bayonet] came out the other side. I was in shock. I couldn't speak because I knew that if I called for help, the Japanese would kill me too. So I kept silent, and my uncle died from his wound. The Japanese then shot the American and he died with my uncle on the same spot.'

It is believed that between 5,000 and 10,000 Filipinos and 700 Americans died on the march. Some were killed outright, but the majority – already ill, wounded and malnourished – simply perished from exhaustion, thirst and starvation. The Japanese also slaughtered several hundred Filipino officers near the Pantigan Bridge. Captain Pedro Felix received four severe wounds in the chest, yet survived the slaughter:

> A Japanese detail stopped our group on the trail and ordered all officers and NCOs to line up on one side and the privates on the other. At 1400 hours... a high ranking officer who alighted from a staff car had a brief talk with the Japanese guard escorts and then left. The privates were ordered to march to Limay while the officers and NCOs were ordered to form three groups. Then the Japanese began tying our hands behind our backs with telephone wire, the wrists of one man linked to the wrists of the man behind. At about 1500 hours, a Japanese civilian interpreter addressed the three groups: 'My friends, we are sorry for you. If you had surrendered earlier, this would not have happened. You gave us no choice. We're going to kill you all because you killed many of our soldiers. If you have any last request before we kill you, say so now.'

When the survivors reached the railhead at San Fernando they were loaded into railway boxcars in which many more of them died of heat and suffocation before reaching the station at Capas and then their destination, Camp O'Donnell in Tarlac Province. Here a further 26,500 Filipinos and Americans died in the immediate aftermath of their harrowing journey: some as a result of extreme hardship on the Bataan march, others from fresh brutality, disease and privation. Many thousands of Filipino non-combatants were among the casualties: caught in the area that the Japanese were trying to clear, they had been forced to join the Bataan march, too. Thirteen-year-old Maria Cervantes lost two brothers and a sister en route, but the worst sight she saw was the gratuitous slaughter of a stranger:

We saw a woman on a bridge, crying because she was about to give birth. One of the Japanese soldiers was annoyed because she was making so much noise, and he stabbed that pregnant woman. She died along with the child in her womb... I was very angry. I said to myself: these are just foreigners – why are they doing this to Filipinos? They've just shown up here. Why are they hurting us? It's not as if she was a soldier. She was a civilian, and she was giving birth. I pitied that girl so much, but we couldn't do anything.

The last Allied colonial stronghold in the Pacific to fall was the fortified island of Corregidor, just off the southern tip of Bataan. Its defenders took shelter from Japanese shelling in the network of tunnels that run deep into the island, but the Japanese were unstoppable. To this day the 'Rock' is covered with ruined buildings and huge guns. Visitors stroll through the Malinta tunnel, the island's main fortification, which once contained the command centre, barracks and the hospital where nurse Madeline Ullom worked through the constant shelling. She recalls her feelings of frustration and despair as the inevitable was announced: 'When General Wainwright broadcast the surrender, everyone was standing around, the tears just flooding down their cheeks because they had worked so hard and had fought so gallantly. And then to think that they had to surrender – but there was nothing else to do.'

US Corporal Erving Strobing broadcast the last transmission from the island. His signal, sent in Morse code, was picked up by an army listening post in Hawaii and subsequently broadcast to the American people. His last words speak for all those across Asia and the Pacific who had already stood on the brink of captivity, shocked and fearful:

We've got about fifty-five minutes and I feel sick at my stomach... I am really low down, they are around now smashing rifles, they bring in the wounded every minute, it is a horrible sight, we will be waiting for you guys to help... shells were dropping all night faster than hell, damage terrific, too much for guys to take... I can't say much, can't think at all, I can hardly think... the white flag is up, everyone is bawling like a baby, they're piling dead [and] wounded soldiers in our tunnel, I'm vomiting, arms weak from pounding, long hours, no rest, short rations, tired... I know now how a mouse feels caught in a trap waiting for guys to come along finish it up... my name is Erving Strobing, get this to my mother, Mrs Minnie Strobing, 605 Barbie Street, Brooklyn, New York – they are to get along OK, get in touch with them soon as possible... hope they be there when I come home, tell Joe wherever he is, give 'em hell for us. My love to you all, God bless you and keep you...

5

WE'RE GONNA HAVE TO SLAP THE DIRTY LITTLE JAP

Kill a hundred rats for every boy that fell,
Remember Pearl Harbor,
Wipe the Japs from the map – give them hell.
Dawn on the Sunday morning, dawn on the wide blue sea,
A warrior isle of sunshine, lay so peacefully.
Then from the sky without warning, the vultures swarmed to
attack,
Hiding behind their peace talks, they stabbed our boys in the back.
'REMEMBER PEARL HARBOR' – American popular song

PEARL HARBOR WAS THE THUNDERCLAP that woke up America. Two hours of Japanese bombing had done what two years of war against Hitler had failed to achieve: US entry into the Second World War. Those with long memories heard the echo of 1917, when America declared war only after German U-boats threatened her shipping in the Atlantic. Overnight on 7 December 1941 the nation again renounced isolationism. But this time, Americans bayed for blood. They wanted revenge.

It suited America best to see Pearl Harbor not as a failure of national defence, or intelligence, or planning, or governance, but as a simple case of Japanese treachery. At one stroke it avoided undue introspection and self-flagellation. Admiral Husband E. Kimmel and Lieutenant General Walter C. Short, Hawaii's naval and military commanders, made handy scapegoats but the Japanese were nothing less than diabolical. What sealed their perfidy was that Japanese diplomats were blithely discussing a peaceful way forward in Washington while their fleet bore down on Pearl Harbor. Roosevelt clearly could not tell his people that his code-breakers had read most of the Japanese final note before their ambassador did. Not that the note was a declaration of war. Its author, Toshikazu Kase, had discussed the matter with the Emperor himself: 'It was his opinion that we should declare war. However, the army and the navy didn't want the Emperor saying that. It is still discussed today whether we should have declared war, or if the situation was that we wanted to but couldn't. Well, we couldn't.'

It was given to US Secretary of State Cordell Hull to ram treachery down the throats of Japan's ambassadors just before they were packed off home. He fixed on Toshikazu Kase's note, which Ambassador Nomura had only just had decoded, and which he had had the apparent gall to deliver while Pearl Harbor was burning: 'In all my fifty years of public service I have never seen a document that was more crowded with infamous falsehoods and distortion... on a scale so huge that I never imagined until today that any government on this planet was capable of uttering them.'

Roosevelt had no way of knowing that neither Ambassador Nomura nor Toshikazu Kase in Tokyo had been told that the surprise attack was under way. Indeed, Toshikazu Kase was present when their boss, Shigenori Togo, Japan's Foreign Minister, learned about the attack – after it happened.

> It was a phone-call for the Minister from Oka, the chief of the military services... The Minister seemed very surprised, and I heard him say, 'What? Pearl Harbor?' loudly. He was very surprised because he didn't know about the sneak attack on Pearl Harbor; they didn't let him in on it. Having heard that they had success-fully sunk several warships, the Minister said, 'Congratulations. I will see you at the meeting.' After he put the phone down, he told me about it and still seemed absolutely shocked.

Togo and Roosevelt perhaps had one thing in common: total surprise at the sudden attack on Pearl Harbor, but the hunch that something like it must have been on the cards. Roosevelt's Secretary of War, Henry Stimson, had summed up the problem only twelve days before: 'The question was how we should manoeuvre them into the position of firing the first shot without allowing too much danger to ourselves. It was a difficult proposition.'

On 8 December 1941, the post-mortems could wait. When President Roosevelt addressed Congress and the world, breast-beating was not on his agenda:

Yesterday, December seventh, 1941 – a date which will live in infamy – the United States of America was suddenly and deliberately attacked by naval and air forces of the empire of Japan... Always will be remembered the character of the onslaught against us... this form of treachery shall never endanger us again. I ask that the Congress declare that since the unprovoked and dastardly attack by Japan on Sunday, December seventh, a state of war has existed between the United States and the Japanese empire.

Yet in the final days of campaigning before the presidential elections of November 1940, Roosevelt was forced to offer isolationists what seemed to be a 'no war' pledge to boost his candidacy. He declared: 'I have said this before, but I shall say it again: your boys are not going to be sent to any foreign wars.' Roosevelt won an unprecedented third term in office but faced a tough struggle weaning America off isolation. His device for trying to defeat Hitler without committing US troops was Lend-Lease, whereby $7 billion was made available to supply weapons to nations fighting the Nazis. Yet it took fifteen months to put into practice this idea to make America the 'arsenal of Democracy'. A fleet in flames and some 2,400 dead Americans changed everything. Now, when Roosevelt called for all-out war, there was not a single dissenting vote and only one abstention. Fixing on Japanese treachery kick-started the hatred necessary to fight a vicious war to its bitter end.

Eugene Sledge joined the Marine Corps 'to kill Japs because they had bombed Pearl Harbor... I wanted to do my part in making them pay'. He and his father had gone out quail hunting early that historic December day; they turned on the radio for the drive home. Neither knew much about Japan but Eugene can still remember his father's response: 'they were very aggressive and savage people... Just because they wrote nice poetry and had nice flower arrangements it didn't meant that you could trust them.'

Rod Steiger, then not even an actor, let alone a movie star, recalls the tremendous anger and indignation people felt: 'It was like you were having an argument with a man and suddenly he slapped you three times rapidly across the face, you can't wait for the fourth slap.' Al Fernandez, who had watched the Japanese pilots attack Pearl Harbor, shared the outrage: 'Somebody snuck up on you and hit you on the head from the back... or stabbed you in the back... As far as we were concerned it was very treacherous.'

Winston Churchill did not waste time crying foul when Japanese troops stormed the north-eastern coast of Malaya a few hours before their planes appeared over Hawaii. Certainly, unlike at Pearl Harbor, intelligence had given fairly accurate advance warning. Also, no one dreamed it would lead to the fall of Singapore. Churchill's response was a mixture of relief and rejoicing. To him, Pearl Harbor was a godsend: Japan's attack meant America was in, and if America was in, then Britain could not lose the Second World War. He wrote in his memoirs: 'so we had won after all'. Later that night, '...being saturated and satiated with emotion and sensation, I went to bed and slept the sleep of the saved and thankful'.

Churchill's joy was based on the knowledge that America's industrial and military might now underpinned their prior commitment to a 'Europe First' policy. This strategy assumed that Germany was a far more immediate and dangerous foe than Japan. In the event of war against both powers, Japanese advances would be checked but the main war effort would be focused against Germany, whose reach now extended to the outskirts of Moscow.

The people of America had yet to acknowledge such strategic considerations. Disgust and hate translated into action, as young men joined up in droves. Nancy Potter was in high school when war was announced. Throughout the school, the boys talked of enlisting. Few of those old enough to join up gave more than a passing thought, she recalls, to the dangers of war:

Consciously we must have realized that it was going to hurt, and that some people were going to get killed, but not the people we knew, they were going to manage to get through, and it was going to be very valiant and quite beautiful. Some people enlisted in the navy because they thought it was a prettier way to die. Somebody once told me you don't get dirty, you just go down into the water.

Sitting in a restaurant, George Peto saw a smartly dressed US Marine who looked like he had stepped down off a recruiting poster, and went off straightaway to sign up. 'We were going to have fun, travel and adventure; we had no thoughts about what was going to happen... it turned out that we should have been paying more attention.' Sy Kahn saw it as 'a great adventure. I came to the conclusion that wars were good for poor people, because it gave them an opportunity to travel.' Lester Tenney had already done some travelling: he was in the US army in the Philippines and saw the Japanese destroying the American air force on Clark Field just hours after the attack on Pearl Harbor: 'We had no idea that this war would ever go on. We figured a week or two weeks and it would be over.'

The widespread expectation that America would triumph quickly was built on the back of ignorance and prejudice. One of the very few to realize the extent of American racism at the time was Beate Sirota. Born in Vienna of Russian Jewish parentage, Beate moved at the age of five with her family to Japan where her father, the renowned pianist Leo Sirota, taught at the Imperial Academy of Music. She lived in Japan for ten years before going on to the United States for her college education. She can still remember her first impression of the Japanese: 'I looked around and I saw all these people with black hair and black eyes and I said to my mother, are they all brothers and sisters?' By the time she left Tokyo she had a far better understanding than most outsiders could ever hope to have of Japan. She now saw its people as civilized individuals, not clones. But in America she encountered the same ignorance that she had displayed as a young child. Beate Sirota felt that most Americans saw 'the Japanese as a primitive people who knew nothing... they practically thought that the Japanese were living in trees. They didn't realize at all that this was a very cultured country.'

Such preconceptions were based on deep-rooted popular belief in white superiority over all other races. During the war these views were reinforced and manipulated by extensive anti-Japanese propaganda. Studs Terkel lived through the war on the home front, worked in radio, honing powers of observation that would make him America's leading oral historian. He saw the Japanese portrayed as 'subhuman, different and slanty-eyed'. Their cultural homogeneity was perverted to present them as monotone and mindless, all alike and all the enemy. This was particularly clear in cartoons of the time: 'The Germans were ridiculed, Hitler especially, and Mussolini with his jutting jaw, but in the Japanese case it was tribal, it was collective... you know: the grin, the slanty eyes, the glasses, the Jap, or the Nip.'

Allied definitions of the Japanese zigzagged between extremes: before Pearl Harbor they were written off as short-sighted, ill-equipped buffoons. Then they became treacherous supermen – unbeatable in their natural simian environment: the jungle. Next – after the battles of Midway, Guadalcanal and Kokoda and such horrors as the Bataan death march – they would be instantly redefined as beatable, but morbid, sadistic monsters. Throughout this propagandistic slalom, one factor remained constant: the Japanese were seen in terms of race. They behaved the way they did because they were Japanese. There were no 'good Japanese' as there were 'good Germans', and the only good Japanese, Admiral Halsey observed, was one that had been dead six months.

Studs Terkel watched these ideas take root in wartime USA: 'It was easy to hate someone who in addition to being your enemy militarily was also different racially. I think in all societies, as a group, you hate someone that's different from you [as] the dominant people of the society.' Racial hatred became an American weapon of war.

The Japanese were routinely presented in print, speech and cartoons as animals, lesser men or vermin. The use of these images helped spread and maintain a view of the enemy as subhuman. Cartoons frequently portrayed the Japanese en masse as monkeys, rats and vultures. When portrayed collectively by a single creature, the most common choices were the ape, monkey, viper or octopus. Examples of such work include the *Time* magazine cover of 26 January 1942, depicting the Japanese invasion of the Dutch East Indies as an ape-man hanging from a tree over the island. The *New York Times* in March that year used a similar image of a monkey dangling by its tail, holding a bunch of coconuts with one hand and reaching for more with the other: representing Japan's attempts to expand its empire to include Australia and India. Japan's invasion of British Malaya was depicted in *Punch* in January 1942 with a drawing of monkeys, with helmets and machine-guns, swinging through the jungle.

One of the more obvious forms of anti-Japanese propaganda was the 'spoof' Japanese hunting licence. There were many versions, but just one theme: the Japanese are pestilent animals who must be killed. One licence entitles the bearer 'to hunt or trap any yellow Japanese slant eyed rat' and goes on to state 'No bag limit, no closed season'. Another declares 'Open season for that vile stinking viper known as Jap snake' and is accompanied by the warning: 'Do not turn your back as this animal is noted for back stabbing'. Licences are also marked 'No Yellow Belly Japs', 'Bag limit: Tokyo' and 'Viper Exterminating Society'. Anti-Japanese paraphernalia included badges, T-shirts, pens and car stickers – all with racist slogans. One particular brand of matches had a slant-eyed soldier printed on each paper matchstick and the accompanying slogan 'Strike 'em Dead!'

Popular songs similarly denigrated and caricatured the Japanese. Examples include 'We're Gonna Have to Slap the Dirty Little Jap (and Uncle Sam's the Guy Who Can Do It)', 'You're a Sap, Mr Jap' and Frank Luther's 'Remember Pearl Harbor', from which the quote at the head of this chapter is taken. It managed to combine racism, revenge, hatred, mawkish sentiment and ringing patriotic fervour – and was a big hit.

Nancy Potter bears witness to the success of the propaganda:

The propaganda conducted... against the Japanese was much more insidious and much more successful than it had been against the Germans... It caricatured them in gross ways as a mass of teeth, as a mass of bayonets moving at one... who were threatening and frightening and who took no prisoners, who killed without provocation. They came, it seemed, almost in one size and one type, and we were able to lump them together. It was easy for the propaganda merchants... to turn us totally against Japan. We became completely and totally and unabashedly anti-Japanese.

Stigmatizing the Japanese because of their race had complex repercussions for minorities within the USA. Racial mistrust of the Japanese was officially sanctioned by the President on 19 February 1942 when Roosevelt signed Executive Order 9066 and authorized the internment of 'any or all' Japanese Americans. In the following months some 110,000 Japanese Americans were expelled from their homes in California, Oregon and Washington. Men, women and children of Japanese ancestry were considered enemies of the state. Without trial and without appeal they were removed from their livelihoods, their schools, their communities and put behind wire in the deserts of California, Nevada, Utah and Arizona.

The *Los Angeles Times* applauded the incarceration, writing in an editorial: 'a viper is nonetheless a viper wherever the egg is hatched – so a Japanese American, born of Japanese parents, grows up to be a Japanese not an American'. While the press used rhetoric to present the Japanese as bestial, the government used their new housing to make the same analogy. Japanese Americans from Washington State were lodged in converted pigpens, and in California they were forced into stables just hours after the horses were removed. Thousands were kept in these conditions for weeks and months before being taken to internment camps.

The man administering the purge was Lieutenant General John Dewitt, head of the Western Defense Command. In his view, Germans and Italians could be treated as individuals but 'a Jap's a Jap – it makes no difference whether he is an American citizen or not'. Testifying a year later before a congressional hearing as to why law-abiding Japanese Americans still could not return home, the argument was the same: 'A Jap's a Jap... we will be worried about [them] until they are wiped off the face of the map.'

Studs Terkel believes the incarceration was one of the most shameful periods in American history: 'There were different internment camps they were sent to and they called them relocation centres. We love euphemisms... A threat? They were so law-abiding it wasn't even funny. Was there a protest? I didn't, I'm ashamed to say. But it is astonishing, the lack of protest. It was obscene, and we accepted it.'

Ted Tsukiyama is an American of Japanese ancestry. His 'face, name and physical characteristics resembled that of the enemy but I was, and thought of myself, and acted as, an American'. Both his parents came from Japan but he was born in Hawaii, making him a second-generation descendant, or *nisei* in Japanese. His future wife and her family in the USA suffered the humiliation, economic loss and miserable disruption of internment camp. Ted and the other Japanese Americans in Hawaii were not interned, for the simple reason that there were too many of them. They made up 40 per cent of the total population and the island's economy could not have survived without them. Yet the way in which Ted Tsukiyama suffered speaks for many who found their devotion to America challenged on the basis of a racist assumptions about their 'real' loyalties.

At the start of the war Ted was in the Reserve Officer Training Corps at the University of Hawaii in Honolulu. Within an hour of the Pearl Harbor attack, he was in uniform and at the ROTC barracks. 'I responded to the call of our country. There was no other thought in mind but that our country has been attacked and I have to defend our country.' He was horrified that Japan was the aggressor but did not feel that his loyalties were divided. When he heard the devastating news that 'the enemy was Japan, the country my parents come from, the country of my ethnic racial ancestry, it was just a terrible, terrible realization'. But his reaction to the strike remained that of 'incredulous disbelief': 'Who do they think they are, that they can attack a great country like the US and try to get away with it?'

Although Ted's response was as patriotic as that of other Americans, he nevertheless quickly realized he was in a depressingly uncomfortable situation: 'There may have been a feeling of embarrassment maybe – I wouldn't say shame because we were guiltless, we had nothing to do with it. But yet the fact is that there is this racial linkage between us and the enemy. And I'm sure that every person of Japanese ancestry who at that moment of truth realized who the enemy is, that they must have had this terrible down feeling.'

With time, this became fear as he tried to weigh the consequences: 'What's going to happen to people of Japanese ancestry, especially people like our parents – we thought they were totally innocent and blameless.' Ted Tsukiyama soon had problems of his own. As the country readied itself for war and young men were lauded for signing up, he was kicked out of the cadets. The company was on the rifle range when their commander came over to announce that all men of Japanese ancestry were to be immediately discharged.

It was just like somebody had dropped a bomb in our midst, and to me this news was worse than the Pearl Harbor attack, because for the first time my ancestry is being held against me, it's being not only questioned or challenged, but they were rejecting us. In effect, you may be American, but you can't be trusted... because your name and your face are the same as the enemy... [My] feeling at that time was like the bottom of my world just dropped out. There's just no words that can really adequately and fully describe what kind of depth of despair that I experienced at that time.

No longer wanted in the fight against Japan, Ted Tsukiyama found himself in a struggle against racism: the 'battle of distrust and fear and suspicion at home, the battle against the mentality that a Jap's a Jap'.

The racism that Ted now faced was not new to Nelson Peery. A young black man from Minnesota, he had endured racism, segregation and discrimination since birth. But his labour and sweat were wanted by the US military. The army needed black men to dig and carry and unload ships, but was not at all comfortable with the idea of letting them fight. The problem was summed up by the phrase: 'Negroes with Guns'. It had several facets. Blacks given combat training would be better prepared for an armed struggle against whites. They would also learn how to be organized, how to give orders as well as take them. Dangerous stuff. But there was another worry, which went to the heart of a country's obligations to its fighting men: that black men willing to fight and die for America would demand equality on their return. If this was not freely granted, then their experience in the front lines might encourage them to fight for their rights. By then, fighting was something they would be rather good at.

A few blacks had rejoiced at news of Japan's early victories, relishing America's colonial losses and humiliations. Some saw the war as irrelevant to them; they had few rights in white America so

Successfully ambushing Pearl Harbor, but barely filming the event, Japan's propaganda machine had to re-enact the attack with models for cinema audiences.

For dive-bomber pilot Zenji Abe the Pearl Harbor strike 'felt like a breakthrough, a victory from the frustrating ambiguous path we had been pursuing'.

The aftermath of Japan's 'unprovoked and dastardly attack': lined up like sitting ducks, eight US battleships were hit during the ambush.

In the first ever raid of its kind, sixteen B-25 bombers prepare for take off from a US aircraft carrier. Their mission – to bomb targets in Japan and avenge Pearl Harbor.

Navigator Chase Nielsen (left) was euphoric: 'the pilot and I were singing "I don't want to set the world on fire, we just want to start a little one in Tokyo".'

Lt Col. James Doolittle (below) under-scores the aim of revenge: he pins Rising Sun medals to the fin of a 500-lb bomb, then scrawls 'Returned with interest' down the side.

Allied soldiers on the Bataan death march. Between 5,000 and 10,000 men died after surrender on this 65-mile march.

Death of a POW. One in three of all white Allied prisoners of war died during captivity.

Dick Gordon endured the Bataan death march, a torpedo attack on his POW 'hell ship', and almost three years of slave labour in Japan.

First published in *Life* magazine this photograph reveals the pervasiveness of America's race hatred of the Japanese. The original caption reads: 'Arizona war worker writes her Navy boyfriend a thank you note for the Jap skull he sent her.'

Australian military nurse Pat Darling survived shipwreck and captivity: 'We actually did envy the girls who... were massacred. We thought [they] were luckier than we because it was all over so quickly.'

The Imperial Army forced as many as 200,000 local Asians to become sex-slaves, calling them 'comfort women'. Few outlived the war.

American troops surrender the Malinta tunnel, Corregidor Island. With them the last Allied stronghold in Asia falls, May 1942.

US flame-throwers burn out an enemy position. 'As a flame-thrower man your life span is very, very short, ... You stick out like a sore thumb, [with] two tanks, and a Buck Rogers gun in your hand, they know what's coming' – Marine Steve Judd.

Dead Japanese soldiers on Guadalcanal.
The battle for the island raged for six bloody months.

A US camp on Guadalcanal. Marine Kerry Lane went on to fight in Korea and Vietnam but 'never experienced the conditions we had to endure on Guadalcanal'.

Christmas Day 1942, New Guinea. Raphael Oembari leads wounded
Australian Private George Whittington away from the front line.
Whittington died from his wounds a few days later.

The Kokoda Track – a tortuous jungle path fought over by Japanese and Australian troops. 'It was a war without rules... it was a case of kill or be killed.'

US Marines on Guadalcanal carry a wounded comrade away from the front. The war was fought in places that looked like paradise – and turned out to be hell.

why should they fight a war to defend the status quo? Others, like Nelson Peery, were vehemently opposed to the racism in America but recognized that the foe, particularly Nazi Germany, was far worse. Peery recalls that 'when the Germans declared themselves the master race of Europe it sounded the same to me as the American white saying that this is a white man's country, which they said over and over and over again'. He was 'not ready to fight for the segregation and brutality that we had known in America; on the other hand we recognized that if Germany won this war we were going to be in worse condition'.

What Nelson Peery – and many blacks in the army – wanted was a double victory: victory at home and abroad. They displayed this by means of a two-handed salute: the left hand raised in a 'V' meant triumph over 'the segregationists and the fascists in the United States'. The army soon responded by making it an offence, punishable by court martial, for any man to make such a gesture. There were also, Peery remembers, pressures exerted the other way: 'There was a very big push on the part of a certain section of the American political establishment to democratize the army. The army had become a southern army, and there was a lot of pressure in the north to recapture that army... and that would involve the development of equality within the army for the black soldiers.'

Some liberal politicians were struck, as were America's blacks, by the paradox of a country proclaiming its fight for democracy and freedom abroad, but denying both to a section of its own population at home. There were two more hard-headed factors: America could not afford to confine so many men to solely rear-echelon tasks. And America could not afford to have large numbers of whites die in combat, leaving vast numbers of young blacks back home, alive and kicking.

In the end, both African Americans and Americans of Japanese ancestry went into combat and fought with great distinction. The latter provided the most heavily decorated American unit of the Second World War. Nelson Peery recalls with laughter his own journey in 1943 to the Pacific:

There were about 7,000 of us on this one ship, the Lurline, *and [she] was such a fast ship that they decided that it would go unescorted to Guadalcanal, and so it took us twenty-one days to go from San Francisco to Guadalcanal, zigzagging across the Pacific, and every one of those black soldiers was absolutely convinced that we were running without escort so that the Japanese could sink us and get rid of us.*

Three thousand miles of ocean and heavy censorship spared American civilians the immediate horror and indescribable carnage of the fighting in the Pacific. For the first two years of the war, no shots of dead Americans were shown on the newsreels. The bodies of the enemy on the beach at Guadalcanal were acceptable – they were, after all, dead Japanese. In November 1943, Norman Hatch was one of a handful of combat cameraman on Tarawa who filmed dead US marines floating in the sea and lying on the beach. He remembers the debate that took place at the highest level about whether to show these images to the American public:

Apparently there was some slippage in some of the defence work that was going on; people were a little too comfortable back here in the United States and so the question was sort of brought up to the President, whether or not he should release this Tarawa film... he wanted to send sort of a jolt to the public and say hey look, what you're doing here is in support of these guys that are dying like this over there, and I think it had a very serious effect on the home public.

The effect was not perhaps entirely what the President wanted: the sale of War Bonds was boosted, but Marine recruitment fell by 35 per cent. Control of what was shown, and when, remained tight throughout the war. Not until 1945 did *Life* magazine show American blood being shed. Shots of men with shell shock – the '2,000 yard stare', as it was known in the Pacific – and images of mutilated or broken American bodies were withheld during the course of the war. Japanese atrocities such as the Bataan death march and such crimes as the execution of downed American airmen were not made public until long after the event. They then became material for proving how alien the enemy was and intensifying civilian hatred for him.

As the public was exposed to more and more of the war's horrors, in the press and at the movies, a process of national desensitization took place which now seems morbidly grotesque. *Life* magazine carried a photograph of twenty-year-old Natalie Nickerson gazing at a skull sent her by her fiancé; newspapers talked of Japanese ears being nailed on to American front doors; letter openers carved from thigh bones became treasured souvenirs. The kind of objects which would in 1945 be regarded as proof of the Nazis' bestiality became a bridge, for some, between the Pacific battlefront and the American mantelpiece. They seemed to symbolize the lengths to which the whole nation was prepared to go, together.

Nancy Potter knew that Americans were collecting Japanese skulls and personal, intimate items such as photographs of loved ones. She finds it hard, even now, to be judgmental, given the American soldiers' age and the nature of the war they were fighting.

I look back at it from the perspective of an older person, and I'm trying to remember how seventeen- and eighteen- and nineteen-year-olds felt about a life and death struggle, a struggle in which they were fighting against a people for whom they had no sympathy at all, and no reason to have any kind of decorous concern, so they are not going to be gentle and sweet and kind. When I was an older woman and I did see an ear brought back from Vietnam by one of my students. I was probably shocked at that point, but not entirely because I could remember what it was like being eighteen.

Not everyone was so understanding. Beate Sirota received a letter from a young Marine she had dated just before he was sent to Saipan. He wrote to her to ask 'whether I'd like to have a necklace made out of the teeth of Japanese corpses... and I was terribly shocked and surprised that someone that I'd gone out with could even think... of such a thing... And so I did not even answer the letter.'

She was in good company. President Roosevelt declined the gift of a letter opener made out of Japanese bone. Yet British singer Vera Lynn, the 'Forces' Sweetheart', was not squeamish when she was given a keepsake on her trip to entertain the troops on the India–Burma border in 1944:

> I think they are important, souvenirs. I mean, you don't really always need these things to make you remember, but they do bring the situation vividly back in your mind. Like one day I inadvertently walked into a little tent [and]... discovered that it was an operating room. I very quickly said, 'I beg your pardon, I'm sorry,' and hastily went out another door, for the surgeon to follow me out and say, 'I thought you might like this as a souvenir,' and he gave me the bullet that he had just taken out of this boy... He said, 'I apologize, it is a bit messy,' but I've still got that bullet.

Movie audiences at home witnessed the machine-gunning of Japanese soldiers bobbing in life rafts out at sea. The attacks were carried out by American and Australian pilots following the destruction of a fleet of troop transports heading for New Guinea on 2 and 3 March 1943. The audiences were treated to dramatic footage, filmed from the cockpit past the pilot's head, of the planes going into action against the survivors. The commentary is even more explicit than the pictures:

> ...the fun begins... the lads will do a great shooting up job on ships and barges crammed with Jap soldiers seeking escape... there's trouble brewing for Tojo today, all right... The Nips have had this coming to them for a long, long time. There they are! Those American bomber boys certainly know their stuff. Let 'em have it, buddy! This is it, boys, give her the gun. Here we go!... The convoy carried 15,000 Jap troops... there's plenty of them left in barges and lifeboats dotted over the sea. There's a boat! Tiny speck, centre screen... Miss! One tiny boat in a wide sea isn't so easy to hit! Bullseye! and more Japs meet their ancestors. The show's over, boys...

As John Dower has noted in *War without Mercy*, this operation was criticized in a letter published in *Time* magazine, describing the attack as a 'cold-blooded slaughter'. The lone voice of dissent was not supported by other letter writers and instead solicited a flurry of correspondence in support of the killings.

The practical, as well as moral, support given by the American public to the military was crucial. Less than a month after Pearl Harbor, Roosevelt had committed the US to the largest armaments production effort the world had ever seen. He announced in his January 1942 State of the Union address plans to produce 45,000 aircraft, 45,000 tanks, 20,000 anti-aircraft guns and 8 million tons of new shipping in the coming year. America would outbuild and outfight the enemy. Her military might was based on vast industrial capacity. By mobilizing huge sections of the populace that had previously been excluded from the workforce, notably women and blacks, industrial output was increased by 15 per cent a year during the war. The propaganda campaign featuring the wholesome, hard-working fictional character of Rosie the Riveter helped propel 6 million women into factories and construction yards.

On the West Coast, shipyards started to roll out prefabricated mass-produced Liberty ships as if they were cars. The 10,000-ton standardized vessels took six months to build at the start of the war, but in less than a year were being completed in under a month. In a publicity stunt, the Liberty ship *Robert E. Peary* was launched with her paint still wet just five days after keel-laying. The overall result of civilian effort and investment was an incredible doubling of GNP from 1940 to 1945, and the establishment of America as the economic dynamo of the world by the end of the war.

Although rationing was never on a par with that in England, the American war production board banned the manufacture of some 300 consumer items in early 1942. Toothpaste tubes, beer cans and automobiles were taken out of civilians' reach almost immediately; later, sugar, coffee and meat supplies were restricted. Nancy Potter remembers it as a time of unique national commitment: 'It was a tremendously intense involvement which I have never felt afterward in terms of the solidarity of the nation. There was an incredible effort that pulled this country rapidly from a dozing depression-ridden, rather rural and somewhat isolationist economy into an intensity that has never been duplicated.'

In high school by day, she was a volunteer at night in a Boston hospital. She served as blackout warden for her residents' hall, turned down the thermostats on the college radiators and promoted 'meal-less meals' to save money for orphans. Several of her girl friends left school at three in the afternoon and worked an eight-hour shift until eleven at night in factories. It was a time of tireless work and turbulent emotions. Young people, even half a world away from the front, lived close to death. Nancy Potter will never forget a friend swallowed up in the bloodbath of Iwo Jima:

I remember him as if it were yesterday, in a high-school sweater with our school letter over the front of it... I remember coming in from lunch and there was a letter from my mother with the death notice in it. It was under my door in the residents' hall, and I remember that I was going to go out immediately after and attend a class, probably in Renaissance drama. I'm trying to figure out why we were studying Renaissance drama when people were dropping off like this.

The sacrifice of life was huge and seemed without end. As we will see later, instead of the Japanese war effort tailing off, they seemed to fight with ever wilder persistence. The closer that American forces got to Japan, the less likely it looked that the Japanese would lie down and roll over. The prevailing mood was that the war must be brought to a rapid conclusion – whatever the cost to the enemy. The stage was set for the world's first use of nuclear weapons.

It was a measure of the potency of the nation's hatred for Japan that many Americans thought it a shame that Japan surrendered so soon after Hiroshima and Nagasaki were reduced to dust, and before more such bombs could be unleashed on them.

6

RETURNED WITH INTEREST

It was a sweet revenge, and of all things it was an ambush. An ambush is a dirty term anyway, but we did to the Japanese just what they had done to us: we ambushed them. It was wonderful.
RICHARD BEST, dive bomber pilot at the Battle of Midway

JAPAN'S SWEEPING VICTORIES IN ASIA had left the Allies with almost no toe-hold in the Pacific, tens of thousands dead, several hundred thousand men and women behind barbed wire and an overwhelming sense of humiliation. It was, Churchill said, 'a cataract of disaster'. In fighting spirit, technical prowess and sheer audacity, the Japanese had proved themselves the masters by March 1942. Perhaps their propaganda was right after all: perhaps America and Britain *were* fatefully soft.

Yet Japan's triumph had masked the extent to which she had gone into war without a unified plan. Her ruling elites, military and civil, had no single answer to the question: what do you do after you suddenly find yourself ruling a slice of the world? How do you hold it? What kind of war industry, logistical infrastructure, supply delivery systems will you need? Will it be an empire held by force or in collusion with its far-flung, disparate peoples? The lack of coherent vision reflected a surprisingly fragmented power structure. Despite her increasing totalitarianism, war had imposed no real unity on the governance of Japan. As historian Akira Iriye has noted, 'The country lacked a powerful, political force exercising leadership, articulating new ideals, and putting them into effect.'

Japan's early successes had blinded the nation to her own unpreparedness, both material and philosophical. They had also bred longer-term danger. Some called it 'victory disease': early wins endorsed Japanese belief in their innate superiority, their natural invincibility. The Japanese did not need to think about conventional planning, strategy and support – even to worry about these practicalities could be construed as defeatism. It was their destiny to become *Sekai Dai Ichi* – first in the world – thanks to *Nihon Seishin* – Japan's innate spirit. Japan's victories had elevated abstract self-faith over dull realities, whereas defeat had plunged America and Britain into fundamental reconsideration of the need for new ways of fighting, innovative weapons, fresh thinking about strategy and supply.

The result was that over the following twelve months the Allies mounted a series of tightly focused operations from carriers (Doolittle's Tokyo Raid and Midway) and on islands (Guadalcanal and New Guinea), which ate at the foundations of Japanese assumptions. These initiatives forced Japan to reassess the war they were fighting and changed the course of history.

The first strikes at Japan were not triggered by solely military agendas. Raw emotion also impelled Allied action in 1942. The American public wanted a general turnaround of national fortunes and specific revenge for Pearl Harbor. Roosevelt desperately needed a propaganda coup in the Pacific to boost American morale and take the war to the Japanese people. At meetings with his military chiefs he regularly asked when it would be possible to hit back. He got his answer in April 1942. By chance, there was a new plane in the US arsenal just small enough to take off from a carrier, just big enough to carry the necessary bombs and fuel. The Doolittle Raid was born.

On paper the mission looked almost suicidal, but specialist pilot Lieutenant Colonel James Doolittle, who led the team, was convinced it could work. Sixteen B-25 bombers would take off from an aircraft carrier as close to Japan as possible; undetected and unescorted, they would fly to their targets, make their bombing runs and then escape over Japan to land in eastern China, which was in pro-Allied Nationalist hands. The plan relied on advanced technology, surprise and fierce fighting spirit; it could almost have been a Japanese operation. Given the risks involved, there would not be another raid against the home islands of Japan for two and a half years. It would be 'volunteers only'. One of the volunteers was navigator Chase Nielsen.

We didn't really know what the mission consisted of, but it was a chance to get into combat... The next day, after we'd sailed out into the Golden Gate and we were far enough out, I guess, so people on the shore couldn't hear the bull horn, we were told this flight is bound for Tokyo. And then there was a big hooray went up. And then about the first thing the pilots did, well, they decided if we're gonna go bomb Tokyo I want to bomb the Palace.

Doolittle heard that the pilots were cutting cards for the right to flatten the Palace – and went ballistic. He issued a formal order: 'Whatever you do, stay away from the Imperial Palace... Bombing military targets is an act of strategic warfare but hitting the "Temple of Heaven" or non-military targets such as hospitals or schools would be interpreted as an inexcusably barbarian act. It could mean your life if you are captured.' Given that US long-range planning was predicated on retaining the Emperor, it is possible that Doolittle was thinking as much about a specific order from Washington as about the fate of his men. The operation had other aims, as Chase Nielsen recalls:

We knew that we weren't gonna do any material damage, we didn't have enough bombs on board to do that. We didn't have enough aircraft to do it. But the idea was really... to deface or downgrade the morale of the Japanese and show them that they were vulnerable, that they might stop their steamroller drive down through the Pacific and take some of that equipment back to Japan for home defence. And, yeah, we were a bunch of egos – we wanted revenge.

On the deck of the aircraft carrier *Hornet*, watched by his eighty men, Doolittle ceremonially endorsed the motive of vengeance by pinning Rising Sun medals (donated by a former naval attaché in Tokyo) to the tail fins of a 500-pound bomb and scrawling 'returned with interest' along the side. However, as the log of the *Hornet* shows, the plans for delivering that bomb were dramatically brought forward:

07:45   *All hands to battle stations. Sighted enemy ships on*
        horizon
08:05   USS Nashville *open [sic] fire on enemy patrol boat*
08:07   *Prepared to launch planes*
08:15   *First army bomber left ship*

Launching 400 miles off the coast of Japan would have given
the B-25s a good chance of making it to friendly China. A picket
line of Japanese fishing boats at 700 miles destroyed all margins of
safety. The *Hornet* edged a few precious miles closer while crews
scrambled, and planes and destroyers raced to sink the enemy
lookouts before they could radio home. Tom Cheek was flying an
F4F Wildcat fighter plane: 'We spotted this little ship bobbing
along. The sea was extremely rough that day, and we had seas that
were running 30, 35 feet high, and it was just like a little cork
bouncing around down there. And we peeled over and strafed it.
And at the end of two runs from the four fighters, the ship was
visibly sinking. We'd holed it that much.'

Rod Steiger remembers his destroyer bearing down on
a sampan:

That I will never forget or feel good about, until the day I die. I
watched, I wasn't shooting, but I watched as the 40 millimetres hit
them, and the women screaming and the children running around
and the men, until they were sunk... they are shooting at these
defenceless people, and inside of your mind you think what the hell
happened to the ten commandments. You know what I mean?
We're not supposed to do this to one another.

In fact the Japanese knew a large fleet was approaching. They
had been eavesdropping on radio traffic between the two aircraft
carriers, but assumed the *Hornet* was carrying single-engine short-
range naval aircraft as usual – not twin-engined bombers. A
Japanese intelligence officer later recalled, 'Even if we had known
it, we would not have believed that they [could] fly from the
carrier's deck. That would have been impossible in our view at
that time.'

It seemed a little impossible to the sixteen aircrews lined up on
the pitching deck of the *Hornet* which stretched such a daunt-

ingly short distance in front of their rain-battered windscreens. In fact the storm came to their aid, giving the planes 55 miles per hour airspeed before moving an inch. Chase Nielsen will never forget the next moments:

It wasn't really a good day to fly... The navy men... were trying to help us get to our aeroplane and get on board before we got blown overboard... We watched the flag-man off to the side, rolled the engines up as high as they'd go, it felt like they were gonna shake the whole aeroplane apart, and finally he dropped to the deck and gave you the forward motion, and we started to roll, and there was no problem. The next thing we knew, we were in the air.

After that, getting to his target was easy. Nielsen just tuned his radio direction finder into Radio Tokyo and flew down the beam all the way. Even though one of the Japanese fishing boats managed to send back a warning, preconceptions about American 'softness' seemed to have worked in Doolittle's favour: it never occurred to the Japanese that their enemy would dare bomb them – even if they could. 'There was no doubt about it... it was a total surprise,' Chase Nielsen remembers. 'The Japanese were out working in their rice-paddies, and even had their water-buffalo out there, and they'd take off their hats and wave at you as you flew overhead.' When they dropped their bombs on a Tokyo steel mill, Chase and the rest of the crew were elated: 'I think the pilot and I were singing "I don't want to set the world on fire, we just want to start a little one in Tokyo".'

In a telling echo of the Pearl Harbor eyewitnesses, Japanese journalist Kay Tateishi watched two of the Doolittle Raiders swoop overhead and leapt to the same conclusion that so many had done a few months before in Hawaii: 'It looked like some daring manoeuvre. A commuter nearby said, "It looks real, doesn't it? Just like a foreign aircraft breaking through Japanese air defences. I guess the imperial forces want to impress the people that they are fully prepared." Then the planes released their bombs and the people became frightened. Someone shouted, "Hey, that's real enemy bombing!"'

The Japanese death toll amounted to well over fifty people, including children at play and patients in a hospital. The surprise attack was naturally fiercely condemned. Japanese newspaper editors reached for the same lexicon of outraged disgust used by their American counterparts on 8 December 1941. The *Asahi Shimbun* headline read 'Enemy Devils Strafe Schoolyard' and called it: 'an inhuman, indiscriminate bombing attack on the sly'. Other papers reported the raid as 'bestial', 'crazed' and 'evil'.

The Doolittle Raiders had bombed four cities – Tokyo, Yokohama, Nagoya and Kobe – and the Yokosuka naval base, and headed for China. Then they paid the penalty for launching early: the planes had to fly much further than planned – making up distance in the air, not riding on the deck of the *Hornet*. One after another, the bombers ran out of fuel. A single plane managed to land in Russia, where the crew was interned before escaping to Iran. Eleven were abandoned in flight, their crews bailing out. Four planes crash-landed or ditched off the Chinese coast. Three men died and eight, including Chase Nielsen, were captured by the Japanese. The Japanese executed two pilots and a machine-gunner, Harold Spaatz. Before he was put in front of the firing-squad, Spaatz managed to talk to Chase, giving him a clue as to why he had been condemned to death: 'He told us, he said, "In my interrogation they asked me if I had used my machine-guns," and he said, "I told them, yes, and if I ever got another chance, I'd do it again." So he signed his own death warrant.'

Seventy men, including James Doolittle, had made it to safety, relayed from village to village and across mountains by pro-Allies Chinese peasants and soldiers. Perhaps a quarter of a million peasants paid the price for this over the following weeks, as the Chinese Nationalist leader Chiang Kai-shek informed the United States by telegram: 'Japanese troops attacked the coastal areas of China where many of the fliers had landed. These Japanese troops slaughtered every man, woman and child in these areas – let me repeat – these Japanese troops slaughtered every man, woman and child in those [sic] areas.'

In America, the Doolittle Raid had the effect Roosevelt desired. The audacious and, above all, victorious attack lifted flagging morale. The raid also had enormous repercussions on Japanese strategic thinking. A fierce debate had been raging as to whether to advance south into New Guinea and the Solomons or concentrate on smashing the American fleet once and for all. The

Doolittle Raid played into the hands of those urging decisive action, and Admiral Isoroku Yamamoto – mastermind of the attack on Pearl Harbor – was given the go-ahead for a massive and complex operation to lure the US Pacific fleet to its destruction. Other Japanese operations did go ahead too, although on a rapid timetable: notably an attempt to land at Port Moresby on the Papuan Peninsula of New Guinea (foiled by the naval battle of the Coral Sea) and the move to establish a base on the Solomon Islands. But these moves played second fiddle to Yamamoto's gamble at Midway. He knew that the longer the war went on, the more vulnerable Japan would become. He had lived in America and knew time was running out before its industrial might kicked in. Better, he thought, to force America to the negotiating table before the problems Japan really faced caught up with her.

Yamamoto designed a trap to take the Midway Islands – two tiny coral patches dead in the centre of the Pacific and a key US outpost. A decoy attack on the Aleutian Islands would force the Americans to split their resources. The American fleet racing to Midway's defence would be pounced on by a lurking Japanese armada that included no fewer than four aircraft carriers and the biggest battleship in the world, the 64,000-ton *Yamato*. Japanese intelligence myopically ignored the lessons of the Doolittle Raid and complacently reported that Americans 'lack the will to fight'. The results of Japanese war games conducted during planning for the Battle of Midway were skewed to give Japan victory. Victory disease had struck again.

There was a further, decisive, problem in store for Yamamoto: the Americans had cracked the Japanese code, and knew the whole plan in advance. Everything, that is, except for the target itself. They only knew that as 'AF'. Code-breaker Lieutenant Commander Joseph Rochefort had a hunch that AF signified Midway. He came up with a simple ruse to verify it. The garrison commander on the island was instructed, by secure cable, to put out an emergency radio call in plain English that the base's water distillation plant had broken down. Less than twenty-four hours later, listening posts intercepted Japanese signals reporting AF short of water and ordering the invasion force to take extra supplies. The next day not only was the Commander of the Pacific Fleet, Admiral Chester Nimitz, told to expect an attack on

Midway, he was given an accurate Japanese order of battle. Nimitz immediately set about planning the operation that would rob the Imperial Navy of its Pacific supremacy.

In the days that followed, Japan's navy led a sophisticated and elegant dance, choreographed to lure the US Pacific Fleet into their trap. Meanwhile a hastily assembled US task force slipped secretly into position off Midway. In a squadron briefing, dive bomber pilot Dick Best had been told the moves the Japanese were going to make and watched in glee as they duly unfolded and the prospect of a reverse ambush became a reality: 'It was lovely, it was the scenario that we were writing. We were going to hatchet them. The Japanese was going to come waltzing in the garden gate with a flower in his hand and we were going to be behind the gate with an axe. We were going to goddam well cut his head off.'

The Japanese fleet off Midway initially failed to detect the presence of America's navy and launched their planned air-strikes against the island base. They caused heavy damage but Midway's runway was still intact. The Japanese planes returned to their carriers for refuelling and rearming, intending a second strike. Then Admiral Chuichi Nagumo learned of American ships within striking range. The second attack on Midway was suspended; Nagumo ordered a switch of armaments to attack ships rather than land targets. In the ensuing haste, safety precautions were abandoned; open fuel lines, ammunition and high explosives littered the carriers' decks. The US task force bore down on the Japanese fleet but several US aircraft attacks were beaten off with nearly total losses. With the Japanese scenting victory, there came a dramatic reversal of fortune.

American Dauntless dive bombers, searching the vast expanses of the Pacific and almost out of fuel, spotted the three Japanese carriers. It was the chance Dick Best had been praying for: 'All the way down there wasn't a gun turned on me, nobody saw me coming... I pulled up and saw the first hit... There was a solid column of smoke from bow to stern, at least 200 feet high above her... it must have been an inferno below deck... A carrier under destruction. I can see it in my mind right now, the most impressive sight of the day.'

Another pilot saw the same view, but with very different emotions. Pilot Iyozo Fujita, veteran of the Pearl Harbor attack, was attacking US torpedo-bombers when his Zero fighter was struck by ack-ack:

The tank was hit and the plane caught fire so I jumped. I had to parachute from dangerously low down, but I survived. The parachute opened with a bang and I hurtled to sea. When I looked around, I saw three pillars of smoke far away. I later learned that our three aircraft carriers, Akagi, Kaga and Soryu, had been destroyed... I thought it was all over. We had no carriers to counter attack. There was nothing we could do.

Dick Best's day got better and better. In the afternoon he and his colleagues found and sank the fourth carrier, *Hiryu*. 'I have never been as exhilarated in my life... That was a good day. It was the best of good days.' It wasn't all good news for the Americans; the carrier *Yorktown* was sunk, 147 aircraft were lost (thirty-eight based on Midway), and 362 men perished. Yet the 3,500 Japanese deaths had an importance beyond their numbers: Japan had lost 385 aircraft and many of her experienced pilots. Yamamoto's gamble had failed. The most decisive single naval battle in US history was also Japan's first major defeat at sea for 350 years. It marked the end of Japanese naval dominance in the Pacific. Army Chief of Staff General George C. Marshall described it as 'the closest squeak and the greatest victory'.

THE END OF JAPANESE NAVAL DOMINANCE did not mean the US now ruled the seas and skies. A dangerous period of semi-parity ensued, during which America launched her momentous bid to claw back land from the Japanese. They chose an obscure island in the Solomon group, 1,100 miles off the north-east coast of Australia: Guadalcanal. The war was to be studded with examples of tiny islands suddenly deemed vital because they had a deep-water inlet that could provide safe anchorage, or an area that could be levelled for an airstrip. Guadalcanal had a runway almost completed by the Japanese, which would be finished by the Marines, then wrangled over for six bloody months.

It was Guadalcanal's position on the Allied life-line to Australia that put it on the war-planners' maps. Australia was the Allies' key supply, logistics and assembly point in the southern Pacific. Japan needed bases from which to interdict America's build-up of men and matériel, and extend and consolidate their hold on the Solomons and New Guinea. The Japanese saw Guadalcanal as 'the fork in the road which leads to victory for them or us'. It had another feature it would share with those other patches of volcanic ash or coral which, overnight, became so precious that men died in droves for them. It looked like paradise, and turned out to be hell.

The landing was easy. Nothing else was. Older Marine sergeants, heavily decorated in previous conflicts and an inspiration in training to their men, faltered in the heat and humidity and had to be retired off the line. Marine hero Kerry Lane was a sergeant at seventeen. He is able to make a comparison denied to most: 'It was the most difficult time in my life. Although I fought in two other wars [Korea and Vietnam] I never experienced the conditions we had to endure on Guadalcanal.' Everything about the experience was alien. Everything had to be learned.

The weird noise is the first thing I remember about the jungle... The birds sounded like dogs barking... and the men were jittery initially when they first got there, they were shooting at everything that moved, but I finally convinced my squad that we didn't have much ammunition, they couldn't waste any. I even emphasized the fact you had better start sharpening your bayonets...

The shortage of ammunition – and everything else – was a result of the continued presence and strength of the Japanese navy. Two days after the landings of 7 August 1942, the US fleet, fearful of a Japanese counter-attack, pulled out. The Marines watched first carriers, then transports and escorts vanish over the horizon. They had been abandoned, and now had to endure incessant shelling and bombing by the Japanese. 'Any amphibious operation must have air and sea support... it was a terrible feeling to think that we were on that island with no support,' recalls Kerry Lane. Some Marines wondered if they faced a repeat of Bataan.

It would have been unpleasant enough with just the jungle and swamps and hunger and malaria. But there were also the Japanese. According to Kerry Lane, 'They were the greatest fighters in the world... they were ferocious fighters, and they were skilled, they were masters of their weaponry... they were terrific jungle fighters.' The Marines had to acquire a new range of skills to combat them: 'General Vandegrift [said] we will have to throw away the rule book and learn to fight the enemy on their own ground, on their own turf, with their own tactics, man to man in the jungle... hand to hand combat, in order to defeat them.'

Hard fighting against tough enemies in hostile environments was what being a Marine was all about, but the Japanese possessed lethal qualities that modified a crucial element in the soldiers' outlook: respect for his enemy. The Japanese fought as if willing to die, showed scant regard for the rights of the wounded and prisoners, and many were morbidly devious. Some Marines had prior warning of this. The American journalist Richard Tregaskis accompanied the task force, and in 1942 published a best-selling account: *Guadalcanal Diary*. In his strolls around the deck, Tregaskis notes the lads' concern that the enemy might play dead, and observes the men being given specific 'dirty trick' warnings: '"You might see a Jap sniper hanging from the top of a tree, lookin' dead," the lieutenant continued, "because they tie themselves in with ropes. He might be playin' possum. So don't hesitate to throw another 0.30 [bullet] up there, bounce him off the tree again. That's good stuff."'

Few were prepared for the variety of Japanese ruses, and many of those who experienced them were inevitably unable to pass back a warning. Kerry Lane lost several men through tricks that were predicated on what seemed to the Americans to be an alien valuation of life: 'You would think they were all dead and they would lay there in the sand and when the Marines would walk by they would jump up and stab them with a rifle or throw a grenade. Of course they would end up killing themselves too, but they would take some Marines with them.'

Six days into the campaign, a group of some twenty Marines under Colonel Frank B. Goettge went up the coast on a mercy mission to bring in a group of starving and wounded Japanese believed to be willing to surrender. When they reached the beach, the Japanese ambushed them. All but three Marines were killed. The last man to escape, Sergeant Frank L. Few, looked back as he swam away to see the Japanese mutilating the dead: 'The Japs closed in and hacked up our people. I could see swords flashing in the sun.'

The fate of the Goettge Patrol was used as the Marines' personal Pearl Harbor: a cautionary tale of vicious treachery. It was passed on to recruits such as Eugene Sledge when he joined a year later: 'This was a humanitarian effort supposedly, and this was the Japanese way of responding to it, and so from then on it was just this intense hatred on the part of the Marine Corps toward Japanese... the mentality became the only good Jap is a dead Jap.'

Yet even before the Goettge Patrol, Richard Tregaskis had seen raw troops on their way to Guadalcanal sharpening bayonets and talking of collecting Japanese body parts as souvenirs. Perhaps the spiral into a war without pity was inevitable; the result of bitter, bloody encounters between charged-up teenagers in fearsome conditions on remote islands, a very long way from Geneva. Certainly, the Marines stopped giving their enemy any benefit of the doubt on Guadalcanal. You could not treat a prisoner as a non-combatant, if he did not share your definition. Kerry Lane was not taking any chances: 'I knew that they weren't going to take any prisoners because they didn't offer any first aid or any assistance or anything else... I didn't intend to... take them for prisoners because it was kill or be killed, and they were trying to kill me and in order for me to survive, I had to kill them.'

Ace pilot Joe Foss operated out of Henderson Field on Guadalcanal. He saw for himself the gulf between American and Japanese attitudes to defeat. A colleague and a Japanese pilot were both forced to bail out over the Pacific after a dogfight in which they shot down each other's plane. The American found himself bobbing about near the Japanese pilot when the US Navy rescue boat showed up, with Joe Foss along for the ride. He saw the Japanese gesture to the sailors to pick up the American pilot first.

Conger just thought this is great, that guy is really a sportsman in this. Here I've knocked him down and he wants to have me picked up first before the sharks get me and all, and so when they came back, old Conger... extended his hand, and of course the guy had his hand gun there and he pulled it out, stuck it right between Conger's eyes and pulled the trigger, and it just went click, this gun didn't go off. So he cocked it again and put it to his own head and it just went click.

The Americans knocked the Japanese pilot out with a boat-hook and packed him off to prison camp. There is a warming postscript to the story. Fifty years after the war, retired Flying Officer Ishikawa tracked down retired Major Conger at a reunion in Texas and shook hands with him – whereupon Major Conger took him off for a round of golf.

The issues the Marines faced in the ground-breaking battle for Guadalcanal would decide the island war. Joe Foss realized the extent to which they were interlinked: 'What we were interested in and what paid off, was that very few [Japanese] supplies ever got to the island – we sunk them all... and of course the poor guys that were there fighting at Guadalcanal didn't have medicine, didn't have food, they were just out of luck, and as a result they couldn't fight as well.'

It would come down to two big questions: who were the better fighters and who had mastery of supply-lines. As the Japanese learned, you could make no lasting claim to be the former unless you could secure the latter.

A fortnight before the Marines hit the beach at Guadalcanal, the Japanese had landed in Papua. Australia viewed Japanese advances across Asia and the Pacific with horror. The fall of Singapore was described by the Australian Prime Minister John Curtin as 'Australia's Dunkirk'. Various Australian writers and politicians have accused Britain of betrayal, of failing to protect Australia from Japan while selfishly trying to hold on to Australian troops in the Middle East. Certainly Britain had given Australia glib and misleading reassurances about its defences in the East, but more out of self-delusion than wilful deceit.

Bert Ward was one of those Australian soldiers, or Diggers, in the Middle East. He then spent six weeks on a troopship criss-crossing the Indian Ocean. His Homeric wanderings mirrored the course of the argument batted to and fro between Churchill and Curtin as to whether Singapore or Rangoon or Fremantle should be his regiment's final destination. Ward talks not of blame, but of simply wanting to defend his homeland: 'We would have been prepared to fight anywhere, we were all volunteers, but the score was that Australia was apparently under such a dire threat that it was quite understandable we did want to get back to play our part in the defence of Australia.'

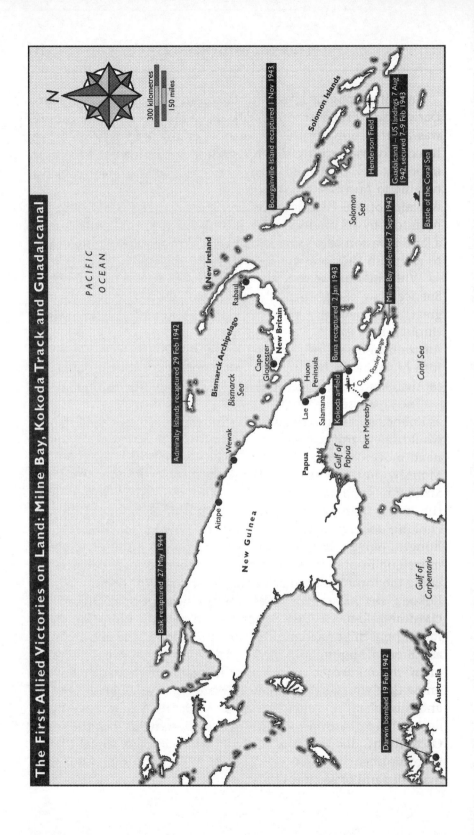

The First Allied Victories on Land: Milne Bay, Kokoda Track and Guadalcanal

Bourgainville Island recaptured 1 Nov 1943

Solomon Islands

Guadalcanal – US landings 7 Aug 1942, secured 7–9 Feb 1943

Henderson Field

Battle of the Coral Sea

Solomon Sea

Admiralty Islands recaptured 29 Feb 1942

PACIFIC OCEAN

New Ireland

Bismarck Archipelago

Rabaul

Milne Bay defended 7 Sept 1942

New Britain

Buna recaptured 2 Jan 1943

Cape Gloucester

Bismarck Sea

Huon Peninsula

Owen Stanley Range

Blak recaptured 27 May 1944

Lae

Salamana

Kokoda airfield

Wewak

Port Moresby

Coral Sea

Papua

Gulf of Papua

Aitape

New Guinea

Gulf of Carpentaria

Darwin bombed 19 Feb 1942

Australia

N

300 kilometres

150 miles

Fear of a Japanese invasion became alarm with the bombing of Darwin on 19 February 1942. Widespread panic across the country was averted only by the imposition of strict censorship, which heavily downplayed the scale of the attack. With Britain an impotent ally, the country looked to America, just as America was turning to Australia. Roosevelt declared the defence of Australia a war aim of the US. By mid-April, the Australian leadership had been told by US intelligence that the Japanese no longer intended a land invasion of Australia – but evidently kept it from the troops to maintain their preparedness and motivation.

With the Australian coast just 300 miles away, Diggers like Bill Spencer saw the fight as personal: 'We knew that the risk was great, we knew the speed with which [the Japanese] moved through the islands, we knew his tricks and we knew that he had Australia in his sights... We had a purpose – he wasn't going to get into Australia, there's no way in the world he was going to get in to Australia.'

The Japanese goal in New Guinea was to capture airfields such as Kokoda and harbours such as Port Moresby and Milne Bay. This would safeguard supply lines, and provide a springboard for the next move. No one expected the Japanese to approach Port Moresby the way they did: overland from Buna across the Owen Stanley mountains. It was nightmare terrain. Japanese veterans of the jungle-fighting in Malaya inched up sheer ravines, through choking undergrowth and cloying swamp, enduring malaria and hunger, muggy days and biting cold nights. Australian forces moved up from Port Moresby to meet them, over razorback ridges along the tortuous Kokoda Track. The two sides met and fought at Kokoda; the Australians were forced back in retreat. Bert Ward's classical role-model switched from Homer to Horatius, as he found himself at one point holding the rear: 'I was called forward as a Bren-gunner to hold the Track... and I was there about fifteen or twenty minutes on my own... it is not the best of feelings to know that you are the most forward Australian between the Japs and Australia.'

Australian cameraman Damien Parer won his country's first Oscar for his documentary *Kokoda Frontline*, which brought home to complacent domestic audiences the extraordinary suffering, mateship and bravery of the Diggers on the Kokoda Track, and the heroic support given by the native stretcher bearers. Military nurse Meg Ewart had survived the Japanese bombing of Darwin, and was now working at the field hospital in Port Moresby. She remembers the wounded coming in off the Track:

The Fuzzy-Wuzzy angels were the native boys of New Guinea. They didn't have any time for the Japanese... and they were so gentle that this is the nickname our boys gave them... because they were the only ones that could bring them out. It was terrible terrain that they were fighting in... so you can imagine the terrible state they were in, those that we did get into hospital.

The Japanese almost got within sight of Port Moresby, when their advance ground to a halt. Their supply lines had stretched and snapped. The men were running on empty. Masaru Moriki was at Regimental HQ in Papua:

We faced the enemy on the ground and in the air... Our other enemies were nature, disease, and shortages of food and ammunition... We fought these tremendous foes, and the fight sometimes seemed worse than death itself... At one stage each person was given just sixteen grains of rice to last the whole day. I think it's possible that more people in New Guinea died from hunger than from bullets.

The Japanese turned and limped back along the Kokoda Track, with the Australians now at their heels. Kokoda was to pass into Australian war mythology as perhaps her only Second World War battle to approach the iconic quality of Gallipoli in the First World War. Mythology does not here suggest fiction; the accounts on both sides confirm the epic quality of the struggle. Masaru Moriki praises Australian fighting capability as 'outstanding... I think the Australians fought more bravely than the Japanese did.' However, Bert Ward adds another dimension, which sits uncomfortably with a portrait of undiluted glory: 'It was a war without rules, possibly that's the best way to describe it, because it was a case of kill or be killed. The true jungle factor. It was just the same as animals, and I must say that we did think of the Japanese basically as animals.'

Bill Spencer fought in the repulse of the Japanese attack at Milne Bay, and the horrific battles for Buna and Sanananda. His view of the New Guinea campaign is as unromantic as Bert Ward's:

We didn't have an opportunity to take many prisoners; we had other things to do with them, we had to kill them initially, and that's what happened, very few prisoners were taken. But they weren't butchered in cold blood, they were killed in action... Those that we hadn't cleaned up in Milne Bay were cleaned up on the northern beaches. They didn't have many left when we'd finished with them.

Masaru Moriki is one of many Japanese never to reach the northern beaches. In mid November 1942, cut off from the main Japanese force and completely surrounded, his unit gathered for a night attack in a final attempt to reach the sea. With no ammunition and no food, his group of around 120 men was ordered to make a desperate charge.

Lieutenant Morimoto, who was at the front of our line, shouted 'Fire!' The answer came back, 'We have no bullets!' Without bullets there was nothing we could do. He shouted, 'Charge!' Each person charged in whichever direction he happened to be facing... I had drawn my sword and run five or six steps when I got shot in the right leg. I fell head over heels.

Masaru Moriki was one of just three survivors. To his great shame, he now became a prisoner of war. In camp, he learned from others captured in New Guinea just how desperate the Japanese on New Guinea had become: 'I heard men using phrases like "black pig" and "white pig". "Black pig" referred to eating a black man, and "white pig" meant eating a white man. I also heard they ate the flesh from dead Japanese soldiers as well.' The men at the front were paying the price for 'victory disease': the myth of their own invincibility was no substitute for food.

For the Allies, something had happened on Guadalcanal and in New Guinea which had less to do with the short-term issue of who controlled that runway, or this ridge. A crucial notion had been implanted in the minds of the Allied forces: the Japanese were not invincible. A clerk from Brisbane, a coal-miner from Durham and an Iowa farmboy could take on a Japanese soldier 10,000 miles from home – and walk out of the jungle as victor. Bill Spencer speaks for many:

> The Japanese had never been defeated or held up anywhere at all before during their incursion into the islands... The fact [was] we had... defeated a first-class regiment of soldiers and thrown them off New Guinea... We had virtually thrown them off of Australian soil, and that really gave us backing and up our spirits went and we thought well, we'll do it again if we have to, which we did.

Ambushes, killing prisoners and preparedness to fight to the last man had been forced into the Allied battle repertoire. Soldiers such as Kerry Lane were learning how to win an increasingly vicious war: 'We could see the light; we knew eventually, we wouldn't stop until we landed in Tokyo as we stepped across, island to island across the Pacific... we would continue to fight until every one of the damn SOBs were annihilated.' No one who fought in those early battles on Guadalcanal and New Guinea had any illusions how tough that would be. A lone Japanese prisoner stood on Guadalcanal among his slaughtered comrades, warning the Marines: 'Make no matter about us dead. More will come. We never stop coming. Soon you all be Japanese.'

7

SUP WITH THE DEVIL

I was never sorry that we joined the Japanese, though I had diametrically opposed views to them on many things, and especially on their treatment of women, but I thought I could hold my own and I wouldn't give up any of my ideas. I only wanted their help for a limited period and after that... we would turn against them, we would have no compunction at all in turning against our allies.

CAPTAIN LAKSHMI SWAMINATHAN, Commander of the
Women's Volunteer Regiment of the Indian National Army

THE EXPERIENCE OF THE PEOPLE of Asia and the Pacific under Japanese rule varied from partnership to slavery. The empire was too big to rule solely by brute force, so a balance had to be struck between subjugation and collaboration. A host of factors determined the nature of the relationship. Much depended on each country's previous history and her state of development. Korea had her culture, language and national life colonized and her people put to the yoke. There are islanders from the Palau group, east of the Philippines, ceded by Germany after Versailles, who look back on Japanese rule as a time of prosperity, education and growth.

The Philippines was content under American domination, especially as it had a time limit: independence was guaranteed for 1946. But Indonesian nationalists needed Japan to lever her from Dutch control. As the Indonesian activist (later his country's first president) Achmed Sukarno said: 'If the question concerns a choice between Dutch democracy and Japanese militarism I would prefer Japanese militarism.' Allied – and particularly Dutch – ex-POWs have said that the chances of successful escape in Indonesia were poorer than anywhere else, because of the likelihood that the local people would turn them in to the Japanese.

It is a complex, often paradoxical story: the Japanese settled old scores in Singapore, murdering thousands in reprisal for helping the Chinese in their war against Japan, but many Indian soldiers captured at the fall of Singapore willingly fought alongside Japan across Burma to the gates of India. Japan taught Asia a priceless lesson, as Singapore and Burma veteran David Wilson explains: 'The Japanese soldier did one thing... whatever else he may have done in atrocities and all the rest of it, he set the seal on white dominance in South-east Asia; life was never quite going to be the same again. The white man was not totally unconquerable.' The Japanese in fact fulfilled an old Indonesian prophecy about the coming of 'yellow cocks who overthrow the rule of white men'. But the legend said the freedom-fighting poultry would leave after just three months. The legend got it wrong by three and a half painful years.

Japan expanded her empire with guns and slogans. The propagandists went into Asia and the Pacific virtually alongside combat troops, trying to win hearts and minds. The banners read: 'Japanese action spells construction. Enemy action spells destruction'; 'With firmness we fight. With kindness we build', and 'Fight on until Asia is Asia's own'. One of the men who dreamed up such slogans as these was Junsuke Hitomi, who worked in the Japanese army's propaganda unit in the Philippines. He admits that expediency, not altruism, was the driving force behind their campaigns: 'In order to survive, Japan called upon the Asian countries to recover the Asia that belonged to us: the Asians. So in the Philippines we campaigned to reconquer the country back for the Philippines, and it was agreed that such slogans would prove effective... We were trying to think of ways to gain advantage in Asia.'

Yet there were clearly some Japanese who believed that co-operation, not conquest, was the goal. Carmen Guerra Nakpil recalls the genuine dismay of the Japanese that she and her Filipino countrymen could racially betray their fellow Asians: 'They would take their arms, I remember, and put them beside our arms and say, "Look, we're the same colour, why do you prefer the white men?... We are fellow Asians; we have to work together to make Asia great together"... They were enraged by us.'

Japanese newsreels showed Asians cheering the armoured columns snaking through their towns, setting out jugs of water for thirsty troops in tropical heat. The notion of Asian solidarity led to deep concern in America and substantial fears in Australia and Britain. For the first time in history, South-east Asia was unified under the rule of a single authority. What would happen if this vast empire became united in a holy mission to proliferate their race, and annihilate all others? Might the war become a war of races, the Orient versus the Occident? When Britain's ally, the Chinese Generalissimo Chiang Kai-shek, visited New Delhi in 1942, Churchill feared a 'Pan-Asian malaise [spreading] through all the bazaars of India'. President Roosevelt, who suspected the skull and brain of the Asian were less developed than those of the European, was not immune to such alarmist tendencies, saying shortly before his death in 1945: '1,100,000,000 potential enemies are dangerous.'

In Japan, Kanji Suzuki was on the receiving end of propaganda to persuade the Japanese people of their country's philanthropy in uniting Asia. He saw it not as cynical opportunism, but as something to be proud of: 'We were told that we were fighting a righteous war for the establishment of the Greater East Asia Co-Prosperity Sphere. We believed that right from the beginning. Otherwise, we couldn't fight the war.' Yet the idea at the heart of this league of Asian nations in fact ensured Japan's supremacy.

Launched by the Foreign Minister in August 1940, but following ideas that had been common currency among Japanese radical ideologues and politicians for years, the Greater East Asia Co-Prosperity Sphere was an umbrella organization for the mutual benefit of the nations of Asia. But it was the other countries that were holding up the umbrella, and Japan that was enjoying the shade. Lakshmi Swaminathan, who led Indian women troops into battle alongside the Japanese, remembers the contemporary joke: 'They are the Prosperity and we are the Co-.'

A secret Japanese report compiled between 1942 and 1943 makes it clear that, in historian John Dower's words: 'The subordination of other Asians in the Co-Prosperity Sphere was not the unfortunate consequence of wartime exigencies, but the very essence of official policy. It was the intention of the Japanese to establish permanent domination over all other races and peoples in Asia – in accordance with their needs, and as befitted their destiny as a superior race.'

So while 'Asia for the Asians' was the message to the people of the Philippines, Indonesia, Thailand and the rest, at home the war was seen as restoring Japan to its proper place as 'the leader of Asia, the protector of Asia, the light of Asia'. The Imperial Army and Navy would restore the natural, preordained order under the divine Emperor. Kanji Suzuki recalls the myth that governed Japan's attitude to her neighbours: 'Unlike other nationalities of the world, the Japanese had always been pure-bred, of a single race. We believed we were a superior nation, ruled always by the Emperor.' An organization called the Imperial Rule Assistance Association stated in March 1941: 'Although we use the expression "Asian co-operation" this by no means ignores the fact that Japan was created by gods or posits automatic racial equality.'

The central contradiction of the Co-Prosperity Sphere – the dichotomy between Japan's slogans of Asian liberation and the conviction that Japan must rule Asia – was never resolved. Nor was there any consensus within the military hierarchy on how co-operation or co-prosperity might be achieved; no single blueprint for the future was ever agreed. As the historian Keni'ichi Goto has explained: 'Japan's southern occupation policies were never thoughtfully planned or firmly carried out.' Any civil servant charged with running the policy who took the benign view of its purpose would inevitably lose out against military administrators facing wartime realities. The result, as Carmen Guerra Nakpil remembers, was a catalogue of suffering:

> The Japanese army fed off the Philippines. They didn't bring any supplies; they ate up what we had grown for us to eat, so there was a lot of hunger and despair, and they commandeered every-thing that could be used for raw material, and they were very cruel, even to passers-by in the street. They would slap you down if you didn't greet them, if you didn't bow profusely enough, and there was a lot of hardship.

Lack of firm leadership stunted the Co-prosperity Sphere's development – but the idea was kept alive. Familial analogies were used to explain away the inequalities while maintaining a façade of solidarity. Just as a younger brother must respect and obey his elder brother, so it followed that the countries of South-east Asia must submit to Japan. Thus Colonel Tsuji's booklet 'Just Read This and the War Is Won' stated: 'To the natives... the British, the Americans, the French, the Dutch are mere armed robbers, while we Japanese are brothers. At least we are indubitably relatives.' It was not the first time the military employed such supposed ties of blood or common culture to justify their actions. General Iwane Matsui attempted to rationalize Japan's invasion of China by seeing its people less as beasts, and more as brothers:

> *The struggle between Japan and China was always a fight between brothers within the 'Asian Family'... It has been my belief during all these years that we must regard this struggle as a method of making the Chinese undergo self-reflection. We do not do this because we hate them, but on the contrary because we love them too much. It is the same in a family when an elder brother has taken all that he can stand from his ill-behaved younger brother and had to chastise him in order to make him behave properly.*

In her new colonies Japan quickly replaced the superiority myth of the old colonial masters with xenophobic ideas of her own. The racism that had wreaked devastation in China and Korea was now exported across South-east Asia. Lakshmi Swaminathan regrets the way the Japanese squandered their chance to win over the hearts and minds of neighbouring peoples:

> *The Japanese had a wonderful opportunity when they launched this Greater East Asia Co-Prosperity Sphere because all the local colonized peoples were thoroughly against their colonizers, and only needed a little support to overthrow them. So they all fully supported the Japanese, but the Japanese didn't take full advantage of that. Instead of being the liberators they also became oppressors, and their way of oppression was much worse and more drastic than any of the previous colonizers. I mean they didn't just*

throw people into jail, they killed people, they raped women; they committed all other kinds of atrocities, and they seemed to be also grabbing whatever they could.

JAPAN WAS PUSHING AN OPEN DOOR in the Dutch East Indies. Many Indonesians came out on to the streets to welcome and salute the shock troops of the invading army. In several places, most notably the Muslim province of Aceh, local people actually rose up in advance of Japanese landings. They prevented the Dutch from carrying out a scorched-earth policy and arrested those trying to flee. The commander of Japan's army in Java, General Hitoshi Imamura, wrote in his memoirs: 'Many natives gathered round us far and near, the way country people in Japan run to the road when soldiers are marching during manoeuvres. The natives... brought coconuts, bananas and papayas to the Japanese... I wondered, "Is this really a battlefield?"'

General Imamura's idyll was soon over. The Japanese academic Shigeru Sato estimates that as many as 10 million people in Java alone were forced to work for the military, digging in for a protracted war against the Allies. Many of the projects were worthless, either because of poor planning by the Japanese or because they were overtaken by the war. The Javanese constructed airfields for aeroplanes that never arrived and built sea defences that were never attacked; 200,000 people laid a railway 75 miles long between the coalmines of Bayah to the railhead of Saketi – the idea was to make Java self-sufficient in coal, given the extent of Japanese shipping losses.

We will never know how many thousand slave labourers, known as *romusha*, died building the line, nor how many died working in the mines themselves. Local legend indicates the project had a nightmarish death rate. The Indonesian revolutionary Tan Malaka, who stayed in the area, reported: 'Few were the *romusha* who emerged from that place uninfected by fatal diseases such as ulcerated boils, dysentery and malaria. The *romusha* were provided with insufficient food, very few medicines, and inadequate nursing staff; in particular no care at all was given the sick and dying.'

The bitter irony is that the mines never produced enough coal to justify the cost of building the line, let alone to solve the island's coal shortage. Indonesians were also drafted into an auxiliary military force known as the Heiho. By the end of the war they numbered around 50,000; some were sent abroad to supplement Japanese forces in the Philippines and Vietnam. Arifin Marpaung joined up, wanting to avoid the horrors of forced labour, and to better himself:

> *I knew I had to work for the Japanese. Faced with the choice of being made a* romusha *or joining the Heiho – becoming either a slave or a soldier – I chose the latter. A slave had no status and little food. A soldier is given a gun and taught how to fight... I was very proud to get a uniform, to be given a gun. Everyone else was poor but I was not. I was so proud. In those days I had no political upbringing. I believed Japan would win the war.*

With so many able-bodied people across Indonesia taken away from the land, there were fewer hands left to tend crops. Intervention by centralized Japanese-run agencies only made matters worse and farming yields plummeted. At the same time the military commandeered ever-increasing amounts of rice from rural farmers. Such meddling and mismanagement of the local economy probably killed more people than the labour projects, as hunger and starvation gripped the country. According to Indonesian figures, as many as 4 million of their countrymen died as a consequence of Japan's occupation, including non-labourers killed for suspected resistance activities.

It is worth remembering the first decree of General Imamura, the man so impressed by the respectful reception of his troops when they first landed. He declared on 7 March 1942: 'The Japanese army shall seek to promote the welfare of the people of the East Indies who are of the same race and origin as the Japanese and also ensure the coexistence and co-prosperity with the local inhabitants in conformity with the guiding principles of the co-operative defence of Greater East Asia.'

Lee Kuan Yew lived through the Japanese occupation of Singapore and laughs at the idea that Japan came to Asia with peaceful partnership in mind: 'It's a joke. I don't know, maybe a few who had actively collaborated with them – spies or fifth columnists – may have believed this, but they came in as conquerors and as superior beings. There was no doubts that they were the masters... They left nobody in any doubt that they were here for the next thousand years.'

Just two days after the colony's capitulation, the Japanese began systematic punishment of Singapore's Chinese community for having sent funds, men and equipment home to help fight the Japanese, while boycotting Japanese goods. Every man of Chinese descent was rounded up and paraded past a series of hooded informers and Japanese agents who, in seconds, determined the fate of each individual. The unlucky were taken to a beach on Singapore's east coast. At the war crimes trials after the cessation of hostilities, Wong Peng Yin recounted what happened next: 'We were then driven about 200 yards from the shore... the Japanese opened fire on us with machine-guns and rifles. I had managed to struggle out of my ropes and swam away.' For days and weeks bodies were still being washed ashore. Human remains littered the beaches. The Japanese were reluctantly forced to dispose of the dead, this time by burial in mass graves. After the war several of these sites were unearthed. Some 50,000 were murdered in a process that brought untold grief, fear and stomach-churning anxiety to the entire community, many of whom simply did not know what had become of their loved ones. Elizabeth Choy, one of the heroines of that period, remembers the universal distress:

I went into the street, you know, where angels fear to tread, and I met groups of women in tears saying, 'Oh, I don't know what's happened to my son,' and some saying, 'I don't know what's happened to my husband' and some saying 'I don't know what's happened to my father'... My grandfather lost one son... his eldest son lost a son, his eldest daughter lost a son, and they all nearly went out of their minds, it was very, very pitiful... I remember their sadness, their hopelessness... Even today I don't know what happened to my brother, and that is the saddest part...

In addition to their brutal tactics of coercion, the military attempted a process of 'Japanization' to encourage the collaboration of local people. It was scarcely more subtle. Singapore was renamed 'Shonan' – Light of the South – and run on Tokyo time and the date changed to 2602 (the seventeenth year of Hirohito's reign). Japanese language lessons were played on the radio and repeated in the newspaper. Raffles Hotel was renamed but, tellingly, locals still could not enter – now it was reserved for Japanese. Local women who worked in Japanese firms were employed only if they were shorter than their boss; school-children were made to sing the Japanese national anthem. These changes did little to foster love for Japan. Nor was violence ever far away; the omnipresent Kempeitai, the secret police, made sure of that. They arrested Elizabeth Choy and her husband as British sympathizers:

> *They stripped me to the waist and tied my hands and my feet, tied me in such a way I couldn't move... That day they brought my husband to kneel beside the frame to watch me being tortured, and they applied electricity on my bare back you know. Oh, I screamed and I had tears coming down, nose running, it was terrible... the Japanese asked, 'Now you tell us, give us names [of those] who are anti-Japanese and then we will set you free at once.' My husband said, 'We don't know anybody,' and so I said, 'I don't know anybody...'. 'All right, you won't tell us, tomorrow [that's to my husband] we take you to Johore Bharu to be executed at nine o'clock. At ten o'clock we will take you [that's me] to Johore Bharu to be executed.' So they told us to say goodbye. So my husband said, 'Goodbye, Elizabeth. Don't worry, we die, we die an honourable death.'*

Elizabeth only learned that her husband was still alive – and he that she had survived – when the war was over.

AS THE WAR PROGRESSED, Japan's demand for labour sucked ever more Asian people into slavery. To a European, the infamous Burma–Thailand Railway invariably conjures up the vision of emaciated white POWs building bridges in sweltering heat. In fact, perhaps five times as many Asians (300,000) worked on the railway as whites (60,000). Worse, it is estimated that as many as three-quarters of the Asians died, compared with about a fifth of the POWs. The POWs, whose terrible plight we discuss in Chapter 8, confirm that on this project, and on many others, Asians suffered much worse Japanese brutality than they did. Most forced labourers working on the Death Railway were Malays, Tamils and Burmese although Indonesians and Chinese were also recruited by the thousand. Few were Thai, because of the Thai government's extensive collaboration with the Japanese.

Disturbingly, a large number, perhaps as many as half of all forced labourers on the line, were women and children. Professor Michiko Nakahara has spent years collecting the testimony of Asian labourers who did survive. One woman, called Sada, was interviewed in 1993 (because she was orphaned at such a young age Sada does not know her family name). Sada went with her father from Kota Bharu in Malaya to the railway when she was just five or six years old, because her mother had already died and there was no one else to look after her. When her father died in a jungle camp by Takanun (approximately midway along the railway), Sada buried him in banana leaves. She then remained working at camps along the line until the end of the war. When surrender came she was too small to climb into the lorry taking workers away from the camps, and it was years before she managed to return to her home village.

Soon after the Japanese started to bring Asian labourers on to the Thai side of the railway, cholera erupted along the line. The POWs still had a degree of military organization, which facilitated food and sanitation arrangements, plus a sprinkling of doctors. The Asians had neither, and cholera cut a devastating swathe through them. The secret diary kept by Dr Robert Hardie, a POW also at Takanun, records the conditions of the Asian labourers:

There must be thousands of these unfortunates all along the railway course. There is a big camp a few kilometres below here and another, two or three kilometres up. We hear of the frightful casualties from cholera and other diseases among these people, and of the brutality with which they are treated by the Japanese. People who have been near these camps speak with bated breath of the state of affairs – corpses rotting unburied in the jungle, almost complete lack of sanitation, a frightful stench, overcrowding, swarms of flies.

Tan Choon Keng saw the suffering at first hand. He had studied medicine in Singapore for several years but had not qualified as a doctor. The Japanese needed medical personnel and forced him to go to the railway. He was a skilled worker, so he was comparatively well treated. One day he was summoned to a camp in which around 200 men, women and children were in the final stages of cholera. The Japanese ordered him to burn the whole place down, even though the occupants were still alive, in a merciless, desperate attempt to contain the epidemic. Tan and his men poured kerosene around the camp buildings, along the raised sleeping platforms and over the very bodies of the dying:

> I told my men, I said, 'Look, this is going to be terrible,' I said, 'but either they die or we die. If you don't do it – we die.' We set fire to the camp... All these people, most of them were Malays or Indians [Tamils]... started screaming, shouting, because they knew they were going to die, but there was no chance of them escaping because they couldn't move. Their wives were the main sufferers with the babies, some of them were with babies you know, crying and shouting, but what could we do?... This was the only way to survive... to destroy them or we be destroyed. God forgive us.

ONE OF THE MOST DISTRESSING manifestations of Japan's racist and superior attitude towards the people of South-east Asia was the military's system of forced sex slavery. During the course of the war, an estimated 200,000 women were forced to become so-called 'comfort women'. They were drafted from local populations across Japan's empire but the majority, some 80–90 per cent, were Koreans.

These women were forced to endure the most appalling life. Typically, they were raped thirty to forty times a day; as many as sixty rapes in a day were not uncommon. Many of the women were virgins before being seized and many were so young that they had yet to begin menstruating. The use of children as sex slaves is confirmed by the Japanese veteran Kiyoshi Sakakura:

> I went to the comfort station camp and a girl, of about fourteen – she still looked like a child – was sent to me. She wouldn't stop crying. I thought it was strange and so I called for the manager. He told me that she was new, she didn't know anything, she couldn't understand Japanese. I asked for her to be replaced... the

manager sent in another girl. But that first one was clearly no more than a child.

Narisa Claveria was just eleven years old when she was seized by the Japanese. The soldiers entered her village in the Philippines on a patrol to search and locate guerrillas. Because Narisa's father was the village headman he was tied to a tree and questioned. As his answers were not to the soldiers' liking, some of the men skinned him alive while others raped his wife. Three of Narisa's siblings who tried to defend their tortured parents were bayoneted – the youngest thrown in the air and impaled on the blade. Two others escaped and two, Narisa and her sister Emataria, were taken away by the soldiers who burnt down their house before leaving. They were kept, along with many other women, in the soldiers' barracks. Here they were gang-raped on a daily basis:

Whenever the Japanese thought about it, they would just rape us… We women couldn't say no, we couldn't refuse them; we had to go along with it – otherwise they'd hurt us. We had a terrible time. We almost couldn't get up from our beds because of the pain. Because it's not just one Japanese, there were loads of them. They would just rape anybody they wanted to.

The women lived in total fear. They were not even allowed to speak to each other. The Japanese used a horsewhip on them or stubbed lit cigarettes out on their arms. Of the two sisters only Narisa talks about the experience. Her older sister Emataria has not been able to speak about this period in her life for sixty years: 'It was my sister whom I really pitied at that time. She fought the Japanese when they tried to rape her… They really punished her… She lost her mind because of what the Japanese did to her. That's what happened to my sister, because she spent a very long time in the barracks. She was the one who suffered most there.'

It is estimated that only 30 per cent of all the women and girls forced into sex slavery by the Japanese survived the war. Because of their proximity to the front lines, many were killed in bombing raids and caught in cross fire. Many others were killed by soldiers when forced to retreat and some even after surrender – when their presence was considered an embarrassment. Others died from sexually transmitted diseases, were shot while trying to escape, were murdered for refusing to submit any more, or simply killed out of vindictiveness. Some were killed because they became pregnant. Remedios Estorninos Felias, then a fourteen-year-old Filipino girl, describes how she escaped from the Japanese when American forces landed on Leyte:

Suddenly one day, the garrison was bombed and the Japanese soldiers ran. I began to run too, fearing I would be hit. I saw Manang [a friend] fall when she was hit in the face. I dropped into a foxhole. There were three other Japanese soldiers inside. We were trapped inside the foxhole for days without food and water. But even though we were all trapped, in the same situation, the three Japanese soldiers still raped me. When the firing sounds died down, the soldiers forced me to go up – 'Go, go,' they said – so that I could test if it was safe. I climbed up and saw Filipino and American soldiers. They tried to shoot me but one Filipino shouted not to, that I was a Filipino girl.

EVERYONE IN OCCUPIED ASIA faced tough decisions about how to survive. In the Philippines, Carmen Guerra Nakpil remembers the divisiveness of the times: 'There were families who had turned one against the other because one was pro-Japanese and the other was pro-American, or because someone had joined the guerrillas and the others didn't. Families were divided, the towns were divided.' To many, collaboration was just a form of self-preservation. Lee Kuan Yew recalls the trade-off people were forced to make: 'Once you are in occupied enemy control you have to accept that your life is in their hands. They can deny you food, medicine, they can starve you to death or they can kill you outright, so you have to compromise.'

Leocardio de Asis had been a Filipino army officer fighting alongside the Americans in Bataan. He was one of a number of officers chosen to go to Japan for study and training so as to form a leadership cadre that could then return to the Philippines: 'We were really under a very awkward position... we were officers of the United States Armed Forces of the Far East – we had sworn allegiance to the US Army, you know, and at the same time we were going to Japan as guests of the government of Japan. A really awkward position, you know, but what can we do?...It was in a way an adventure for us, so we went.'

He was treated well, and that in itself forced him to rethink his attitude to the Japanese: 'All that hatred for the Japanese changed also into more understanding. We felt that, after all, people everywhere are the same. Basically people are the same; not everybody is cruel. Stripped to bare essentials, they are all human beings, and that changed our concept of Japan.'

Some national leaders subsequently defended collaboration as the only way to ensure the survival of their people; others used it as a stepping stone to independence. Aung San, Burma's most famous nationalist leader, declared: 'British imperialism is the real, decisive enemy for Burma... we must use other devils to drive away the vampire that is imposing itself on us.' The key to exploiting the temporary coincidence of interest with Japan was the formation of national armies to fight alongside the Japanese: the Indian National Army, the Burmese Independence Army and the Army for the Defence of the Fatherland (PETA) in Indonesia – all of which played a crucial role in their respective countries' pursuit of real independence at the war's end.

The leader of the Indian National Army (INA) was Subhas Chandra Bose. Unlike Mahatma Gandhi and Jawaharlal Nehru, Bose believed India could win its freedom only through an armed struggle. As president of the Indian National Congress, he toured the country openly denouncing British imperialism and urging civil disobedience, until his arrest in July 1940. Impatient to turn the war in Europe to India's advantage, Bose escaped house arrest and fled to Moscow. Failing to secure Stalin's interest, Bose flew to Berlin where Hitler gave him a tepid welcome and minimal support. In early 1943 he headed for Tokyo. Lakshmi Swaminathan was one of Bose's key subordinates; she explains his opportunist approach to international relations: 'Subhas Chandra Bose's theory or belief was, that nations don't have any permanent friends or permanent enemies, only permanent interests.'

The Japanese flew Bose to Singapore where he resurrected the INA, dormant since its formation during Japan's initial invasion of Malaya and Singapore. At first the ranks of the INA were filled by captured Indian soldiers: they were offered a chance to join the army just two days after the fall of Singapore at a mass rally attended by some 60,000 Indian prisoners. Many refused and remained steadfastly loyal to the British Raj, but thousands eagerly enrolled. It was a turning point in Hari Ram's life: 'OK, we were British servants to this point. Now that's finished and we're Japanese prisoners of war. Now we're getting a second chance to fight for our country and its freedom... And we did not think it a bad thing. In fact we thought it good that we had the opportunity to serve our country. A lot of my friends had died in that war. What if I had died too? So, let me serve my nation while I'm still alive.'

With the arrival of Bose, some 18,000 civilians joined the INA from Malaya and Singapore's Indian community. Lakshmi Swaminathan commanded the Rhani of Jhansi regiment, comprised entirely of women volunteer soldiers. She had absolutely no compunction about siding with the Japanese:

The most important thing for me was the independence of India, irrespective of fascism, of Japanese imperialism or anything... We were willing to fight with the Japanese because they were the only people who were prepared to give us all-out military help...We had no illusions at all about the Japanese, about their character, about their atrocities and things that they were capable of, we had absolutely none. Bose himself at many public meetings said, 'I give every Indian soldier the full liberty to train his gun or his bayonet on a Japanese if he finds him in any way misbehaving with any of our people, especially women.'

When it suited the Japanese to treat Asian women and men decently, they clearly did so. Leading units of the INA advanced through Burma, albeit as decidedly junior partners to the Japanese, but attracting much Japanese propaganda newsreel coverage. This was, after all, the Greater East Asia Co-Prosperity Sphere in action. They momentously crossed the border into north-eastern India in the early spring of 1944. For Lakshmi Swaminathan, it was 'one of the most thrilling moments of my life in the INA, and I felt that now that we had established a foothold, however small, that we would somehow progress and reach Delhi finally'.

But at Imphal and Kohima they encountered Britain's 14th Army, two-thirds of whom were Indians. Hari Ram addressed

them: 'We called to them... on our loudspeakers saying: "Move
back. We're Indians. We're a freedom army. Netaji [Subhas
Chandra Bose] is our commander. What are you fighting for?
We're fighting for our freedom. You're fighting for slavery.
Surrender!"' Few switched sides, in what now bore the hallmarks
of a civil war. British soldier Bhim Singh had qualms about killing
fellow Indians fighting with the Japanese, but he overcame them:

> You are not treating it as your own country, if you want to hand it
> over to someone else, to help aggressors. So we didn't think of
> them as Hindustani. This soil is like our own mother. How we would
> suffer if someone carried off our mother! How much we'd grieve.
> And they were selling their mother... It is a tragic tale. We had no
> choice. We had to kill them. We didn't kill them thinking of them
> as our countrymen. We killed them as Japanese.

On the opposite side, Hari Ram similarly rationalized the
killing of fellow Indians:

> Even if it had been our own brother facing us, we would still have
> had to fight him. We were for our country. A few Indian men were
> up against us – India is a huge nation. Even if they had all been
> killed, they don't count for much in a nation's freedom... It was not
> relevant to hold our fire because you're confronting your brother.
> We had to fire. We were there to fight.

Ironically, the last great campaign of the Indian Army before
partition was to kick the Japanese and INA out of India and push
their tattered, dying remnants back across Burma. Bose's hopes
that the INA would set India ablaze in spontaneous uprisings were
dashed by British skill at preventing all news of the INA reaching
the people. It was not until after the war that treason trials at the
Red Fort in Delhi achieved what Bose, in the jungles of Burma,
had been unable to. Far from encouraging the people of India to
damn the INA leadership as traitors, the trials carried across the
country the story of those who dared all for independence. India's
first Prime Minister, Jawaharlal Nehru, who ruled after partition
and independence in August 1947, subsequently wrote: 'Those
men, whatever they were as individuals, became symbols of

India's struggle for freedom.' The academic Joyce Lebra confirms the crucial role the INA played in undermining British rule: 'Despite the military defeat of Japan, and with it the INA, popular support of the INA finally precipitated British withdrawal from India.'

Almost in spite of itself, Japan had played a crucial role in the evolution and emancipation of South-east Asia. Although Tokyo never intended to put into action its rhetoric of Asian independence, the very discussion of it, coupled with the expulsion of the former colonial occupiers, spurred the region into fighting for its own liberation. There was even an indication at the very end of the war that the 'Asia for the Asians' slogan had found its mark: on the point of surrender, a number of Japanese soldiers made sure they handed their weapons over to local nationalists – rather than to the British or Dutch. Japan had let the genie of independence out of the bottle, and there was nothing the returning war-weary white colonists could do to trick it back in. Within five years of the war's end, India, Burma, Indonesia and the Philippines were all free self-governing countries.

8

HELL'S TEETH

I remember this one guy came up and he tried to knock this gold tooth out of a Jap's mouth and the Jap wasn't dead yet... and he started kicking his feet around and mumbling all these awful sounds, and so that character took his K-bar knife and slashed his cheeks open back to the ears and then you could hear the man gurgling in his own blood, and I said, 'Why don't you shoot him and put him out of his misery?' and the guy looked at me and said, 'Why don't you shut up?'

EUGENE SLEDGE, US Marine veteran of Peleliu and Okinawa

VICTORY IN WAR HAS A WAY of retroactively purging the winners of all sin. We were in the right. God was on our side. We fought fairly. They were in the wrong. They fought dirty. They committed the war crimes. Ticker-tape parades, medal ceremonies and slaps on the back greet the winners, not tribunals into what exactly you did with that flame-thrower when you entered a village on a patch of coral half a world away. Victories wipe slates clean. The less a nation backs a war, the more questions get asked about its soldiers' conduct, as the British learned in the Boer War and America found out in Vietnam. The revelation of atrocities increases public doubt in the war as a whole, which in turn speeds the dissemination of undermining evidence about how it is being fought.

On 16 March 1968 a unit of the 11th Brigade of the Americal Division entered a suspected guerrilla village in Quang Ngai Province, Vietnam, and killed 357 unarmed women, children and old men. It took a year for news of the My Lai massacre to leak out; it thereafter heightened popular disapproval of the war.

The protest movement, Vietnam Veterans Against the War, conducted their own investigation in which a hundred veterans testified that atrocities were part and parcel of usual conduct in Vietnam. The war in the Pacific between 1941 and 1945 enjoyed virtually total support from the public, and yet many front-line troops returned home certain there were things they could never discuss. Second World War veterans who followed the course of the war in Vietnam may even have heard the news of the massacre at My Lai with a faint nod of recognition.

Lester Tenney was in the fighting in the Philippines in 1942: 'We would go in with a machine-gun, which we had in our tank, we would go into a village, and start firing the machine-gun. And if we saw somebody that looked like it could be Japanese, we would shoot. Now, it could have been a Filipino for all we know, it could have been Chinese. But, if we saw them, we would shoot, on the grounds that we just didn't know.'

Recognizing the enemy in Tobruk or Anzio or Normandy was comparatively easy: they conveniently wore German and Italian uniforms. In the Pacific War, the cliché 'they all look alike' was compounded later on in Saipan and Okinawa by the presence of hostile Japanese women, with their children, on the battlefield. There is film of machine-gunning and torching village huts in Saipan, echoed a quarter of a century later by images from Vietnam that shocked television audiences.

'Gooks' was not coined by GIs as a nickname for the Vietcong; it was inherited from the Pacific War. Napalm is a weapon that will always be associated with the Vietnam War: a petroleum gel shot from a flame-thrower or dropped from planes. It adheres to the body, burning at a temperature of about 2,000 degrees Fahrenheit. Napalm was in fact used in the First World War, but came into its own in the Pacific. It became the preferred way of dealing with the Japanese in bunkers and caves: the flame consumes oxygen, killing by asphyxiation. Japanese positions on Bloody Nose Ridge on Peleliu in 1944 were turned into balls of flame hundreds of feet high by napalm bombs. The American-held airstrip was so close to the target and the pressure to burn out the Japanese so great, that the Corsair bombers did not bother to raise their undercarriages, but went round after dropping their load, landed, rearmed with more napalm and took off again.

The Pacific War had its public face: its long roll of landings made, airfields secured and harbours seized in the painful push towards Japan. Some of these battles were crucial to the outcome of the war. Others were less decisive. And some were simply irrelevant. But for the men on the ground such strategic considerations were of little consequence. Shrapnel or a sniper's bullet would kill them just as surely on a useless bit of ground that took the war no closer to Tokyo.

If survival was a fluke – or an act of God – there was also something arbitrary about whether a campaign was noticed back home. Tarawa became famous in the US because film and photographs taken here were the first images of American war dead to be shown publicly. Anywhere MacArthur went, film crews seemed to go, though the lasting impression the world was given was of a jutting-jawed general striding safely ashore clenching a corncob pipe, rather than that of his men – days before – pinned down on the same beach, clinging on to a carbine for grim life. A photograph of half a dozen Marines raising a flag became one of the iconic images of the Second World War and ensured eight square miles of volcanic sand and rock called Iwo Jima will never be forgotten.

By contrast, Peleliu, an island 500 miles east of the Philippines and defended in depth by the Japanese, was almost totally ignored. Yet the fighting here lasted nearly two months and saw over 1,250 Americans killed and all but fifty-three of the 10,900 Japanese garrison. Peleliu's relegation to the margins of popular consciousness can be traced to two factors. First, the press corps was told the battle would last only four days; few went ashore to cover the critical early phase and several of them were killed including the brilliant Australian combat cameraman Damien Parer. Secondly, word of the assault on Peleliu reached the world's news rooms just as stories were coming in about the ill-fated airborne invasion of the Netherlands at Arnhem, where, during the advance into Germany, thousands of Allied paratroopers were trapped trying to take a bridge over the River Rhine. On Peleliu it was difficult enough to know what was happening 20 feet away. Little wonder that an Allied disaster 7,300 miles away grabbed the headlines.

Yet it did not matter what degree of publicity a campaign received at home; much of what happened would remain the

secret of those who were there. This was not so much to conceal
atrocity, but arose out of the soldiers' realization that what they
had to do daily in combat would horrify civilians. The point at
which behaviour becomes atrocious is neither fixed nor easily
defined; we have to understand the norms before the aberrations.

GOING INTO COMBAT for the first time is a seminal experience. It
is clear from talking with Marine veterans that their fears before
going in – Will I let my buddies down? Will I reveal myself to be a
coward? Will I live? – are tempered afterwards by a certain understanding, a knowledge of what it is like to live amid death. US
Marine Eugene Sledge's first assault, on the island of Peleliu, was a
revelation: 'It was such a momentous event that I knew I would
never be the same afterward, and everything in my life that had
gone before just paled into insignificance compared to this moment,
and from then on I knew that I was expendable, and that's not a very
happy thought, but you had to learn to live with it.'

When Eugene Sledge came ashore, men he knew and men he
did not were dying all around him. The scale of it, the suffering
and the waste, were horrors that Eugene could never have
imagined: 'I just simply could not conceive of what kind of
madness this was.' His introduction to war became all the more
personal when a close friend was killed: 'He wasn't on the beach
two minutes, and that was a real blow... I thought what kind of a
killing machine is this, that takes these people of this age and just
smashes them up.'

In his first ever experience of combat Stan Dabrowski, a
medical aide (known as a corpsman), hit the beach on Iwo Jima
and immediately saw his first casualty: 'I ran over to this fallen
Marine, turned him over and my God, it's my friend Stan Sanders.
He was hit by multiple machine-gun bullets, he was dead, his eyes
were already glazing over and that was a tremendous shock. Right
there on a beach. I mean... you were almost ready to crack
yourself, but... you had to go on with your unit and do what you
were trained to do.'

For Marine George Peto, the loss of a close buddy on Okinawa
made killing the enemy a lot more personal: 'My friend's name
was Henry Vastine Rucker, and he got hit with a piece of shrapnel
real bad, his intestines were all messed up... and he died the next

day aboard ship. And that sure did put a different perspective on my part in the war. That's why killing the Japs was no problem at all, in fact at times it was an outright pleasure.'

The sight of dead colleagues was both debilitating and galvanizing; the transformation of raw recruits into battle-hardened veterans was swift. It did not take long for the war to grind down soldiers on both sides: the danger; the waiting; the way it never seemed to end; the heat; the food – or lack of it; the stomach-churning sights and horrific smells. The trouble with Peleliu was that it was made of coral, too hard to dig latrines or graves. Eugene Sledge remembers the consequences:

There were dead Japs and you couldn't bury them because of the rock, and so they were lying all around there, and at night these land crabs would come up out of the swamp and climb up into the ridge, and you could hear them crawling all over the dead vegetation and you absolutely could not tell whether it was a man slipping up on you or whether it was these land crabs crawling around, because they were crawling up there to feed on the dead Japs.

Conditions in the Pacific were appalling. Add to the conditions the brutality of the fighting and the constant fear of death. Men had to adapt to survive. Boundaries between right and wrong became blurred and obscured by the constant strain of war. At the sharp end, anything went. Nelson Peery, a veteran of Biak, Morotai and Bougainville, reflects on how men far from home, in an alien and deadly environment, become stripped of their humanity:

Men in combat... cease being individuals; they become part of a machine that kills and that bayonets people, that sets fire to people, that laughs at people when they're burning up from getting hit by a flame thrower. They're running down the trail screaming in agony and you laugh at them. It's because you're no longer an individual, you're part of a machine, a killing machine.

Nelson Peery is not talking about a dispassionate machine, but one with the capacity to laugh at others' agony. There is little doubt that the Allies hated the Japanese much more than they hated the Germans. One study, conducted on a US infantry regiment still in training, reveals this distinction. Asked 'How would you feel about killing a German soldier?' just 7 per cent gave the answer 'I would really like to' from a list of possible answers. When the word Japanese was inserted into the question, the percentage really wanting to kill the soldier jumped to 44. Bill Spencer is in a position to compare the Germans and Japanese; he fought them both:

> The Germans that we encountered in Tobruk, Rommel's men, they were honourable soldiers, they fought as honourable soldiers, they treated our wounded well, they looked after them, fed them and nurtured them, not the Japanese, he had no soul whatsoever... The German was a gentleman soldier, I mean he was from the old school, he fought as a soldier should fight; he wasn't a butcher.

It came down to race. The German treatment of 'Aryan' Allied troops in North Africa and on the Western Front was one thing. Jews, Gypsies, Slavs and so on saw little or nothing of the gentlemanly German. Dachau bore no resemblance to Colditz. The Japanese did not have this schizophrenic two-track attitude to their enemies. By 1941 no one was regarded as their racial equal. By extension, Allied propaganda played down the racial dimensions of the war against Germany, but the Japanese were targeted with virulent racism, as veteran Sy Kahn recalls: '[There was a] substantial background of being propagandized into thinking of the Japanese as being subhuman.' Senior figures, such as General Blamey, Commander of Allied land forces in New Guinea and Commander-in-Chief of the Australian army, routinely advanced racist views. He told his troops in 1943: 'Your enemy is a curious race, a cross between the human being and the ape... he is inferior to you, and you know it.' He went on to conclude: 'You know that we have to exterminate these vermin.'

What the soldiers found at the front confirmed everything the propaganda had told them about their enemy, and seemed to justify correspondingly brutal responses. Yet 'he started it first' may not cover all questionable behaviour during the war. It is possible that some Allied soldiers used examples of Japanese atrocity to avoid some share of responsibility for the bilateral escalation into extreme grimness. Other elements played their part: fear, propaganda, racial hatred, and ignorance. A lot depends on what is classified as an atrocity. Australian Bill Spencer has no doubt after fighting the Japanese in New Guinea: 'The native women weren't spared, they were raped and mutilated, I mean it wasn't just a question of sating their lust on women, they mutilated them for no reason at all. It was shocking. That again acted as a spur, and it wasn't going to happen to us or ours.'

Australian nurse Meg Ewart, working in a New Guinea field hospital, saw so many ghastly wounds and watched so many young men die that she acquired a belligerence that now seems shocking: 'I really formed a hatred for the Japanese because of what I saw they had done to our boys. I had always been very, very frightened of guns, but I'm quite sure if I had been faced with a Japanese and had a gun, I would have shot him – which seems a terrible thing for a nurse to say, but it was quite true. I had that feeling.'

Australian infantryman Bert Ward was also in New Guinea. He was horrified by the Japanese use of the corpses of their own war dead to build up the height of defensive parapets; it showed 'their complete indifference to death'. However, in countless wars soldiers have sought protection behind corpses, feeling bullets thudding into the dead that were aimed at the living. Is this indifference to death, or a commitment to life? Is it the systematic piling up of dead comrades that is shocking? The disrespect for the body itself? Are there different cultural traditions about the sanctity of the human body in death, which explain why Bert Ward was shocked by the parapet of corpses? If so, how could British troops use Japanese corpses as defences during the siege of Kohima in north-east India, where fewer than a thousand British and Indian soldiers held out against a Japanese force at least 12,000 strong?

If there are cultural differences, why did Japanese soldier Ei Yamaguchi look shocked and puzzled when asked about the American practice of removing gold teeth from dead Japanese? It was something he clearly knew nothing about. Most Japanese were unaware of Allied atrocities. Ei Yamaguchi fought opposite Eugene Sledge on Peleliu, but he spent his time falling back from one cave to the next. You have to advance to discover what the enemy has been up to. Very few Japanese will ever have recovered enough ground to come upon the bodies of dead comrades with gaping gashes in their mouths where gold teeth had been ripped out, and then survived to relate what they had seen.

Eugene Sledge had no illusions about his fellow Americans' absolute lack of consideration for the enemy. As the desperate fight on Peleliu drags on, he records the ever-rising level of indifference in his unit to their humanity. One day they were resting near a dead Japanese still seated behind his machine-gun, with the top of his skull blasted away:

> A heavy shower of rain had fallen after he had been killed... and one of my buddies was picking up little coral pebbles and just tossing them – like you try to toss them into a bucket – he was trying to toss them into this skull, and every time he would get one in to the Jap's skull there would be a little water, it would go plop... and he did that with as little emotion as you would throwing acorns in a puddle on the roadside, and I guess it just showed how we had just become almost insensitive to the fact that these people really were human beings, but they were our enemies, and they were so savage that we just didn't see anything wrong with that kind of thing.

Is Eugene Sledge's pebble-throwing colleague so unlike the Japanese who topped their parapets with corpses? Some might argue that he was worse – for using a dead body for an idle game rather than to save lives. Hiraoka Hisashi was a medical orderly in the Philippines and recalls a desperate conversation with his starving colleagues near the war's end. They found the dead body of a soldier and debated whether to eat it:

> Some argued that if we left him there, he would just turn to dust, whereas if we ate him, it would give us blood and meat. We seriously considered it. In the end, he was eaten by some other people. This is what happens when people are pushed to the extreme limit. Humans are savage beasts. It's easy to talk about morality and ethics when your belly is full. You can't argue ethics with a starving man.

Clearly, no one is obliged to collect gold teeth, but even Eugene Sledge found himself tempted, until the unit corpsman Doc Caswell made him think twice:

I said, 'Doc, I think I'll get me some gold teeth and start my gold teeth collection like a lot of the guys.' And he came over to me and tugged me by the sleeve of my dungarees and he said, 'Sledgehammer, don't do that. You don't want to fool with those things,' and I said, 'Well, a lot of the guys do it,' and he said, 'Yeah, but just think of the germs,' and I didn't know anything about germs then, so I hesitated and he said, 'And think about what your parents would think'... So I never took any gold teeth, and in retrospect I think Doc was just trying to help me retain some veneer of civilization and decency, rather – not that I imply that my buddies were indecent when they took gold teeth – but some of them today kind of cringe at the thought of what they did.

Allied troops often blame the Japanese for initiating the spiral into horror. Charles Lindbergh, America's record-breaking pilot (who in 1927 became the first man to fly across the Atlantic), was troubled by the callous behaviour of his fellow Americans. Too old for active service, Lindbergh nevertheless flew for several months in the Pacific as a 'civilian observer', taking part in over fifty combat missions. On 21 July 1944 he wrote in his diary about American double standards of behaviour:

What is courage for us is fanaticism for him. We hold his examples of atrocity screamingly to the heavens while we cover up our own and condemn them as just retribution for his acts. A Japanese soldier who cuts off an American soldier's head is an Oriental barbarian 'lower than a rat'. An American who slits a Japanese throat 'did it only because he knew the Japs had done it to his buddies'.

Yet the longer Lindbergh spent in the Pacific the less certain he was that responsibility for atrocities should be equally shared. By 11 August he wrote: 'barbaric as our men are at times, the Orientals appear to be worse'. One wonders what his view would have been had he fought on the ground. As a flier, Lindbergh was spared most of the sights with which the Marines and infantrymen had become familiar. On Peleliu, Eugene Sledge had come across the bodies of three Marines, two of whom had been decapitated and had had their penises cut off and placed in their mouths. The third had been chopped up and grotesquely rearranged. If these displays were intended to frighten the Americans, they had the opposite effect. Sledge's response was: 'The more of those Japs I can kill the better it's going to be.'

American troops committed similar acts; to black soldier Nelson Peery these mutilations were all too familiar: 'It was a projection of the lynch mob. After they'd lynched a black man they always cut off his fingers and his penis and his ears for souvenirs, and that's exactly what they did to the Japanese in these jungles.'

Gurkhas and pro-British Naga tribesmen fighting on the Burma Front simply continued old traditions: chopping the ears and heads off their Japanese enemies and bringing them back to display their achievements. Some Gurkhas had strings of ears, just as some Americans had little sacks of gold teeth. Nigerian soldiers used Japanese heads to adorn their fox-holes. Trophies were proof of fighting prowess, but as the quote that opened this chapter makes clear, they may show only how good you were at finding victims who could not fight back. General Slim wrote after the war, in a light-hearted tone, of men who took souvenirs from the battlefield: 'The Gurkhas... presented themselves before their general, proudly opened a large basket, lifted from it three gory Japanese heads, and laid them on his table. They then politely offered him for his dinner the freshly caught fish which filled the rest of the basket.'

But while some men collected teeth, skulls and other body parts for reasons of triumphalism, boastfulness or simple hatred, others did so for more complex motives. Sy Kahn served in the US Army's transportation corps. He spent much of his time unloading ships, but the job was far from safe. Enemy action, disease, breakdowns and accidents took approximately half the men in his company out of the war. On New Guinea, he found a skull.

I wince a little because I kept a skull... It wasn't done with the motive of desecration, it was done with, I think, a kind of curiosity.

I've thought a lot about this incident... It was a way of taking the horror out of death and becoming familiar with it, of making it more ordinary... It was a way of looking at that skull and truly saying, 'There but for the grace of God go I, that's what I'll look like, it's not so horrible to become a skull. If that's the end game, if that's part of the end game so be it, it doesn't horrify me, it's sort of interesting'... To understand it you have to see it in a spectrum of ghoulishness. By that time we had seen so many ghoulish things, we had seen badly wounded people, mutilated people, scarred people, crazy people, you know, the whole fog of war, that having a skull did not seem as outlandish in that context as it would have in other contexts. It was almost an emblem of who we were, because so many of us were committed to death.

The treatment of enemy wounded had its own moral complexities. They were often the only easy source of prisoners for interrogation, and they can be seen in newsreel film near beach-heads being carefully looked after and taken out to hospital ships. Deep in the jungle, the situation was different; expediency ruled. Nelson Peery recalls a patrol in New Guinea in which a firefight left him with two wounded Japanese soldiers on his hands:

Now we have our option, we could leave them there to suffer or we can kill them... We have no way to carry them back, we need to have our rifles in our hands... and no matter how much we feel for them, you have to kill them. And of course at the same time, between men in combat you don't really look upon that enemy soldier as a human being, this is an enemy, this a rat, this is somebody that needs to be killed. Now once they're in your care your attitude towards them changes, but on the battlefield they're vermin, they're trying to kill you. You're the hero, they're the enemy, so nobody looked upon it as an atrocity to kill wounded soldiers who were dying, and many of them were begging to be killed. They would point to their gun, they would point to their head, they were suffering, you know, and they knew that if they were allowed to lay there they were going to suffer terribly for two or three days and then they would die. We couldn't take them back... One of them was begging us to kill him, the other one was begging for mercy...

The problem of how to handle the wounded far from base became acute if they were your comrades. When evacuation was impossible or would severely threaten the lives of others, both sides killed their own – rather than allow them to fall into the enemy's hands. It was a problem often faced by the British in the hills of Burma, where lines of communication were stretched thin. The British 14th Army was mostly composed of Indian troops; Khajan Singha recalls a typical scenario: 'If our friends were wounded, we tried to bring them back – but it we failed in our attempts to carry them away because we were under fire, then we shot them and moved on.' In 1943 the British launched a pioneering guerrilla offensive deep behind Japanese lines in northern Burma. Named after the dragon statues fronting Burmese temples, the Chindits were told in advance by their messianic leader Orde Wingate that the wounded could not be airlifted out and that nothing would be done for those too injured, or too sick, to move. Approximately 800 men, of the 3,000 who set out on the first Chindit campaign, were left behind or shot by their comrades.

Having to kill colleagues added a particularly distressing pressure to the combat troops. Veteran Bhim Singh was on a night reconnaissance patrol when the lead scout was shot:

> I was about ten yards behind him. When he was shot he said: 'Brother Bhim Singh, I've been hit. I'm not fit to walk. Shoot me.' I said: 'No, Brother. We'll carry you back. You'll be fine.' He said: 'I can't get better. I've got to die. I can't even walk.' So I crawled across and took his weapons. And I shot... I was forced to shoot him... When a friend goes, you do feel pain. I suffered a great deal. But I had no choice. I had to shoot him.

Fighting on comparatively small islands often surrounded by their own ships, US troops could generally evacuate, or at the very least treat, the vast majority of their wounded. But it was not always possible. Eugene Sledge recalls an incident when a Marine went insane during a night patrol. Fearful that the enemy were all around them (it was later discovered the noises were coming from crocodiles, not enemy soldiers), they had to stop the man's screams from giving away their position:

All of a sudden out there at night in that pitch black dark in that swamp we heard this most horrible screaming and yelling and he was having a nightmare... his mind simply had had all of the stress it could take – Peleliu was his second campaign... and so I heard either the lieutenant or the sergeant say to the corpsman, 'Give him a shot of morphine, maybe that will quieten him down,' so they gave him a shot of morphine and it didn't faze him. They gave him two more shots of morphine and he still didn't get quiet, so somebody hit him with a fist and that just seemed to stimulate him. So then finally one of them said, 'Hit him in the head with that entrenching tool,' so they hit him in the head with an entrenching tool, and it was a sickening sound, and the next day that boy was dead.

Kiyokazu Tsuchida recalls a similarly heart-breaking incident on a burial party after his squad killed a comrade to prevent him from surrendering: 'As we were carrying the body, one of the soldiers was crying and speaking to the body, saying, "Please forgive us, please understand. I am sorry, I am sorry. I cannot imagine how crushed your family would be if they heard about this, Ei. I can't imagine what would happen if they were to know."'

Those in the front line faced the most severe stress. Men soiled their pants from fear; trapped by artillery fire with nowhere to dig in, they trembled so badly they could not stop shaking; they were so on edge at night that it was advisable to whisper to a buddy to wake him up when it was his turn to keep watch: if he was touched, he might come up fighting with his K-bar knife. They collapsed from heat exhaustion having fought for days, in searing heat, without receiving any fresh water supplies; and through it all they endured the stench of putrefying flesh and the sight of maggots devouring the dead. The numbers of men who cracked under such intense pressure grew as the war rolled towards Tokyo and encountered ever more fanatical resistance. The battle for the tiny volcanic island of Iwo Jima, in which close to 6,000 US Marines died, had approximately 4,000 evacuations for battle fatigue (out of a total 18,000 evacuations). Later that year on Okinawa, the most bloody island invasion of the war, some 26,000 men were evacuated as neuro-psychological cases.

The Marines described the look in the face of a man who had snapped as the '2000-yard stare'. Corpsman Stan Dabrowski knew that the men he tagged as combat fatigue cases and sent back down to the beach for evacuation were not faking any symptoms: 'You are ready to scream but you can't, your spirit just gives out and you just crack.' Marine George Peto remembers the warning signs: 'After a fellow is there so long, and if it starts to get the best of him, he starts wandering around looking lackadaisical and he's got this wild look in his eye and he's about to lose it, you can pretty much tell he's right at the end of his string... And sometimes he will sit down and cry, just sit down and cry...'

What kept Allied troops going? A few took solace from broad aims such as patriotism, defeating fascism, or protecting democracy, but the ordinary soldier knew all too well that war was a vast project, within which he was a small, probably irrelevant, and certainly expendable cog. Considering the larger picture only highlighted one's own insignificance. The most common retort to the news, given to the Marines on Okinawa, that Germany had surrendered was: 'So what?' The Japanese troops only yards in front were at the limits of their horizon. As Eugene Sledge recalls: 'As far as we were concerned, Nazi Germany might as well have been on the moon because we made an attack that same day and the company got all shot up.'

Hatred and revenge motivated many, but was not what men clung to in moments of desperation. Stan Dabrowski explains: 'You didn't fight for your mother's apple pie or something – you fought to keep your buddy alive, protect each other.' Marine George Peto is even more adamant: 'There is never no thoughts about "I'm doing this for my country", that's a lot of crap. You're doing it because you're there and you can't leave your buddies, and they wouldn't leave you either.' Trapped in an arena of hate, men still managed to respect, admire and even love their comrades. Dabrowski had wounded men, on occasion, insist their buddy be treated before them. Some even gave their lives for their friends: 'They were in a foxhole with their buddy, a Japanese lobbed a grenade in there. He saw it, he dove on it, protected his buddy with his body and got killed, OK. This was not rehearsed, nobody said he had to do this, this was just done.'

God offered comfort to many men. There are no atheists in fox holes, went the saying, but George Peto disagrees:

I never was too religious in my life, and so I thought well, you know, this is a good time to get with the act, so I said, 'Lord, if you can help me now is the time,' and that was the exact words I used. And nothing changed, them mortar shells kept coming down and the machine-guns were just lining that beach, you couldn't stick your head up... and I hate to say this, but I went through that war not believing in anything but myself and my buddies.

Eugene Sledge and his friend Snafu were at opposite ends of the religious spectrum. Both fell back on what they knew best as they secured the open ground of Peleliu's runway – Eugene's worst combat experience of the war: 'When we crossed the airport I couldn't tell you how many times I recited the 23rd Psalm and the Lord's Prayer, and I could see Snafu's lips moving, and when I got close enough to him there was just this voluminous amount of cursing coming out of his mouth. The harder I prayed, the more he cursed.'

Some battles led to sudden increases in attendance levels at church services. Chaplains would offer communion and mass right up to the front line, with men falling back just a few yards to take the holy sacrament. On Iwo Jima attendance nearly quadrupled. But other battles had a different effect. Months of brutal fighting in New Guinea had hit Australians like Bill Spencer hard: 'The church parade was held after the Buna turn out, and the men just walked away from it... seeing all the death and desecration around you – it's enough to turn you off religion and say there is no God, he wouldn't let this happen.'

There is a danger of overestimating the degree to which the soldiers were dehumanized. Even with the war raging around them, men on both sides did discuss the moral implications of what they were doing, whether it was Hiraoka Hisashi and his colleagues arguing if it was right to eat the dead soldier, or Doc Caswell gently talking Eugene Sledge out of collecting gold teeth. Yet moral squeamishness could put lives at risk.

On Saipan, Marine Steve Judd was ordered by an inexperienced lieutenant to get the Japanese occupants out of a cave alive. Judd and his demolition team felt that, given the tendency of the Japanese to kill themselves and their captors with grenades, their own safety overrode that of whoever was in the cave. His story has two lessons, one aimed at the irresponsible young officer, the other at all of us today: 'We told the lieutenant don't tell us what to do, so we took it and we just blew it up, and we don't know if there was women and children or whatever, we just blew them up. We just didn't have time to waste, you know. Some people will tell you today it was cruel and inhumane, but you weren't there, we were.'

9

CAUGHT

We were captives, we weren't prisoners of war. They told us we were dishonourable; we were captives, and therefore we were despicable... As far as the Japanese were concerned, we were non-persons.
TOM MORRIS, an Australian prisoner of the Japanese

We had received excellent medical treatment and kind hospitality. Our Japanese idea of the enemy had been completely overturned. But we were still Japanese. No matter how much kindness we received, we still had to die.
MASARU MORIKI, a Japanese prisoner of the Australians

THE MOMENT OF CAPTURE BRINGS the intense pressure of clashing emotions down on a soldier. Shame, guilt, anger, fear – and perhaps a measure of relief – hit exhausted minds and bodies. Worrying questions about others – Have I let down comrades? The regiment? What will my family think? – vie with immediate personal anxieties: will my captors torture me? What should I tell them? The Pacific War spared its soldiers none of these torments, and added a few more: both sides killed enemy prisoners on the battlefield; Allied POWs were subjected to brutality, sickness and death in Japanese prison camps; captured Japanese faced years of mental anguish at having betrayed their Emperor and country. Some Japanese prisoners killed themselves, by hanging or by biting their own tongues and bleeding to death.

One of the terrible features of being a prisoner of war is that you have time to think about your position. Most find it hard to get it out of their minds for the rest of their lives. Fred Seiker, a

Dutch captive of the Japanese, speaks for many prisoners of war: 'It doesn't finish there, and it doesn't finish here today, ask my wife, it doesn't. It's still with me and all the others. I am no exception, they are all the same. People say, "After sixty years, you have nightmares?" Yes, and so does Charlie, so does Jimmy, so does Harry, they all have.'

The majority of Allied POWs were captured in the initial phase of the Pacific War, when Japan was rapidly expanding her empire. Around 200,000 Allied POWs were Asians. Most were released after just a few months' captivity – although for some it was already too late. Over 60,000 Filipino soldiers taken on the Bataan peninsula were subjected to the death march, and the survivors imprisoned in Camp O'Donnell. Here they suffered similar privations – but in far larger numbers – to the Americans also surrendered on Bataan. Over 30,000 lay dead when the Japanese decided to release them later that summer. Those Indian soldiers, captured in Singapore, who refused to switch allegiance and join the Indian National Army never enjoyed the amnesty granted to most other captured Asian soldiers. Some 35,000 of them spent the duration of the war in captivity.

Around 133,000 POWs held by the Japanese were white: British, Dutch, Australian, American, Canadian and New Zealanders. These men, as guests of the Emperor, faced survival odds little better than three to one. Although Japan's Foreign Ministry promised the country would abide by the Geneva Convention of 1929 – signed but not ratified by Japan – in practice, the western rules of war did not apply, as historian Gavan Daws explains:

> By the mid-thirties, the Japanese were saying that whenever and however the white man's way of doing things conflicted with the Japanese, Japan would go ahead and do things its way. The way the Japanese read the 1929 Geneva Convention, an enemy prisoner of war in their hands would be entitled to a softer time than a Japanese fighting man in the field with the Emperor's army, and to them that was absurd.

Captives of the Japanese could not look beyond the barbed wire for protection or justice, as Chase Nielsen, the navigator captured in occupied China after the Doolittle bombing raid on Tokyo, discovered when brought before a Japanese officer:

I said: 'According to the Geneva Convention, all I can tell you is my name, rank and serial number.' And he said: 'What's the Geneva Convention?' He said: 'We're fighting a war. Don't you know that?... We're making our rules as we go.' And he said: 'I'll tell you something else,' and he put his finger right up in my face, 'I can kill you this afternoon and no one will ever know who did it.'

At the heart of the tragedy are the very different attitudes of the two warring sides towards prisoners and surrender. The Japanese had been long educated to believe they owed unquestioning loyalty to the Emperor, and that had to be discharged by fighting to the death. Surrender was a state that brought only dishonour. It was unthinkable. So when Allied troops surrendered in vast numbers, they forfeited their dignity and much of their humanity in the eyes of the Japanese soldier. Twenty-one-year-old Hiroshi Abe was the engineer responsible for the tortuous 30-kilometre section of the Death Railway at the Burma–Thailand border.

Some men in the Japanese army lacked all understanding. It was a collection of people from all sorts of backgrounds. Those brought up in a rough, ignorant environment resorted to violence whenever they didn't like anything. And the Japanese army indulged them – there was a widespread attitude that because these were prisoners who had been defeated in battle, they deserved to be badly treated.

The academic Ikuhiko Hata summarizes the view of those at the very top: 'At the heart of the matter lay their belief that their own troops on being taken prisoner should forfeit all human rights. Inevitably this attitude was applied with equal vigour towards enemy POWs.' It was a lethal cocktail: army authorities who had strict deadlines for slave labour projects did not care about prisoners' conditions and kept their own men short of food and medicine; engineers and guards on the receiving end of exacting targets from above had contempt for POWs and were conditioned to use violence as the solution to problems.

We saw in Chapter 3 that a key feature of training and life in the ranks of the Imperial Army was the NCOs hitting the soldiers; the second-year recruits hitting the first-years and so on. As historian Saburo Ienaga argues: 'An army so brutal to its own people would hardly refrain from atrocities against enemy forces or civilians in occupied areas.' Both ex-POWs and former guards have explained the brutality in the prison camps in these terms: the guards beat the prisoners because they were themselves oppressed by their officers, who were themselves under intense pressure from headquarters. The prisoners were simply the last in a long chain of violence and received the accumulated momentum of brutality. Fred Seiker does not agree:

I have heard people say that because they were so badly treated by their superiors in the army they took it out on us. Bullshit, not true, not true at all. I just do not agree with it, because they tortured for pleasure many, many a time. They didn't torture because they were mistreated by their superiors, they tortured us because that gave them satisfaction, or they felt totally superior to us as a race, totally.

Certainly, there are many stories of sadistic guards across the prison camp system, which play into the argument that certain temperaments seek out certain jobs. Korean guard Lee Haku Rae argues that they had no choice in the matter: 'If I had turned it down, our rations would have been stopped and my family would have been in trouble from day one... It was really an enforced recruitment. In that way three thousand and several hundred men were recruited from Korea.'

Former engineers on the railway tend to blame disciplinary excesses on the guards, but some ex-POWs, such as Tom Morris, maintain that the railway engineers were as capable of cruelty as the guards:

Don't swallow that one about the engineers, because one of the most feared jobs on the railway was to work on a bridge with Japanese engineers, where you could be knocked from the bridge with whatever weapon... whether it was a bar of bamboo or iron or steel or a pick handle, whatever, baseball bats they carried...

and it wasn't for arrogance or disobedience. If you just didn't understand what the Jap wanted you to do, what he wanted you to hand him, he could knock you off – knock you off a bridge.

The strongest argument to refute the notions that the guards and engineers had no choice but to be brutal – they had all been brainwashed, it was in their genes, and so on – is that almost every surviving prisoner can remember at least one good Japanese in their camp. Lester Tenney was an American prisoner in Japan, working in a coalmine in Fukuoka, where a guard called Sato 'brought me sweetened condensed milk, which most probably cost him a fortune, or he most probably could have lost his life if they ever caught him giving that to me, you know. But he was very, very kind.' A Japanese sergeant on the Burma–Thailand Railway scrupulously shared food and cigarettes with Duncan Ferguson when they worked together stringing telegraph wires down the line. He also saved Ferguson from beatings at the hands of another guard: 'That was one of the finest men that I've ever met.' Dick Gordon worked on dam construction in Mitsushima, Japan, and recalls with gratitude a guard, a civilian contractor and a camp commandant, all of whom went out of their way to treat prisoners with compassion. The good were the exceptions, but they demolish the racist arguments and show that there were choices to be made, even in the intensely pressurized worst Japanese prison camps.

Character, peer pressure, ignorance, boredom, sadism all played their part in determining the behaviour of the Japanese who dealt directly with the prisoners. Hiroshi Abe exempts neither himself nor top brass from responsibility: 'I felt all those with the title of a general should have been executed at the end of the war. As for myself, I was prepared to be killed on the coast of Changi when we were made to line up to be shot.' The first director of the POW Information Bureau, Lieutenant General Mikio Uemura, actively wanted white prisoners to be treated severely, used as labour to support the war effort and exploited across the region as testimony to Japanese superiority. A conversation between Uemura and Prime Minister Tojo during a conference of the Heads of Army Ministry Directorates in July 1942 (recorded in a wartime diary) demonstrates their complicity:

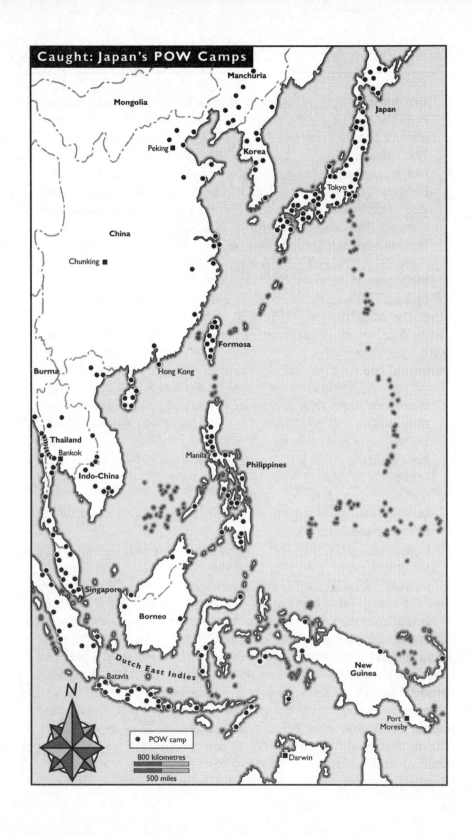

Caught: Japan's POW Camps

Uemura: 'We rejected a British offer to send relief goods to the POWs at Hong Kong and now the Americans are making a similar offer for the POWs at Bataan.'
Tojo: 'Where Japanese troops are facing hardships... there is no need to pamper POWs.'
Uemura: 'The Red Cross wants to send quinine...'
Tojo: 'Reject them all. There's no knowing where this might end.'
Uemura: 'The Red Cross want to send their delegates to the areas that we have occupied. We'll turn that down too.'

Medicines and food parcels from the Red Cross were stockpiled, or pillaged for use by the Japanese and Koreans working on the line. The almost total lack of medicines not only resulted in men dying from preventable diseases but meant they did so in agony, with rarely anything to alleviate their pain. Dick Lee remains furious at the suffering men had to endure before they died:

When they [the POWs] died it was release, but it was the suffering them people had for the weeks and weeks beforehand. I'll never see the same suffering here, never. You can have cancer, you can have anything you like, you name it, there is always a jab here or something to ease that suffering. Not them – they suffered till unconsciousness took over from them... and it was hundreds upon hundreds it was happening to in our camp. What about all the other camps? Just the same, all up the line, all had the same experience: suffering. And them bastards would not let the Red Cross come and bring stuff. I mean they [the Japanese] were animals.

It is almost impossible to generalize on the experience of being a prisoner of the Japanese. Although no camp was 'good', some were better than others, and some were absolutely terrible. According to Japanese figures there were 170 main camps and 214 branch camps in all. The death rate in each depended on numerous factors: the health of POWs when they arrived at the camp; conditions in the camp; the work they were forced to do; the temperament of the camp commander and his guards; the skill of the interpreter (if any); the weather; the amount of supplies the camp received; the number of medical staff among the group of POWs; the ability of POW officers to stand up for their men; and the ability of POWs to organize and look after themselves. Even the course of the war itself could be a factor, as Lester Tenney recalls: 'The Americans can bomb Tokyo, and that day in the mine, the civilian workers would beat the devil out of us with pieces of wood, with pickaxes, with hammers. Break your nose, break your head, knock your teeth, anything.'

The Burma–Thailand Railway was the biggest slave labour project undertaken. It was a desperate act by Imperial Army Headquarters to provide a supply route for Japan's Burma forces, who by 1944 threatened India itself. A pre-war estimate reckoned it would take five years to build some 250 miles of track. But Tokyo gave its native and prisoner work force just sixteen months, toiling through the dense jungle and ragged hills separating the frontier region of the two countries. Nowhere else in the Japanese empire did as many Allied POWs die: out of the 60,000 (over half of them British) sent to work along the track, some 12,000 men died.

The engineers overseeing the project treated their charges as tools. Fred Seiker was told by an officer: 'You belong to me. I have the power to kill you any time I like.' Completing the railway was all that mattered. The lives of the men, POWs and Asian slave labourers alike were of no significance. Otto Schwarz was present when Colonel Yoshitada Nagatomo first outlined the task to the assembled prisoners:

> He told us that we were the rabble of lost army. He told us that they had a railroad that they needed built for them to continue their campaign on the Burma–India border. He told us that while we had no status as human beings, the gracious Japanese would treat us fairly and kindly. He said that we were expected to work hard and we would be treated well. He then told us that they intended to build this railroad over the white man's body and that's exactly what they did.

In desperate conditions and with almost no mechanized tools, the men were set to work. It did not take long for the shortage of food, long hours of hard labour, random beatings and woefully inadequate medical supplies to have disastrous consequences. Dysentery, beriberi (a painful wasting disease caused by malnutrition), malaria and tropical ulcers (that destroy both skin and bone) set in. Soon the labour force resembled a parade of sick men more than anything else. Korean guard Lee Haku Rae had to provide a fixed number of workers every morning for the engineers – regardless of how many were fit for work:

The Railway Regiment was based near our camp – every evening they sent over a messenger, telling us how many workers they needed the next day. If they needed 300 workers, and we only had 270 fit enough to work, what choice did we have? We simply couldn't tell them that. So we got together however many they wanted, including some in the 'mildly ill' category, and sent them off. Whatever we felt, that didn't count.

'Mildly ill' included people who would nowadays be rushed to hospital. Forced to work when sick, many men died at the side of the railway. Duncan Ferguson was in F Force – perhaps the worst affected POW contingent to go up into the jungle. He worked on the line until the completion ceremony itself, and saw the callous lengths both guards and engineers were prepared to go to meet their schedules: 'The stretcher cases were taken out and laid at the side of the railway with a hammer to break stones. True. The stretcher cases! And they were carrying them in at night – dead.'

Misery was compounded even further when Imperial Headquarters in Tokyo increased the pace of construction work from June 1943 onwards, coinciding with the wettest monsoon in memory, and a savage, uncontrollable outbreak of cholera that killed thousands up and down the line. The effect on the Asian labourers has already been discussed in Chapter 7. The POWs fared only slightly better. They could no longer be buried: the dead were too numerous and too contagious. Hiroshi Abe, the Japanese engineer, was not blind to the torment the prisoners were forced to endure:

There were about ten people whose job was to burn the bodies. Their faces were full of despair. I knew what was in their minds because I too was in despair. But who was to blame for all this? There was no point in blaming God. We were up against reality. People were dying of cholera, and so many bodies were piling up that we couldn't keep pace with the burning. But I had to complete my mission, no matter what. I had to meet the deadline to finish the bridge. The worst times were between June and July in 1943. There was heavy rain every day; the trees we cut down were too damp for use. There were 7,000 POWs from Australia and Great Britain. Within a month, 3,200 of them died. 1,200 died in my unit.

The puzzle for many prisoners is why, if the Japanese wanted railways built or airfields levelled, it wouldn't have been expedient to provide the necessary shelter, food and medicine. As Fred Seiker says, 'Had they treated us properly, which they could have done with the resources of the countries where we were working, we would have built this damn railroad for them.' The sad truth was, the one commodity the Japanese thought they had to spare was slave labour. With food, medicine and qualified medical staff in short supply for their own men, some Japanese commanders seemed to treat POWs as disposable. They were, in a sense, dead already.

Some men went mad; one Japanese response was to hang a wooden sign around their necks and give them a wide berth, as Duncan Ferguson remembers: 'The Japanese wouldn't touch these people... you know, they are crazy men, no they wouldn't... I don't know why, but they steered clear of them. There were two or three that laid it on and got away with it. Hahahaha. Crazy – till the war finished! They were OK then! Hahahaha. I know two or three did that.'

Lester Tenney took drastic steps to get out of work in the Mitsui-owned mine, which had been closed before the war because all the coal that was safe to extract had already been taken out:

Sometimes you'd just say I can't go on. You'd say to yourself, if I go back in that mine tomorrow, I'm dead... So, I may pay [a buddy] five rations of rice over a period of a month, to break my hand. Then he would take a steel pin that would be holding the coal cars together... 12, 14 inches long, about an inch and a half in diameter. And then when it's ready with your foot, your hand, whatever it was, you'd put it down there, and he would take one good whack at it, whammo, and that would break it... And I'd be out of work for maybe two or three days. A broken hand, two or three days, a broken arm maybe five days.

The one consistent, tangible lifeline to humanity was friendship. Few prisoners can now talk about it without shedding tears. Australian Tom Morris is no exception: 'I remember sitting in a little running creek... trying to cleanse myself. I had just fouled my pants and I tried to clean myself up the best I could, and being helped back to my bunk which was two tiers up by a friend, with his arm around me to help me get back to my quarters... mateship was a terribly important factor.'

Duncan Ferguson agrees: 'Oh, you had to have muckers. A man on his own just let himself go.' For Dick Lee, 'To have pals was worth a fortune.' Late in 1944, after the railway had been completed, Dick's friend Tony Mansi was brought into the main camp near Kanchanaburi on the Burma–Thailand Railway racked with disease and covered in rotting ulcers. Tony had once saved Dick's life; now Dick tried to save his.

I've washed his front down... but he's lying in mess now, his dysentery, the smell. So I gets hold of him, I said, 'I'm going to turn you over, Tony'... You've got to remember you're pushing over a bag of bones, the spine is all showing through the back, the flesh is so thin, it's all bone you're moving, but here's a man still alive, talking to me... He says to me, 'Would you like to take my personal things?'... his mess tin, his mug... some photos of his mother, his sisters, his girlfriend, and a few old letters... So I says to him, 'Tony, you'll be OK... No one will touch nothing. I'll see you in the morning, it will be OK.' He said. 'I'd rather you take them, Dick,' he said, 'because I won't be here in the morning.'

Dick Lee buried his friend the next day, and has not stopped grieving for sixty years. Virtually every prisoner lost friends. Over time, some even tried not to form close bonds because they came to dread the pain of increasingly inevitable loss. But alongside the comradeship was a defensive survivalism among the prisoners which, as Fred Seiker acknowledges, bordered on its own kind of – literal – brutality: 'I hate to say this, but you become an animal... with all the senses of an animal, self preservation. You are marching along or you see something on the ground that is edible, you look around, you pick it up because if you don't somebody else might, that's how you become, and you share it with your mates, nobody else.'

As the months and years passed, living became so painful and death so common, that prisoners debilitated by work, illness and loss could scarcely focus beyond survival. Pat Darling was imprisoned in a civilian internment camp on Sumatra. She remembers how, critical though friendships were, sheer frailty forced a degree of isolation on the women: 'We didn't see a lot of one another because you were just too weak to walk that distance. You could walk and carry the water that you had to carry, you could help carry out a coffin, and half the time that you went out on a funeral, it was because you had to collect wood so you had something to cook your food with.'

She recalls a mordantly comic exchange with an Irish girl named Biddy: 'She looked me up and down from her whole five feet tall and said to me, "Sister, do you think it's worth your while walking back?" – this was walking back from the cemetery. Haha. I said to her, "Biddy, I'll make you a promise if you'll make me the same promise: I promise to carry your coffin out, if you promise to carry mine out."'

The dividing line between black humour and callousness was a fine one for prisoners such as those in Duncan Ferguson's hut, who had to be up at first light, but were kept awake by the distress of others:

> I can't remember the camp we were in, but there was a chap there, oh, he was delirious, and he kept asking for a rope. He says: 'I want to hang myself, somebody give me a rope, I want to hang myself,' and this went on night after night. And somebody this night says, 'Will somebody give him a bloody rope, and let him hang himself, so we can get a bit of peace?' He eventually did.

In the fight for survival, prisoners did terrible things to other prisoners. American POW Dick Gordon characterizes such people as predators, like the American medical orderly who had quinine tablets but refused to give them to Dick, sick with malaria. He would only sell them, for $5 each. In Camp O'Donnell on Bataan, five men jumped the water queue to fill a five-gallon drum for the hospital. In fact, they went behind the barracks and drank their fill. The Japanese severely limited access to water, so five men deprived many more of a life-saving, precious commodity. Dick Gordon is still bitter about those who added to their suffering:

The Japanese brought it about and which is why I have never forgiven them, and I will never forget what they've done. But then the Americans compounded that, and that's the part that I could not accept, no matter who it was. We were Americans, we are supposedly the good guys, and here the bad guys just got through roughing us up; now we've got the good guys doing the very same thing, and that's the difficult part to accept... The predators caused deaths, and we were more or less not only contending with the Japanese, we were contending with our fellow American.

Prisoners sometimes took the law into their own hands. Supplies of extra food were smuggled into Fred Seiker's camp by Thai peasants, thereby risking their own lives. But in exchange for a cushy job in the camp kitchens, a fellow prisoner betrayed the operation to the Japanese. Fred Seiker presided over a kangaroo court:

He was a traitor, he was responsible for one of ours being beaten to death almost. I passed what I call a death sentence. And it was then decided by a majority vote what would happen to this person. This guy goes to the toilet late at night, two chaps go with him, they kick his feet from under him, down he goes, and they watch him not come up. Simple. On parade he's missing, nobody knows where he is. Start dredging the shit pit, out he comes, end of story. There was no bad feeling, there was no ill feeling, there was no sad feeling, there was no feeling. Nothing at all.

The second biggest cause of death for Allied POWs, after the horrors of the camps, was drowning. The Japanese transported their prisoners to new labour camps in the cargo holds of rusty tramp steamers without any markings to indicate they were carrying POWs. America's ever tightening grip on Japanese shipping had an unintentional side effect: at least 10,000 – possibly many more – Allied prisoners were killed at sea. These losses were so great because the guards rarely opened the cargo hatches when a boat was hit. Those who did escape into the sea were sometimes shot for sport by Japanese in life rafts, or on rescue vessels. Only occasionally were prisoners allowed into the boats that stopped to pick up Japanese survivors. Guards caught in the water by prisoners did not last long.

Yet the POWs who escaped America's submarine packs did not have an easy time. They call their vessels 'hellships' for a reason. For up to forty-five days, men were packed into the holds so tightly that they could not lie down; they were desperately thirsty; fed little; and suffered from heat, seasickness and claustrophobia. Frank Ficklin was moved from Java to Singapore in the safer, earlier days of the war:

We had just about enough room to sit with your legs apart, and someone sat right in front of you, so that you really didn't have room to lay down – if you did, you all had to do it at one instant. It was hot, we were right on the equator, there was no air, the only light that came into it was from the hulls above. The latrine was on deck... often times they didn't let you up when you needed to go so we were sitting in our own filth.

As the war dragged on and the journeys became more dangerous, ships increasingly hugged the coastline, taking longer and longer to reach their destination. The more time men spent in the hold, the more chance they had of going crazy from thirst, fear and frustration. A few Americans ended up killing those who went mad, desperate to keep their guards from exacting group punishment for the misdemeanours of one. Richard Gordon, himself a survivor of the Bataan death march, Camp O'Donnell, a hellship from the Philippines to Japan and several years' hard labour once there, knows of one consignment of POWs who left Manila in December 1944:

They were sunk right outside Manila Harbour, and they were put on another ship. That ship got as far as Formosa... and they were attacked by bombers, and that ship was sunk with so many men dying there. So of the original 1,600 aboard that ship, 300 reached Japan, and those conditions were so bad that the men were going mad in the bows of the ship, some to the point that they slashed the wrist of a sleeping American and drank the blood from his wrist to put some liquid into their bodies.

THE JAPANESE TAKEN PRISONER by the Allies were generally well treated. The problem was surviving the surrender process. Marine George Peto recalls the instructions broadcast by loudspeaker to men in the first assault waves attacking Peleliu: 'When we were aboard the LSTs [Landing Ship Tanks] there was a message came through from our colonel, and the word was that we were to take no prisoners.' Soldier Nelson Peery in New Guinea recalls that the killing of Japanese men who wanted to surrender was routine: 'We all saw the brutality and in some instances just plain savagery against Japanese soldiers who were trying to surrender, or who had surrendered, who were shot or clubbed. They were pretty brutally treated.'

Dennis Warner, a soldier turned historian, recounted after the war an incident he witnessed in New Guinea: '"But sir, they are wounded and want to surrender," a colonel protested to [a major general] at the edge of the cleared perimeter after a massive and unsuccessful attack. "You heard me, Colonel," replied [the major general], who was only yards from up-stretched Japanese hands. "I want no prisoners. Shoot them all." They were shot.'

Charles Lindbergh recorded conversations about the shooting of prisoners and other atrocities. His journal entry for 13 July 1944 reads:

It was freely admitted that some of our soldiers tortured Jap prisoners and were as cruel and barbaric at times as the Japs themselves. Our men would think nothing of shooting a Jap prisoner or a soldier attempting to surrender. They treat the Japs with less respect than they would give to an animal, and these acts are condoned by almost everyone. We claim to be fighting for civilization, but the more I see of this war in the Pacific the less right I think we have to claim to be civilized. In fact, I am not sure that our record in this respect stands so very much higher than the Japs'.

Other men he met told stories of machine-gunning Japanese airmen parachuting out of their planes, slaughtering Japanese wounded in a New Guinea field hospital and throwing captured Japanese out of aircraft transporting them to prison, then reporting the deaths as suicides. Another of Lindbergh's diary entries records a revealing conversation with American officers: 'The talk drifted to prisoners of war and the small percentage of Japanese soldiers taken prisoner. "Oh, we could take more prisoners if we wanted to," one of the officers replied. "But our boys don't like to take prisoners." We had a couple of thousand down at —, but only a hundred or two were turned in. They had an accident with the rest."'

According to Lindbergh, one US division was so reluctant to take prisoners that its commanders were reduced to offering a fortnight's leave in Sydney for every prisoner brought in alive for questioning. Then they were snowed under with Japanese POWs. When the offer was withdrawn, the source of subjects for inter- rogation dried up. While, clearly, it was not impossible to take prisoners, it was potentially dangerous: they might try to kill their captors with a concealed weapon. It was invariably incon- venient – guarding them absorbed precious resources. Most important of all, it had absolutely no appeal to troops who hated the Japanese and saw their role as being to fight and kill them, not save their lives.

Eugene Sledge, veteran of Peleliu and Okinawa, sums up the – unofficial – attitude and practice of the Marines: 'We had such intense hatred for them, and they were so tricky about coming in to surrender and then coming in with their hands up like that [he half raises his arms], and then when you got close enough they opened their arms out and out dropped two grenades, one for each armpit, and so we just automatically shot them, unless some officer stopped us.'

Alexander Leighton, a social scientist heading the US govern- ment's Foreign Moral Analysis Division, was charged with the task of investigating ways to convince the ordinary Japanese soldier to lay down his arms. Leighton was convinced that Japanese soldiers could be encouraged to surrender, given the right approach:

The analysts came to the conclusion that the most important single point connected with the obtaining of surrenders was the necessity of convincing Allied troops and local field commanders of the value of prisoners and of training men in the technique of securing them. Without this, surrender propaganda was a waste of time, since it could not overcome the effect of witnessing the fact that men were shot when they tried to give themselves up. Our evidence indicates that this happened time and time again and that many of the desperate hold-outs and banzai charges were based to a significant extent on the conviction that the Americans would not take them prisoner, and that their choice was merely between two kinds of death.

The reality was that Japanese trying to surrender were as likely to be shot as deserters when leaving their own lines. Nor did the Japanese have a monopoly on the 'no-surrender' policy, as Marine George Peto makes clear: 'It became sort of an all-out war... there was no talk about surrender, the word surrender was not in our vocabulary, we never even talked about it.' Yet despite Allied reluctance to take prisoners, and Japanese reluctance to surrender, roughly 50,000 Japanese fighting men did do exactly that. The key was often an independent-minded commander with a realistic appreciation of his force's chances of success, combined with a deep consideration for his men. In Hollandia, Netherlands New Guinea (now Indonesia), over 600 ill or wounded starving Japanese under Major General Masazumi Inada gave themselves up.

Marine George Peto recalls an incident on Okinawa: 'It was a captain, a Japanese captain; he surrendered 200 of his soldiers, and that was almost a miracle, but that happened at the end of the war on Okinawa. And I did go down to look at him, and he was dressed as neat as you can. And he demanded a formal surrender, and he still had an attitude about him, and... we had to form up and give them a formal surrender.'

Some Japanese surrendered as individuals, choosing with great care the moment when they could safely cross over. One man waited in bushes until an American had put his rifle down and was busy using a latrine. On Saipan in August 1944, Takeo Yamauchi tried to talk two subordinates into giving up with him; their conversation provides a rare insight into diametrically opposed notions about where their duties lay in a war they all knew was lost:

The three of us had been hiding in a foxhole on the beach for three days. It was then I approached them, saying, 'Let's not die in this stupid war. This war is not the good war you have been made to believe. It is idiotic for us to die in it. If this war is lost, even if the nation is torn apart... the race known as the Japanese will survive and will simply construct a new society. You think that everything will be over if the war is lost, but it won't be the end. After the war, Japanese society will remain, and a new society will spring from it. So it would be stupid of us to die here in Saipan when we are fast approaching such an important time in our society. So let's figure out a way to survive.' My subordinates replied that my ideas were anti-nationalistic, the ideas of a traitor. They said, 'We will never agree to such thoughts. We will die gracefully as soldiers of the Japanese Empire. There is no other way. Commander, you must rid your mind of such thoughts.'

Takeo Yamauchi gave them the slip, bided his time and then crossed to the American lines. When he looked back he saw he had become a Pied Piper, with a small group surrendering in his wake, although his two colleagues were not among them. Once a POW, even he kept quiet to his fellow prisoners that he had willingly given up: 'Had I admitted that I had voluntarily surrendered, I would have been subject to serious violence.'

The Japanese taken into captivity before the end of the war retained a strong sense of shame over what they had done. Almost to a man, they refused to write home – not wanting to tarnish their families with their dishonour. For the same reason, they gave false names; one camp guard in Hawaii would relieve the tension when taking in a fresh batch of POWs by asking 'Have we Kazuo Hayakawa [a famous film star] here today?' Largely ignorant of the Geneva Convention and never instructed on how to behave in captivity (as their orders were to die rather than surrender), many of the prisoners were remarkably co-operative with their captors, showing no security awareness during interrogation and willingly divulging all they knew.

Yet despite this cooperation, few Japanese settled comfortably into captivity. Masaru Moriki was captured on New Guinea when wounded and was taken to a prison camp in Cowra, 180 miles west of Sydney in Australia. The Japanese POWs were given good food, kind treatment and virtually no work. They spent the day playing sports, particularly baseball, which Moriki organized:

While I was playing, I forgot about everything else. It was a good laugh. I forgot all about being a POW during the game. Then afterwards, the grey feeling would return. I thought, I'm a prisoner. How can it be right to be enjoying myself? The more kindly we were treated, the more tormented we felt... I thought I shouldn't be indulged in this way and should think about dying at the first opportunity.

Faced with growing numbers of Japanese prisoners, camp authorities informed the Japanese at Cowra that officers and other ranks would shortly be separated. This caused dismay. It would undermine the POWs' command structure, thereby threatening their ability to rise up in support of the Japanese invasion of Australia which the hard-liners were convinced was only a matter of time. Their only option was, this militant core argued, a mass breakout. Masaru Moriki was opposed to the hard-liners but, when confronted by their proposal, he like many others found it impossible to reject a course of action dictated by the ideology that they had all been brought up to honour. At a series of meetings the plan was discussed and votes cast. Moriki recalls one of the speeches that convinced 80 per cent of the men to vote for the suicidal breakout:

'Are you really Japanese soldiers? Now is the time for us to die. If the Australian army is going to divide us into two, we should stand up and fight against them until we die, like the fall of flowers in full bloom.' Nobody had any word to throw back at them because as Japanese we basically believed being a prisoner was the greatest shame. Everyone got dragged in by it.

In the small hours of 5 August 1944, about a thousand Japanese prisoners set fire to their huts and charged the wire. The Australian guards opened fire. In the ensuing mayhem four Australians were killed, but the main aim was neither attack nor escape, but death: 183 Japanese were mown down by the guards. A few fanatics had pushed the majority into suicidal action but, under fire, inner feelings and old habits took over with the vast majority, Masaru Moriki included: 'Whether it was human instinct or the result of army training – somewhere deeply ingrained in us was the instinct to take cover in the face of bullets. There were ditches running down the road through the camp. People jumped in the ditches and lay down, and so did I. I stayed there till morning.'

Hundreds made it into the surrounding countryside, without trying to escape beyond. Most chose life; one group of seventy-five simply sat out in the nearby hills having a smoke, surrendering at dawn. But twenty-nine killed themselves, or helped one another to die. Two men threw themselves in front of a train. And some Japanese never even left their huts, but hanged themselves from the rafters, queuing up to use the one rope.

10

SHATTERED JEWELS

Corpses drifting swollen in the sea-depths,
Corpses rotting in the mountain grass –
We shall die, by the side of our lord we shall die.
We shall not look back.

HITOMARO KAKINOMOTO, seventh-century Japanese poet

THIS VERSE, FROM THE EARLIEST Japanese poetic anthology, the *Manyoshu* (Collection of Ten Thousand Leaves) became a defining summation of what Japan expected from her people 1,250 years later in the Pacific War. The soldiers' booklet, 'Just Read This and the War Is Won', quoted it twice, and it became the lyric for the popular martial song 'Umi Yukaba' (Across the Sea). After Prime Minister Tojo gave his radio broadcast announcing the declaration of war, it was this song that was played to the nation.

At the verse's heart lie two ideas which, in the crucible of the Pacific War, took on the power of commandments: that death in war must be accepted as inevitable and that loyalty to authority was an absolute obligation. By late 1944 the words of this poem were being acted out in Burma, in New Guinea, in the Philippines, in Peleliu, in Saipan. Wherever there were Japanese soldiers, there were the corpses of men who had died 'by the side of our lord'. The inevitability of the sacrifice makes it no less poignant.

In the third year of the war – late in 1944 – Japanese forces were in retreat on most fronts. Gradually the Allies retook Pacific islands and clawed back Burma, mile by painful mile. The Japanese in Burma could at least retreat; the island garrisons had nowhere to go.

The story of Japan's soldiers in the final year of the war challenges both understanding and belief. A host of myths have sought to explain their actions in terms of glorious sacrifice or mass insanity; as the flick of a dying dinosaur's tail, or as a last bid for victory. The desperate fight and sacrifices that characterize the final death throes of a long war were part of the daily routine of the Pacific War, taken for granted by Japanese and Allies alike. Both sides' propaganda portrayed the Japanese as 'a billion hearts beating as one', as identical stampings from a single mould. Perceiving Japan's soldiers as individuals with feelings suited neither the Allied will to demonize their enemy, nor the Japanese requirement for an unquestioningly obedient military machine. Many did not survive to record their feelings; of those who did, some still prefer to remain silent. But it is from the testimony of others who survived those extraordinary final twelve months that their humanity emerges: in the awareness of the suffering they both endured and inflicted, in their doubts and guilt, in their anger at their masters and themselves.

As some senior Japanese had foreseen, Japan could not match America in either quantity or quality of weapons production. By 1943, US factories were rolling out a new plane every five minutes. By 1944, submarine attacks on Japan's lifeline, her merchant fleet, reduced vital supplies for Japanese industry to a trickle. Crucial commodities such as oil, rubber, coal, iron ore and fertilizer were all in desperately short supply. The most important of industries was affected: aircraft production fell by half. No single oil tanker breached the blockade after March 1945. Japan had been deprived of the very prizes the military had first used to justify the war and, without control of sea or air, it was increasingly impossible to move men and matériel around the Pacific. The Japanese war machine was virtually running on empty.

This was transformed in the exotic alchemy of Japanese wartime propaganda thinking into a unique Japanese advantage: 'victory-without-weapons'. For the troops actually having to fight against the latest American aircraft, flame-throwers and rocket launchers, this notion fell short of needs. Hiraoka Hisashi in the Philippines recalls high command's insistence that 'mental attitude was all you needed to fight in a war. It isn't true. What you needed to overwhelm the enemy was sufficient firepower.'

Masao Maeda had been fighting since the first day of the war, from the invasion of Malaya and the capture of Singapore; he had chased the British across Burma and all the way to India. He had seen Japanese tanks crushing British armoured cars, and Zeroes demolishing Brewster Buffaloes. By late 1944, for the first time in three years his faith in Japanese superiority and in certain victory had begun to waver:

> *The reason we were defeated was because of the sheer scale of their military resources. We didn't have command of the air at all. They pinpointed our position from aerial photographs, then bombed, shelled and besieged us. Within a day our position in the jungle was completely destroyed and turned into a sea of mud. I was really afraid of their military resources... my thoughts were less about fighting, and more about running away.*

Hiroshi Yamagami was also up against the might of the re-equipped British 14th Army on the India–Burma border: 'Japan had its pride completely destroyed in the Pacific War and was really taught some lessons about modern warfare... and what we learnt was that mental strength is no compensation for material equipment.' While Hiroshi Yamagami and Masao Maeda were being forced back across the Indian border into Burma, Ei Yamaguchi was facing the US Marines on Peleliu: 'We had to fight with what we had, without resupply. The Americans had supplies to spare. So, the two mental attitudes were very different. We were there to fight to the death, but America could, if she wanted, bring in more soldiers, and had time on her side... The Americans were superior in everything.'

The first island the Japanese defended to the death, and a harbinger of struggles to come, was Attu in the Aleutian island chain. Outnumbering the foe more than three to one, US troops landed on Attu in May 1943. After two weeks of bitter fighting, the Americans had effectively pinned down the last 800 enemy troops (of an original garrison less than 3,000 strong). With almost no ammunition left, and no practical option other than surrender, the Japanese commander ordered all his men to charge the enemy on the night of 29 May 1943. Fewer than thirty survived.

In describing what the Japanese soldiers did that night, the English language is restricted to such words as 'suicide' and 'self-slaughter'. Reference to a thesaurus adds the Japanese words *hara-kiri* ('belly cutting') and *seppuku* ('cutting the abdomen'), and the Sanskrit word *suttee*, which applies specifically to a wife who dies on her husband's funeral pyre. Recent history, particularly in the Middle East, has added the term 'suicide bomber', which starts to add the key active element to an act which is generally seen in the West as personal, generally solitary and above all self-destructive. It may have punitive motives – to make others feel terrible – but it is largely directed at the self. Many Japanese did not recognize what happened on Attu as suicide because it was seen as 'active'. It was an attack – one of whose by-products was the death of those taking part. It was not the result of depression but elation; it gave purpose to life, instead of expressing life's purposelessness. That, at any rate, was the theory. The Cowra breakout in the previous chapter revealed that these were not necessarily unanimous acts, and – as we will see – the elation was often supplied out of the mouth of a sake bottle.

English may not have the word, but the concept exists. Going forward under orders when the odds are so impossible that death is virtually inevitable is a proud feature of British military history. It happened with the Charge of the Light Brigade in the Crimea, occasionally in the Boer War, again and again in the Great War and particularly in the Battle of the Somme with its 57,470 British casualties in a single day. It is just that it is not seen as suicide – except by cynics. Probably the histories of most western armies have their equivalents, although the Attu garrison inspired contemptuous repugnance, not nods of approving recognition. Widely divergent cultures were battling it out in the Pacific, and ideas help win wars. What happened on Attu was seen as proof of the enemy's 'otherness'. 'Others' are non-human. The best thing to do with non-humans is kill them. *Time*'s war correspondent Robert Sherrod wrote:

> *The results of the Jap fanaticism stagger the imagination. The very violence of the scene is incomprehensible to the western mind. Here groups of men had met their self-imposed obligation to die rather than accept capture, by blowing themselves to bits... When the Jap*

knows he is beaten he tries to kill himself, after killing as many of us as he can. But in his anxiety he presses the grenade to his stomach before the plotted time. The ordinary, unreasoning Jap is ignorant. Perhaps he is human. Nothing on Attu indicates it.

In Japan the battle of Attu assumed a different significance. The troops' last act was widely reported, but presented as heroic and moving. The Japanese government called it an 'honourable death'. The soldiers had risen above their plight, overcome their numerical and material weakness, and refused to submit to the enemy. It was glorious self-annihilation – not inhuman stupidity. In honour of the men who died on Attu, Japan's media brought into common parlance an old and obscure term to convey the moral authority and purification the troops had achieved through their destruction: *Attu gyokusai*, or literally, 'Attu jewel smashed'.

There were other options. On neighbouring Kiska, the Japanese withdrew without a fight. The garrison commander had realized his 5,000-strong force could not hope to mount an effective defence without adequate supplies and air-cover. Rather than pointlessly waste the lives of his men, he organized their evacuation. On 15 August 1943 the first soldiers of an American force of 35,000 hit the beaches. They were so convinced that the Japanese could not have fled that it took them a week to realize they were alone.

The Japanese military elite cultivated its troops' resolve to die. In the propaganda and training manual 'Just Read This and the War Is Won', men were advised to write a will, and enclose a lock of hair and a fingernail paring in case their bodies were lost and never recovered. Front-line army propaganda units provided additional encouragement as Ei Yamaguchi recalls: 'The soldiers at the time died willingly. Once a week, there was a lecture to raise the spirits of the soldiers. It encouraged the mentality to die for the Emperor.' Takeo Yamauchi noted an almost mindless acceptance of death among his comrades:

Death is frightening but when you are out in the battlefield, your mind goes blank and you merely begin acting by reflex. If you were ordered you just followed... Only a few people indulged in consideration of the deep philosophical implications of death; most gave

little thought to it, resorting to just following orders. If by chance
that led to their deaths, they simply shrugged and accepted it.

The term 'banzai charge' entered the American soldiers'
lexicon. Marine Steve Judd was on Saipan, where they were a
frequent occurrence: 'They would come through drunk...
sometimes they might even have a part of a band out there,
getting them all hyped up and liquored up and everything. And
then they'd come through there, and they'll come through, and
they'll break through your lines... They'll hit the hospitals in the
rear – whoever is in the rear they'll try and hit – and sometimes
they were pretty successful.'

Mitsuharu Noda took part in the biggest 'banzai charge' on
Saipan in which over 4,000 men died:

We drank the best Japanese whisky... we smoked our last tobacco
– Hikari brand. We were even able to smile. Maybe because we
were still together as a group. I even had feelings of superiority, for
we were doing something we had to do... We are not going to
attack enemies. We were ordered to go there to be killed. Some
probably may have got drunk, just to overcome fear, but that last
taste of Suntory whisky was wonderful. It was a kind of suicide...
We had hardly any arms. Some had only shovels, others had sticks.
I had a pistol. I think I was shot at the second line of defence. Hit
by two bullets in my stomach, one passing through, one lodging in
me... I woke up when [Americans] kicked me and they took me to
the field hospital.

Steve Judd witnessed the effects of that charge: '[The Japanese]
went through the 27th Army Division, and we seen the American
soldiers there, they were stacked up by the hundreds, they were all
dead. They finally broke through the army lines and they ended
up by the 10th Marine artillery... and the next morning we saw all
those bodies... stacked up like cord wood.'

Most charges were not so effective. Gradually the Americans
learned to realize they had won a battle when they heard the
characteristic sounds, described by Marine George Peto as 'like the
4th of July going on... a'hollerin' and a'hoopin', and a'firin''. On
Peleliu, the Japanese switched tactics, deciding to exploit the

caves and ridges of the island to dig men in, forcing the Americans to pay dearly rather than offering their machine-gunners a 'turkey shoot'. According to Eugene Sledge, the Japanese now saw themselves as occupying not a foxhole but an octopus pot: 'The octopus pot was by definition a crevice or a cranny or something in the rock, in the coral, in reefs, where when an octopus was threatened by a predator, it could simply back into this place and then have its tentacles out to protect itself, and then stay there until it died.'

Yet in the end, even on Peleliu, the Japanese came out of their octopus pots. Kiyokazu Tsuchida could hear the unmistakable sounds of the *gyokusai* from his cave:

We began to hear men screaming faintly in the distance, and every time we heard this we knew our colleagues were engaging in charge attacks against the Americans. As soon as we heard the yelling, we heard gunfire immediately afterwards... If the order was to sacrifice your life so as to kill a large number of the enemy, then that's what you had to do, and you just prepared yourself accordingly.

In fact, Kiyokazu Tsuchida hid in the caves and jungles of Peleliu until 1947 with others, including Ei Yamaguchi: "I still did not believe Japan was losing. When we formed the last group of thirty-four survivors, I did not believe Japan would ever lose the war. We would hide and keep on the move, and one day our army would come and rescue us.'

The wounded, unless they could walk, were a liability in retreat, and both sides feared for the safety of wounded comrades if they were left behind. As we saw in Chapter 8, there was no thought of abandoning them to be looked after by the enemy. The problem was particularly acute later in the war when whole field hospitals were about to be overrun. Hiraoka Hisashi served as a medical orderly in the Philippines. He recalls the orders he received as US forces were closing in:

I was called in by Commander Togasaki and ordered to proceed east. His orders were to kill the badly wounded and move out fast. I opposed the commander – so did the army surgeon – because I was against the idea. But the commander said the soldiers would rather be killed by their own comrades. I was only twenty-five and the commander was among the most experienced in the army. So I obeyed in the end, although the army surgeon wouldn't give in.

We released those who could still walk and then went round the bedridden, asking for their last wills... First of all, they mentioned their children, their wives, then their mothers, but not often their fathers, unfortunately. I don't know why... [They said] 'Take care', for example, or 'grow up to be a good man'. When they had said what they wanted to say, we told them to rest in heaven and gave them the injection. I just remember how they were all lined up waiting to tell me their dying words, while those who were already dead were being carried out of the room. Imagine how they must have felt waiting for their turn.

Hiraoka could not keep his pact with these doomed men: 'I promised if I returned alive, I would make sure to deliver the messages, which, of course, turned out to be a lie.' In the chaos and haste he hadn't been able to write down their dying words. He and his comrades did try to adhere to the recommendation in 'Just Read This and the War Is Won': 'After they died, we cut their hair and nails and wrapped those in the paper we used to wrap medicine, wrote down their names, the unit they belonged to, their positions, and the date and time, and with those we fled to the east.'

The man who looked after these mementoes clung on to them long after he abandoned everything else he carried. Then he died, and with him went the last identifiable traces of all those men. What makes the story so illuminating is the way it cuts against the conventional, propaganda picture of the wartime Japanese, for whom death is a trifle and humanity an alien concept. The surgeon refused to kill the wounded, the soldier held on to their nails and hair till the very end, and Hisashi Hiraoka has subsequently visited as many of their families as he can find. He has worried about what he did that day ever since, particularly after working in a US military hospital and realizing how considerate their medical care was:

Maybe if, instead of actually killing them with chemicals as ordered, I had sneaked them out behind the hospital and left a sign so they could be found later, they might have lived. It is possible that the US Army might have taken them prisoner and treated them well... Nevertheless, I was only twenty-five then, so I suppose I couldn't have thought of anything other than to obey the orders. I wouldn't have known what the US Army was like anyway... But I still regret it today.

STAGGERINGLY, COMBAT DEATHS ACCOUNT for only one-third of all Japanese troop fatalities. Disease and starvation were the largest killers – not Allied firepower. As US forces island-hopped toward Tokyo, thousands upon thousands of Japanese were cut off and abandoned by their own high command. Not every island was the target of invasion; some were simply bypassed, leaving the Japanese on them to 'wither on the vine' in the US phrase. On Jaluit, Mili, Wotje and Nauru, the Japanese tried to stay alive by farming and fishing. More than one-third died of sickness and starvation. On Wolwei, a force of over 7,000 men numbered fewer than 2,000 by the war's end. One bypassed island, Manus, was even used for training. Raw troops would be sent there to be toughened up, by practising on the Japanese stragglers living in central and eastern parts of the island.

For years, Japanese commanders had been 'solving' supply problems by having their troops live off the land. The phrase was *jikattsu jisen* which, as historian Louis Allen explains, 'was much in use at the time for Japanese forces overseas. It meant subsisting on your own and fighting on your own. No help was to be expected from Japan'. Ordered to attack India's north-eastern border in early March 1944, Japan's 15th Army carried just three weeks' rations. Their offensive met fierce resistance from the British 14th Army at Imphal and Kohima, preventing the Japanese from carrying out their plan of capturing enemy stores. Critically short of food, ammunition and medicine, officers at the front made repeated requests for resupply. Their pleas were ignored by the commander of the 15th Army, Lieutenant General Renya Mutaguchi, who preferred instead to quote glib proverbs such as 'Before a resolute will, even the gods give way'. He seems to have cared nothing for the men under his command, believing extreme circumstances would drive them to secure the enemy's positions.

Three divisional commanders, furious with the lack of support provided by headquarters and Lieutenant General Mutaguchi's stubborn refusal to sanction their withdrawal, were subsequently dismissed. One of the three, Lieutenant General Kotoku Sato, broke off radio communication and ordered his men to pull back, informing headquarters of his effective mutiny with the signal: 'It seems Army cannot grasp the real situation: no supplies and men wounded and sick... I wish to inform you that, according to the situation, the divisional commander will act on his own initiative.'

Six weeks later, on 31 May 1944, Mutaguchi accepted the inevitable and ordered a general retreat. It was the longest, most painful withdrawal the Japanese undertook in the Second World War, a desperately grim echo of the British retreat through Burma of 1942 in the face of the victorious Japanese. Now those glory days were long gone. Hiroshi Abe remembers the rout:

I'd say it was like hell... It was that bad. Of course, no one had a single rifle left. We were in rags, mostly bare feet, with a stick and a rice steamer. You were lucky to be alive and still able to walk. In Burma, many places have been given the name 'Bone Road', where piles of white bones were found. Starving and exhausted soldiers left the front in small groups. Along the way, they sat down and rested when they were tired. Those who had no more strength died on the spot. It's a strange human characteristic that they preferred to sit down by anything that barely resembled a human being, even though it was dead or infested with maggots. They had lost their minds. They sat by those dead bodies, stared into space and eventually died.

Hiroshi Yamagami owes his life to the brave decision taken by Lieutenant General Sato. He remembers walking down one of the Bone Roads, listening to the heart-breaking pleas of emaciated men collapsed on the verges: '"Take us with you!" they begged. There was nothing we could do. All we could say was, "Come on! Walk with us!"... Once a soldier lagged behind the regiment, that was the end of him... there was no other future for him other than to die on the road.'

The Japanese stumbled back with the British at their heels. In the words of Lieutenant General Slim, commander of Britain's forces in Burma: 'Relentlessly we would hunt them down and when, desperate and rabid, they turned at bay, kill them.' Brigadier David Wilson pursued the foe through the monsoon rains: 'They were starving, they had nothing, they were eating grass, they were in a dreadful state. I had never seen human beings in such a dreadful state before. How on earth they had continued fighting under those conditions I cannot think, but you see later on in the retreat they were blowing themselves up with grenades and sitting starving by the side of the road.'

According to Hiroshi Yamagami, patriotism played no part in these suicides: 'I think people decided to kill themselves because there was nothing else they could do. They had been driven to it. The situation wasn't about to change, and committing suicide would end the agony. So they killed themselves with hand grenades.'

He and barely 500 others, out of an outfit that originally numbered 5,000 men, eventually reached the relative safety of the Burmese plains. Three-fifths of all Japanese sent to Burma died there: a total of 185,000 men.

The failure of Japan's military high command to supply their troops with adequate food stocks forced large numbers of men to turn to cannibalism. There were outbreaks as early as 1942 in New Guinea, growing more frequent as the 'self-sustaining policy' of August 1943 took effect. This euphemism for official abandonment meant that almost no supplies reached the troops for the rest of the war. The practice of cannibalism occurred on certain Pacific islands, in the Philippines, and in Burma on the retreat from Imphal. The evidence amassed in affidavits and reports, originally compiled for war trials' purposes, clearly indicates that cannibalism was not just the act of a few isolated individuals. It seems that it was tolerated by some in the Japanese high command as a way of preserving their forces' fighting capability; this is evident from a captured document held in the Australian National Archives. The order, issued by Major General Aozu on 18 November 1944, states that the consumption of enemy flesh is excluded from the military crime of cannibalism and that any soldiers found eating human flesh other than that of the enemy will be guilty of cannibalism, a crime punishable by execution.

There was evidently a degree of teamwork and organization in certain units which allowed Japanese soldiers to continue to fight effectively, while sustaining themselves on human flesh. Some Japanese officers even acclimatized their men before it became a necessity, so they wouldn't have to go through a debilitating period of starvation while wrestling with their consciences and sensibilities. There were also a few cases which are evidence of ritualism; one soldier has described how his commander raped and killed a woman, and then cooked and ate her brain. Such – rare – occasions are not explicable in terms of starvation.

Hatam Ali, an Indian prisoner of war held in western New Guinea, witnessed organized cannibalism in operation:

The Japanese started selecting prisoners and every day one prisoner was taken out and killed and eaten by the Japanese. I personally saw this happen and about 100 prisoners [out of 200 or so held] were eaten at this place by the Japanese. The remainder of us were taken to another spot about 50 miles [away] where ten prisoners died of sickness. At this place the Japanese again started selecting prisoners to eat. Those selected were taken to a hut where flesh was cut from their bodies while they were alive and they were then thrown into a ditch alive where they later died.

Keeping meat fresh by progressively butchering a live animal was a method which crops up in Japanese wartime accounts. Now it was being applied to human beings. Hatam Ali fled the camp rather than face such a gruesome death. He was rescued by Australian forces after two weeks' wandering the jungle.

As Allied soldiers advanced, they sometimes found evidence of cannibalism. Australian Bill Spencer experienced this at Sanananda in New Guinea: 'It was the first area that we had seen cannibalism, the Japanese had been eating our dead parts... They must have been that hungry... That upset us... they cut flesh off the legs and the buttocks of our men, and they had the meat in dixies and they were cooking it in the pots when we moved through the area. Horrible, a horrible sight.'

Here was proof of everything the Allies had been conditioned to believe about their enemies: they were – it seemed – indeed subhuman monsters. Exterminating them was a duty to humanity. Nelson Peery served with the Black American 93rd Division, patrolling deep into island jungles on mopping-up operations:

Our soldiers... had to finish off stragglers, to hunt them down – because these were always a hard core that wouldn't surrender... At Biak they turned to cannibalism, and so you can imagine that we just hated them. They would come down to these villages and they would make off with a child or an older person and butcher them, and we had to go through these hills... blowing up their cooking pots and whoever we found we killed immediately.

This revulsion is easy to understand. The mental state of the Japanese driven to such extremes is almost impossible to imagine. Certainly Allied soldiers endured great hardship in the Pacific War, but they were generally kept supplied with food. This spared them ever having to find out how they would have responded under the circumstances that forced some Japanese to eat other human beings. Certainly the prisoners in Chapter 9 who drank blood from a fellow American in the hold of a hellship had approached that pitch of desperation; who knows what happened to starving Allied men driven mad on lifeboats, or lost behind enemy lines? During the retreat in the Philippines, medical orderly Hiraoka Hisashi saw the effects of hunger on others and on himself and watched thousands of troops die from starvation. He has thought hard about his experiences and is painfully honest about them:

Excuse me for talking about this. When we defecated, we seemed to use so much energy that, afterwards, we had to rest a little. We often saw flies gathering around the faeces – there were lots of flies because of the dead bodies around – and the flies were often then eaten by a lizard. When we saw that happen, we were happy. We'd use a stick to catch the lizard, add some salt to prevent it from rotting and keep it until dinner time, then cut it up and eat it. Having three lizards for dinner was a real luxury. A snake was even better. I know you couldn't possibly understand this...

I have seen people kill live humans and eat them. When I saw someone eat another human being, I thought it looked delicious... This was the reality. I'm sure you would never look at the organs of a cat or dog that had died in an accident and think they look delicious. Well, I did. This is how we humans, in the end, turn into wild animals. I think it was much better to die in battle than die of starvation.

THE LIVING EMBODIMENT of the values expressed in the verse at the head of this chapter – commitment to death and loyalty to the lord or Emperor – was the *kamikaze*. *Kamikaze* is the Japanese for 'Divine Wind'. It was the name bestowed on a fierce storm that destroyed a Mongol invasion fleet in 1281. In the Pacific War, the role of the typhoon was played by young men blessed by a grateful nation, making one-way trips in explosives-filled planes, submarines, motor boats and *kaiten* – human torpedoes. Some Japanese soldiers in Burma would strap wooden bombs filled with picric acid to their chests, and then hurl themselves at British tanks. A British officer was shocked by 'their anguished look of determination and despair'. Divine Wind attacks were not the sole preserve of lone individuals. On 2 April 1945 the giant battleship *Yamato* was sent to Okinawa with only enough fuel for a one-way journey. In what was effectively a *kamikaze* mission, she was sunk with the loss of 2,000 men.

The Divine Wind idea is credited to Vice-Admiral Takijiro Onishi, who realized that with only a hundred planes to defend the Philippines and attack the vast US fleets, he had to make sure that every plane's attack was successful: 'The only way of assuring our meagre strength will be effective to a maximum degree... is for our bomb-laden fighter planes to crash dive into the decks of the enemy carriers.' The *kamikaze* operation would make full use of the 'enthusiasm that flames naturally in the hearts of youthful men'. The idea was in fact, as we saw in Chapter 3, not new to the Pacific War – the Russo–Japanese War of 1904–5 had its 'sure-death' men – but the scale of the *kamikaze* operation was exceptional, as was the way it caught the imagination of both the Japanese and her foes.

In the space of less than a year, almost 4,000 airmen flew these one-way 'body-smashing' missions. By no means all *kamikaze* aircraft (some of which had more than one crew member) success-fully crashed into their targets, but they nevertheless became a potent and feared weapon. Over thirty US vessels were sunk and nearly 300 were damaged – killing an estimated 6,000 servicemen. They worried the Americans so much that, after they first appeared hurtling out of the Philippine skies down on to the decks of US warships, all news of the Japanese tactic was withheld from the American public for six months. Admiral Halsey later wrote: 'The psychology behind the [*kamikaze* attacks] was too alien for us. Americans, who fight to live, find it hard to realize that another people will fight to die.' For Halsey's sailors, watching the last moments of *kamikaze* pilots from gun platforms and ships' rails, the mentality of the men at the controls defied all comprehension. Cy Topol was on the battleship USS *Missouri*:

We saw this guy coming in at us low, just about at water level... and luckily for us, he had a 500-pound bomb which we knocked off of him, out in the water. If that had landed on the back of my ship I'd have been a dead duck... They were crazy, absolutely crazy, they had to be... American people, white people, Caucasian people do not have the same feeling about going to heaven and paying a penalty like that. They had to be brainwashed.

Sy Kahn watched a ship near him explode after a *kamikaze* hit; the air rained down pieces of superstructure and parts of bodies. He realized that the phenomenon had shifted the relationship between enemies:

When you see a kamikaze, *you know that that man flying that plane is going to die, and he knows he's going to die, and he doesn't care if he's going to die, or he doesn't care enough not to, and he's out to kill you with his own body if he must. And that's a strange kind of enemy to be facing, because you're not really on equal ground... emotionally. You're not facing something that's somewhat known to you. The Japanese were really alien to us in many ways.*

Rod Steiger served on a destroyer; he started to see *kamikaze* pilots as fellow members of the human race only when one crashed in the sea near his ship:

The pilot was still alive, and we had to go get him... and every time they got near him the wave took them twelve yards away. This went on and meanwhile he drowned. They brought him aboard, his body, and they put him in the officers' mess on the big table... and they went through his pockets and there were the same things that you and I have in our pockets. There was the photo of the family, there was a religious something, there was some money, you know, and that to me brought everything closer than anything.

To most Japanese, the *kamikaze* pilots were no common mortals. They were portrayed as the superior beings of a race that was already above all others. 'The purity of youth,' said Admiral Onishi, 'will usher in the Divine Wind.' The image with which the men of the Tokkotai – the Special Attack Forces – were usually associated was that of falling cherry blossom: dashing youths wearing white headbands with the red emblem of the Rising Sun. They inspired books and films and a thousand poems. The propaganda films showed them sipping a ritual cup of water and receiving a message of gratitude from the Emperor himself. Crowds turned out to wave off the fearless. Virgin schoolgirls threw cherry blossoms as their planes lifted into the air. Tears streamed down cheeks as the bravest of the brave faded over the horizon towards the fleets of Japan's enemies. Japan's myopic enshrinement of the *kamikaze* as martyrs and the West's morbid fascination with them have done little to dispel these myths. The truth was very different.

The Divine Wind was a wanton waste of human life. Scared young men, who could not say no, flew inferior aircraft at infinitely better trained and equipped Allied forces. Many went through mental hell, and crashed their planes into the ground or sea to end the agony. If a mission was aborted because of mechanical malfunction, the pilots were ridiculed and ostracized as a disgrace to the Tokkotai. Professional pilots such as Pearl Harbor veteran Zenji Abe deplored the way young lives were squandered in the name of military glory: 'I don't think the *kamikazes* were in any sense a strategy. It was more like a desperate lunge... This wasn't war – it was a tragedy. I share my grief with the family of the victims, and I have great respect for them. But I must strongly protest against the officers in charge who made such decisions.'

The propaganda films showing the courageous few applauded by the adoring many concealed the lonely, frightened squalor of *kamikaze* operations. Iyozo Fujita, another Pearl Harbor veteran, had a glimpse of this when he was serving in the Philippines in charge of a conventional air squadron:

When I was in the Philippines, I was told to provide twelve pilots from my unit for the Divine Wind. I rushed to headquarters and said, 'You must have Divine Wind pilots at the base in HQ.' They said they had about a hundred of them. I asked why they didn't just use them, because ours was not a Divine Wind unit. 'Why twelve from my unit?' The answer was that all hundred of them had fallen ill and couldn't fly. I wasn't surprised. Imagine how a criminal condemned to be executed in a few days would feel. He wouldn't feel at all well waiting to be killed. We'd all feel ill.

It is the experience of the pilots themselves that is particularly elusive since most are, by definition, unavailable. Yet a few went on missions and survived. Kanji Suzuki is one of this rarest of breeds:

When they recruited pilots for the Divine Wind, people rushed to join up. Even though they knew they would never return, people wanted to become a Divine Wind because society respected you and it was something to be very proud of... Kyuji Kobayashi, the commander of the 7th Divine Wind unit that took off before us, smiled when he left... As for me, I was a coward – a boy of only sixteen – so I was worried whether I could afford a smile like the others...

Kanji Suzuki put on a brave front, and was terrified inside:

When I left home, with much back-slapping and ceremony, I felt like a hero and behaved like one. But once it had all sunk in, I got the jitters – and I'd feel anxious and scared all day long. There was a constant switch between these two states. When it got closer to the actual day of my mission, this switch occurred every hour or so. People used various ways to get over this. The most effective thing to do was to train one's mind by Zen meditation. Some people read, others drank, or went to look for women.

Kanji sought solace from women. He, like other *kamikaze* pilots, used to visit prostitutes. His squadron was based in Izumi on Kyushu; he would go down to the local brothel area of Hirose-Cho, where one yen bought as much time with a girl as it took a stick of incense to burn down. If the girl liked you – and they liked

Kanji Suzuki – she would lick the incense, to make it burn slower: 'For me, being with women was the only way to alleviate my fears. I didn't drink that much, and nothing else seemed to help. Only when I was with women, could I forget about everything and relax.' He formed a special attachment to the daughter at his lodging house: 'You didn't know when you were going to die, and women then – I know this is unimaginable today – gave themselves to men with the idea that the men were going to die for the country.'

As the time for their mission grew near, he and his two colleagues were billeted in the barracks. On the night before the attack they sneaked out to visit their girlfriends. Kanji did not stay out long because the attack might have been called early: 'I told the other two in my crew to be back in by morning. I really should have stopped them from going out, but I wanted to go myself, so I let them.' Saying goodbye to his girl broke his heart: 'I don't even want to remember the parting. I want to forget about it.'

Theirs was the only plane to take off that day; none of the other crews turned up. There was no word of thanks from the Emperor to send them proudly to their deaths. No last rites. No waving crowds of virgin schoolgirls. In fact, no one at all to see them off: 'There were only the mechanics whom we didn't really know, so their presence didn't give us that much courage, not that I hoped for any. I was more worried whether I could get the plane to clear the pine trees in front of us.' As for his thoughts on the way: 'Well, it's strange how, when facing death, you remember things from your childhood; things you never remembered before. For example, I remembered the face of the music teacher at school playing the organ, and my mother walking in front of a line of people carrying the ashes of the dead. Also, I remembered all the girls I'd ever known, in Ohtsu, Shanghai, and at the base.'

Kanji Suzuki and his two crewmen headed south alone towards Okinawa in the lumbering Ginga bomber. They were sitting ducks. First the rear machine-gun jammed, next one of the two engines was hit. Then Suzuki was wounded, and blacked out. When he regained consciousness he found himself a prisoner on an American aircraft carrier. Evidently, his bomber had crashed into the sea; the 500-kilogram bomb had failed to explode and his two

Punch magazine mocks the Japanese advance on Singapore. These 'subhumans' would soon bring Britain's fortress to its knees.

This leaflet – dropped by the Japanese on Bataan – was aimed at the Filipino troops that comprised the bulk of the US force.

Japanese propaganda depicts an ogre hiding behind a smiling Roosevelt mask. Kikuko Miyagi thought Americans 'were very frightening people who would ravenously kill anybody, anywhere – including civilians – much like monsters'.

American propaganda just after the war redirects the image of the enemy. The Japanese soldier is now less a dangerous animal, more a cuddly pet.

A severed Japanese head (above) attached to a tree in northern Burma, presumably intended as the original caption indicates: 'a symbol of the Japanese defeat'.

A young Japanese POW hangs from a home-made noose. During the uprising in Cowra camp twenty-nine men killed themselves and 183 more ran into Australian machine-gun fire.

Liberated Allied Prisoners of War.

Dick Lee [on the left] with his mate Tony Mansi shortly before the war. Both were forced to work on the Burma–Thailand Railway but only Dick survived.

POW Fred Seiker's painting of water torture he was forced to endure.

Ei Yamaguchi (below) surrenders his thirty-three men to the Americans on Peleliu – two years after the end of the war.

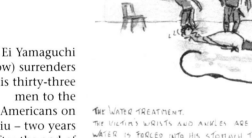

THE WATER TREATMENT.
THE VICTIMS WRISTS AND ANKLES ARE BOUND WITH BARBED WIRE.
WATER IS FORCED INTO HIS STOMACH THROUGH A HOSE.
WHEN STOMACH IS PAINFULLY EXTENDED, JAPANESE JUMPS ON STOMACH
OTHER JAP KICKS VICTIMS HEAD.

Hiroshima survivor Suzuko Numata (left) had this photograph taken for her fiancé just before his conscription: 'the photo was the only part of me that he could look at after that. I still imagine it sinking under the waves with him.'

Filipino Dionisia Carlos Vergara (right) survived a massacre in the local chapel. Her mother, father, two sisters and a brother were all killed by rampaging Japanese troops.

Kikuko Miyagi and classmates (below) in military training, Okinawa. Perhaps a third of all civilians died during the US invasion.

Singaporean Elizabeth Choy recalls the British defeat: 'We thought the sky had fallen and it was the end of the world, it was a terrible feeling'. She was later arrested and tortured by the Kempeitai, the Japanese secret police.

Hiroshi Yamagami [on the left] just before the defeat at Imphal and the retreat down Burma: 'I witnessed what the army could turn into when things became desperate.'

Australian Bert Ward (above): 'We did think of the Japanese basically as animals.'

Kamikaze pilot Kanji Suzuki was shot out of the sky but lived: 'It's strange how, when facing death, you remember things from your childhood.'

A wounded Marine on Iwo Jima. 'You didn't fight for your mother's apple pie... you fought to keep your buddy alive, [to] protect each other' – Stan Dabrowski.

The battle for Okinawa. 'Killing the Japs was no problem at all, in fact at times it was an outright pleasure.' – Marine George Peto.

D-Day on Iwo Jima: 'Complete terror. Your heart was in your throat, your mind was boggled with "my God, what am I going to do?"... I'm liable to get killed, Mum will never, never forgive me for doing this to her'.

A US Marine on Peleliu throws a 'Molotov cocktail' at an enemy position. Out of a garrison 10,900 strong, just fifty-three Japanese survived the invasion.

US troops take cover on Peleliu. Marine Eugene Sledge recalls the battle: 'I knew that I was expendable, and that's not a very happy thought, but you had to learn to live with it.'

Downtown Tokyo after the US blitz. The city burned like 'a paper lantern' and some 94,000 people were killed in a single night.

Pilot Colonel Paul Tibbets waves from the cockpit of the Enola Gay (named after his mother), the day he bombed Hiroshima. 'I don't feel a bit bad. I feel good... I've never lost a night's sleep and I never will.'

The aftermath of the Hiroshima nuclear attack. Survivor Suzuko Numata describes the city as 'a living, unimaginable, hell'.

comrades were dead. He accepts the possibility that none of them had armed the bomb, but rejects the notion that, as an ex-seaplane pilot, he had tried to land on the water instead of seeking a target. He tried to hang himself with his hospital bedsheets, and has never forgiven himself for what happened. He dreads visiting the memorial to the Special Attack pilots, from whose granite honour roll his own name has been sanded off, although he has forced himself to go twice. He is ashamed to face the souls of his two friends:

> How can I stand in front of the war memorial and observe a minute of silence? I feel the dead must have bitter feelings towards me. I don't feel I have the right to stand on the same ground as those courageous soldiers who died in battle; I have lived a coward's life... I can't escape responsibility for the death of my two crew members... Well, there you have it. This is the story of a timid man.

He has not dared revisit the girl, now in her seventies, who spent those last hours with him one April night in 1945 – the girl he left convinced he was a doomed hero.

BY 1945 IT WAS AS IF JAPAN were one gigantic *kamikaze* plane. A slogan described the entire population as a Special Attack Force – never mind that all Japanese hearts were not beating as one, that there were some, as we will see in the next chapter, who did not want to die by the side of their lord. A new slogan appeared in Japan in April: *ichioku gyokusai* – 'the shattering of the hundred million like a beautiful jewel'. It is a moot point whether her enemies played as great a part in smashing Japan's jewels as Japan did herself. As Hiroshi Abe says: 'You had to wonder if the Japanese army had actually come to Burma to fight the enemy or destroy our own troops.' Even as Japan prepared for her final 'banzai charge' armed with sharpened bamboo poles, America was mass-producing B-29s to raze Japanese cities to the ground. And while Japanese soldiers were starving to death on the plains of Burma and in the mountains of New Guinea, the US built a ship that could turn out 5,100 gallons of ice-cream per hour.

11

WERE WE HUMANS?

We looked in the shelter, but it was full of dead bodies and injured people weeping, so we couldn't go in there. While walking around, I saw a woman carrying a dead baby on her back. I came to a temple, with a lot of statues of guardian deities inside, just like the ones outside. I suddenly realized they were really burned bodies, still standing upright.

MIHO YOSHIOKA, survivor of Tokyo fire-bombing

They were shouting. As they stab you, they shout. My sister said they were shouting 'Banzai', but at that point I really don't know what they were shouting. All I know is that they were shouting.

DIONISIA CARLOS VERGARA, survivor of the Rape of Manila

THE TWENTIETH CENTURY'S PARTICULAR contribution to the horror of war was to bring war itself to civilians en masse. It had never been safe to be the medieval citizens of a besieged town, or a shepherdess whose pastures suddenly became a battlefield, but the people of York or Dijon had nothing to fear during Agincourt, except the death of their conscripted sons. Then came the airship bombing of Paris and London in the First World War, and Guernica, Nanking, Shanghai, Coventry, Warsaw, Dresden and countless villages and towns, bombed or pillaged, their populations incinerated, raped, slaughtered, deported to death camps. World war meant not just the world's places, but its peoples. This was Total War.

The people of China had known little peace for nearly a decade after Japan first marched in; since 1941, the peoples of Asia and the Pacific had known only danger. By 1945, Japan was herself within easy bombing range of the great, teeming runways on the recently captured islands of Saipan, Tinian and Guam. Indeed Tinian, just 10 miles long and 4 miles wide, was for a few months the busiest airfield in the world; 1,400 miles to the north, the people of Japan were pounded day and night. In the battles for these very islands, the distinction between soldiers and non-combatants had similarly been blurred, by promiscuously destructive weapons and by Japan's militarization of civilians.

Saipan was the first island invaded by the US to have a signifi-cant Japanese civilian population. Propaganda and rumour had led them to believe that the Americans would rape any women or young girls they caught; that the men would have their legs tied to two jeeps which would then split them in two; that the Americans would crush their victims' mutilated bodies under tanks. In addition to those killed by US shelling, thousands committed suicide rather than face capture and its attendant shame and expected agonies. Takeo Yamauchi, a soldier who did not believe the stories of American vindictiveness, witnessed the military brutality imposed on civilians while hiding in a cave with others. It was the final spur to his decision to get out of the war:

The non-commissioned officer was a little dictator; he ordered the babies to be killed because they were making a noise that could give everyone away to the Americans. At this, one of the mothers got up and walked out of the cave. She said, 'I'd rather die than kill my baby.' But the mothers who were left did strangle their babies to death... the cave went quiet. All I could hear was the mothers crying. My only thought was of surrender; I told myself not to get involved in what was happening around me. But by the third day, the cave had started to stink, from the rotting bodies of the babies. I couldn't bear it any more. That night of 14 July, I slipped quietly out of the cave. I had made up my mind to surrender.

At Marpi Point, where many civilians leapt to their deaths, interpreters up on the cliffs and on navy patrol boats desperately tried to persuade them not to jump. They had little effect. Indeed the waters here were so thick with corpses that boats could not pass without running over the dead. An American officer on a minesweeper watched the tragedy: 'I remember one woman in khaki trousers and a white polka dot blouse, with her black hair streaming in the water. I'm afraid every time I see that kind of blouse, I'll think of that girl. There was another one, nude, who had drowned herself while giving birth to a baby. The baby's head had entered this world, but that was all of him.'

Some Americans had less sympathy. Primed by propaganda to see the Japanese as alien, they had just bitterly fought their way across the island, losing friends. Marine Steve Judd sat with his surviving comrades near the cliffs: 'I think most of us thought that, well, let them kill themselves, it has nothing to do with us, and if you can't get them to give up – let them go. And we couldn't care less, we really didn't care... let them jump, let's get this thing over with already; enough is enough.'

With the fall of Saipan, Japanese propaganda stepped up its portrayal of Americans as demons, bent on a campaign of merciless savagery. The foe were 'barbarians', 'devils' and 'beasts' – not humans. The November 1944 issue of the popular magazine *Hinode* included the photograph originally printed in *Life* magazine showing a young American lady posing with a Japanese skull. The media published accounts of US troops torturing Japanese wounded, killing prisoners, mutilating the dead, and shooting shipwrecked civilians. A drawing in the October 1944 issue of *Manga Nippon* shows a skull-wearing monster, with long claws, sharp fangs and horns, hiding behind a smiling Roosevelt mask. The accompanying article states: 'It has gradually become clear that the American enemy, driven by its ambition to conquer the world, is coming to attack us, and as the breath and body odour of the beast approach it may be of some use if we draw the demon's features here.'

There was a basis in truth for a number of the charges. The brutal hatred with which the war had been fought ensured its exponential progression into new realms of violence. It was easy for both sides to see, in the way their enemy fought, proof of their worst fears. There was nobody on Saipan to report back to Japan the other side of the American coin: the feeding of starving civilians, the medical care for the wounded. The only message the people of Japan, and its outlying island Okinawa, received was clear and unqualified: civilians must expect certain humiliation, certain suffering and certain death from American invasion.

IN TOTAL WAR, THE ENEMY turns civilians into targets, and their own governments turn them into home-front combatants. This then legitimizes them as targets. Japanese plans to mobilize the entire civilian population had begun as early as August 1944 when the government armed virtually every adult on the mainland with bamboo spears. In Hiroshima, Suzuko Numata practised on cardboard cut-outs of devilish Americans: 'Because we were so worried that they might come and land... we practised bamboo spear fighting. We sharpened the end of a stick of bamboo to a point and practised thrusting – shouting "Ei, Ya!" We were made to believe that we could beat the Americans when they landed on our soil.'

Not everyone was so certain. In the town of Kashima, Miho Yoshioka was caught in an air-raid and, looking up, she suddenly realized the vast gulf between Japan and America: 'We were drawing water from a well while huge bombs were being dropped from massive B-29s. I realized the huge gap in the level of civilization, in war capabilities, between them and us. I thought we had no chance. I thought Japan would lose the war and we were going to die.'

In 1939, President Roosevelt had denounced the bombing of civilians:

The ruthless bombing from the air of civilians in unfortified centres of population during the course of the hostilities which have raged in various quarters of the earth during the past few years, which have resulted in the maiming and in the death of thousands of defenceless men, women and children, has sickened the hearts of every civilized man and woman, and has profoundly shocked the conscience of humanity.

By 1944, with experience gained over Germany, bombing Japan had become a key US strategy. Credit for the precise technique which turned Japanese cities and civilians into ashes is claimed by US Colonel Paul Tibbets, better known as the pilot who dropped the atomic bomb on Hiroshima. General Curtis

LeMay, commander of the 21st Bombardment Group, was having difficulty holding B-29 bombers in steady enough formation at high altitudes for accurate attacks. Tibbets, who knew the plane better than most, made a suggestion: 'I said, "General, I know what I'd do." He said, "What would you do?" I said, "I'd strip them out, get some weight out of them, fly them at low altitude and drop fire bombs at night." And he looked at me, he said, "You're crazy as hell..."'

On the night of 9/10 March 1945, 334 aircraft flew at low level over Tokyo, dropping incendiary bombs – devastating against a city whose houses were mostly made of wood and paper. At ground level the temperatures reached 1,800 degrees Fahrenheit. In the air, planes were filled with the stench of roasting flesh; a number were caught in the updraught and tossed over, plunging into the furnace they had helped to light. The target was Tokyo's Shitamachi district, home to countless light industrial 'shadow factories'. It was also the most densely populated area on earth; in terms of immediate fatalities this was the most destructive raid of the Second World War. An estimated 94,000 people were killed that night, a million were made homeless, and 16 square miles of the city were destroyed.

Thousands upon thousands jumped into the Sumida River that runs through Tokyo, only to be suffocated to death as the fire sucked every last breath of oxygen away. Their bodies were then boiled in the steaming water. Captain Shigenori Kubota observed the aftermath: 'The bodies were all nude, the clothes had been burned away, and there was a dreadful sameness about them, no telling men from women or even children. All that remained were pieces of charred meat. Bodies and parts of bodies were carbonized and absolutely black.'

Miho Yoshioka was lucky:

My body caught fire, but I managed to put it out by beating myself and rolling on the ground. I survived because I wasn't hit directly by a bomb... When the air became chilly, we knew we had survived. Then we started to feel cold. I said to my mother-in-law, 'We can't do anything here. Let's find a bomb shelter. We can ask people to let us stay there.' As soon as we started to walk, we saw tons of dead bodies everywhere. Dead bodies. I was so close to death.

Some downed American aircrews were lynched on the spot. There were also instances of outright hostility towards the Japanese military in the aftermath of the bombing. One woman shouted at troops working to clear corpses from the Sumida River: 'You there, you soldiers! How do you feel about all these people? Can you face them?' A group of refugees surrounded a staff officer's car: 'This all happened because of you military men! What's the point of you coming here to look at it?' The officer sensed the mood, and left.

About a week after the first Tokyo raid the Emperor emerged from his vast palace complex to see the damage for himself. An aide later described the public's reaction: 'Victims who had been digging through the rubble with empty expressions on their faces watched the imperial motorcade pass by with reproachful expressions... Were they resentful to the Emperor because they had lost their relatives, their houses and belongings? Or were they in a state of utter exhaustion and bewilderment?'

In a confidential memo, one of General MacArthur's aides, Brigadier-General Bonner Fellers, described it as 'one of the most ruthless and barbaric killings of non-combatants in all history'. It set the pattern for bombing sixty-three of Japan's other cities, although a few, as we will see in the next chapter, were left untouched. In Osaka, Japan's second largest conurbation, over half of all houses were burnt to the ground. In Nagoya, the country's third biggest city, almost 90 per cent of homes were destroyed. In a subsequent meeting with Paul Tibbets, General LeMay showed him 'pictures of burned out cities that he had done with the B-29s, flying them below [normal] altitude... and on the way out I opened the door for him; he stepped out, he said, "Paul, you were right."'

With America bombing the homeland and the Allies advancing across the Asia–Pacific region, the Japanese government exhorted their people to make even greater sacrifices. Propaganda asserted that Japan's spiritual and moral superiority (or 'purity' in the lexicon of the day) would ensure the country's inevitable victory. Suzuko Numata recalls the mood of the nation: 'We had many slogans such as "We don't want anything until we win!", "Extravagancy is our enemy!" and "A hundred million souls, unite and become a fireball!" These concentrated our minds on the war effort. We acted just as we were ordered to. We were not taught the truth, but we believed what we were taught was the truth.'

In Japan's militarized society there were radical solutions to the food shortages caused by the American sea blockade. In June 1945 the Police Bureau Chief for the Osaka area stated: 'Due to the nationwide food shortage and the imminent invasion of the home islands, it will be necessary to kill all the infirm old people, the very young, and the sick. We cannot allow Japan to perish because of them.' Such plans were never carried out, and although the war ended before famine could grip the country, hunger loomed large in the minds – and empty stomachs – of most ordinary people. It caused absenteeism as workers went to the countryside to barter for food, and it created resentment as many in the elite seemed unaffected by the crisis. As the following wartime accounts demonstrate, such disparities were keenly felt:

We couldn't get enough food to live on, yet a family in our neighbourhood whose father was in the Kempeitai [Japan's military police, roughly equivalent to Germany's Gestapo] had sugar candy, canned goods, everything. They were very ostentatious about it.

My brother-in-law was an army major. His family never lacked for anything. It was just as if there was no war on.

It was about the time we had been reduced to eating bread made of bran flour and squash leaves. I was invited to a party to celebrate the birth of a second son to the owner of an armaments factory. I couldn't believe it, there was a sumptuous feast laid out for us. Every kind of food. I thought perhaps I had wandered into fairyland.

Pressures within the social fabric intensified. While popular dissent never approached boiling point – Japan was not ripening for revolution – public dissatisfaction was a major cause of concern for both the government and the Emperor. There were rashes of industrial and tenant-farmer disputes. There was also a surprising level of dissatisfaction expressed in graffiti. Examples include: 'Kill the Emperor. Japan is losing in China. Why does our fatherland dare to commit aggression?'... 'End the war. In the end we'll lose and the people will suffer.'... 'Communism banzai. Oppose the war. Rid Japan of the warmongering military. The sword that kills one saves many. End the war.'

This atmosphere of angry frustration is also found in the files of anonymous letters and overheard remarks. One states: 'Citizens of Tokyo! I think you are all stupid. I'll tell you why: you're giving your lives for that fool who lives for free in the big mansion right in the middle of Tokyo.' Another notes: 'The Emperor looks very carefree in his photograph. He's killed off a million mothers' sons and he sits there looking unconcerned.' Such disparate musings hardly amount to an organized threat to the state. Nevertheless, the aptly named Thought Police considered the situation highly volatile, with one high official comparing the public mood of mid 1944 to 'a stack of hay, ready to burst into flame at the touch of a match'. Their work was so thorough that the US would release nearly a million political prisoners in the first month of occupation. Miho Yoshioka kept a tight rein on her conversation when in public:

I don't know what other people were thinking... I did discuss with my mother-in-law the fact that we would eventually lose... We had to be very secretive. We could only discuss between ourselves how bad the situation was... We couldn't discuss it openly... My cousin was a typist. She was a good friend of a person who believed in pacifism. Somebody heard about their relationship and tipped off the police. As a result she was jailed.

The Thought Police would not have approved of the inner sentiments of even so loyal a citizen as Suzuko Numata, when seeing her fiancé off to war in March 1944. Knowing it was a soldier's duty to die honourably for his country, she could not speak her one wish aloud: that they might see each other again. 'I prayed, "Please come back alive! Please come back alive!" Because you were not supposed to say that kind of thing, I shouted it in my mind.' The proper sentiment for young Japanese girls to express was epitomized by a message sent by a student at elementary school to a soldier at the front: 'Please fight well and die a glorious death.'

THE JAPANESE SOLDIER'S EXPECTATION of his own death – particularly when ordered by his commander and wished for by his family above surrender – could lead to misery and death for countless others. Nowhere was the idea of 'taking others with you into the next world' turned into reality as devastatingly as in the Rape of Manila: one of the most terrible death throes of the Pacific War. It was avoidable; the capital could have been declared an open city like Rome or Paris, but the Japanese commander holed up in Manila decided otherwise. To Carmen Guerra Nakpil the vividness of its horrors are undimmed after fifty-five years:

It was like a scene from hell. It was like one of those lithographs you see illustrating the Bible, it was like the end of the world... The Americans pulverized every square inch of south Manila... everything was flattened by the barrage, and there we were, we were bombed and shelled, we were running like rats. I saw my classmates dragged through the streets, they were raped by the Japanese in Bay View Hotel. I saw my neighbours cut down by sniper bullets, and the killing was terrible. It was just really, I don't know the word for it, it's indescribable... It was a fate that a hundred thousand Filipinos shared. The world doesn't know about it mainly through our own painful silence. It was so painful to talk about it, to remember, that we survived only by trying to forget. I know I tried to forget.

At first it had seemed the capital might be quickly won. The 1st US Cavalry Division reached the city, secured the presidential palace of Malacanang and freed the 5,000 civilian internees in Santo Tomas University. The next day the POWs in Bilibid prison were rescued and just three days later MacArthur proclaimed, 'Our forces are rapidly clearing Manila.' Churchill and Roosevelt sent congratulatory telegrams, but MacArthur had reckoned without the Japanese who still occupied the city.

The Japanese force led by Rear-Admiral Sanji Iwabuchi comprised the naval garrison of 16,000 men, plus 3,750 army security forces. Disobeying explicit orders from General Yamashita, the most senior commander in the Philippines, to withdraw, Iwabuchi ordered these men to fight to the death, declaring: 'If we run out of bullets, we will use grenades; if we run out of grenades we will cut down the enemy with swords; we will kill them by sinking our teeth deep in their throats.'

The troops took the order to fight to the death as an invitation to do whatever they wanted in the days and hours left to them: to break any taboo, to unleash untold hatred and violence. Many seized the chance to get fighting drunk, to rape and torture and take revenge on the people of Manila. Infuriated by the obvious affection so many Filipinos displayed towards America and livid at widespread guerrilla activity across the Philippine archipelago, the Japanese decided Manila would pay the price of their defeat. An order captured during the fighting states: 'All people on the battlefield... will be put to death.' Another reads: 'When Filipinos are to be killed, they must be gathered into one place and disposed of with the consideration that ammunition and manpower must not be used to excess. Because the disposal of dead bodies is such a troublesome task, they should be gathered into houses which are scheduled to be burnt or demolished. They should also be thrown into the river.'

The Japanese divided their manpower between those defending well-fortified positions, machine-gun nests and pillboxes, and those systematically torching buildings and slaughtering civilians. One of many massacres took place at the German Club. Here approximately 1,500 civilians had gathered, hoping its concrete walls and Axis status might save them from the inferno gripping the city and the marauding Japanese marines. When troops block-aded the club's exits, throwing burning furniture and other combustibles inside, a small group of women and girls, some with babies, went out to plead with their tormentors. Francisco Lopez witnessed what happened next:

> The women volunteered to go out and explain that they were civil-ians. They went and knelt before them and begged for mercy, but the Japs ripped babies from mothers' arms and then started tearing off women's and young girls' clothes and raping them. I saw at least twenty Japs abuse one thirteen-year-old girl. I saw at least three girls lying on the ground after being repeatedly raped.

Throughout the city, rape was commonplace. Some 400 young women and girls were separated from their families in Plaza Ferguson, and taken to various locations around the city. During lulls in the fighting Japanese troops would drop back to abuse them. Fifteen-year-old Priscilla Garcia was taken to the Bay View Hotel. She later testified about her ordeal:

He told me to lie on the floor... he wanted to – oh my God. He – then he started to do something to me but he couldn't do anything. So he took his knife and cut me open and then he finally succeeded. He had sexual intercourse. I was bleeding very badly and I was feeling, oh, I was feeling bad... Afterwards another Jap came and took hold of me... I started shouting and screaming.

The crimes committed by the Japanese in Manila were among the worst in the twentieth century. They stabbed babies, beheaded men, violated women, tormented the wounded and left the streets littered with dead. People seeking sanctuary in churches became a particular target, typified by the massacre committed in the Chapel of De La Salle College on 12 February 1945. Sixteen-year-old Dionisia Carlos Vergara and her family had taken refuge there with the Catholic Brothers. Five days before, the Japanese had taken her father away and killed him. Now they returned for the rest:

They told us to line up and then the soldiers started shouting and they started stabbing. The Brothers in front were saying we were Germans – that was to protect us, because they were allies at that time – and it didn't make any difference, they just started stabbing. When that happened and I saw that they were stabbing the second row, I was in the third row, I lay down on the floor and then felt a stab and that was about all that I felt. I became unconscious and I regained consciousness the next morning at about two o'clock, and when I looked around I saw all the dead people around me.

Dionisia crawled out from the bodies. She had been bayoneted twice in the back; one of the cuts went right through her body. Clutching her wound, she went in search of her family:

When I was going up the steps, I was so shocked when I saw my mother hanging on the banister. They shot her and they

*bayoneted her and they hung her on the banister of the stairs. I
got my mother down, and I kissed her. My sister Asela was eleven;
she was also bayoneted, and she died near my mother, also on the
steps. When we came up here I saw my other sister. Cecilia was
nineteen; she was shot – she must have bled to death.*

Upstairs in the chapel the pews were splattered with blood and
among them were the torn bodies of civilians and clergymen.
Lying across the altar rail was her six-year-old brother Antonio.
He had been impaled on a bayonet. Her brother Jose Carlos
Junior was still alive. Brother Baptist had concealed him under a
mattress and was then murdered on top of him. All but two of the
eighteen Brothers were killed. One of the survivors, Father
Cosgrave, recalled after the war how 'sometimes the Japanese
soldiers came in and tried to violate the young girls who were
actually dying'.

The horror of these crimes and the intimate way – almost
eyeball to eyeball – that they were conducted, was not all the
people of Manila had to suffer. Out of consideration for Manila's
700,000 civilians and her beautiful old buildings, MacArthur
refused to use planes to bomb the Japanese into submission. The
artillery deployed to produce the same result was as destructive as
saturation bombing would have been. As Carmen Guerra Nakpil
has observed: 'We survivors sometimes tried to console ourselves
by thinking that maybe he meant well, he could not have wanted
this kind of destruction, but there it was. I think more people,
according to the statistics, died from American shelling than from
the Japanese massacre... Those who survived Japanese hate, did
not escape America's love.'

General Robert Beightler, whose 37th Division was in the
thick of the fighting, seemed proud of his artillery's handiwork:

*We made a churned-up pile of dust and scrap out of imposing,
classic government buildings. Our bombers have done some pretty
fine alteration work on the appearance of Berlin and Tokyo. Just
the same I wish they could see what we did with our little artillery
on the Jap strongholds of Manila... So much for Manila. It is a
ruined city – unhealthy, depressing, poverty-stricken. Let us thank
God our cities have been spared such a fate.*

Two of the buildings targeted were the Remedios Hospital and the Philippines General Hospital. Thousands of refugees had crammed into these buildings, clearly marked with large red crosses. Hundreds were killed by flying shrapnel, explosions and falling debris. The only major battle for a city in the Pacific War ended after a month of street fighting. Over a seventh of Manila's entire population was dead from US shelling and Japanese savagery: an estimated 100,000 Filipino civilians. Their city is believed to have been the most devastated in the Second World War after Warsaw.

A MONTH AFTER MANILA FELL, on April Fool's Day 1945, the Americans landed on Japanese soil. Okinawa is a Japanese island 350 miles south-west of the mainland, with a civilian population then of 450,000. Marines who had survived several other campaigns, far from becoming casual at the prospect, dreaded invading Okinawa. George Peto, veteran of Cape Gloucester and Peleliu, describes the two-week journey there as being 'like a funeral procession'. The customary banter and companionship were gone; everyone knew they were in for a nightmare.

In the event, that proved an understatement. Fresh US troops called up into the line were plunged into a battle more grim than any previous campaign. Marine Eugene Sledge refers to raw recruits as petrified 'zombies'. They were simply too frightened to be of much use: 'The company lost exactly 50 per cent in twenty-two hours, and most of them that were lost were the new men, almost all of them.' Even for a veteran like Sledge the sheer scale of the slaughter was difficult to deal with:

If I had any innocence I lost it at Peleliu, I guess, but at Half Moon Hill at Okinawa I suddenly realized that all of this was just sheer madness. I mean all these boys dying and me scrambling around there trying to keep from getting killed, and what for? It was for an old stinking ridge with rotting Japs all over it and dead Marines lying around the base of it and I mean it was just all so insane I just could never reconcile myself to the fact that it was really necessary after that. But it was necessary... and if we hadn't beaten them it would have been the end of the American way of life.

Marine William Manchester wrote about his fear at Sugar Loaf hill:

Had I not been fasting I'm sure I would have shit my pants. Many did. One of the last orders before going into action was 'Keep your assholes tight,' but often that wasn't possible. We were animals, really, torn between fear – I was mostly frightened – and a murderous rage at events. One strange feeling, which I remember clearly, was a powerful link with the slain, particularly those who had fallen in the past hour or two. There was so much death around that life seemed almost indecent.

The three-month battle for Okinawa saw some of the fiercest fighting of the war. More than 12,000 Americans died and more than 65,000 needed evacuation as sick, wounded, or mentally unfit. At least 65,000 Japanese troops (of whom a quarter had received no combat training) were killed, but it was the civilians who suffered most. Perhaps a third of the entire civilian population were killed: 150,000 men, women and children.

The people of Okinawa had been mobilized into a system of total defence. There were a number of intense pressures on them. Not only was their home being invaded; in the racial hierarchy of Japanese society, Okinawans had been made to feel inferior. They now needed to show that they could do as well as 'proper' Japanese. As one dying soldier said: 'I'm a native of Okinawa. If I hadn't suffered this injury, I would have killed more Americans. I'm ashamed of myself.' Japanese propaganda never let these people forget that everything now depended on the defence of their Japanese island. Okinawa stood between the Americans and Japan.

There was a further agenda: if Okinawa could not be saved, then the battle for it had to achieve one essential result. The Americans had to be made to realize that every inch of Japanese soil would be contested: the price to be paid in an invasion of the mainland had to be set so high in blood that America might think twice – might negotiate a settlement short of unconditional surrender. It was a recipe for sacrifice, pain and tragedy on an epic scale.

Kikuko Miyagi lived with her family in a small shack after their house had been burned down in an air raid. She was one of 240 girls from Himeyuri High School mobilized as assistant nurses in field hospitals.

I told my parents, 'Father, Mother, I'll soon be going on to the battlefield. I'll do my best.' However, when he heard this my father shouted, 'I didn't raise you for sixteen years so that you can go and get yourself killed. Don't go.' My father was a teacher at a local primary school and even though he taught his pupils to 'Work hard, do your best' and to 'Give your life for the country', this is what he was telling me. My mother was in tears; she just held me tight and said, 'Don't go. Let's run away together.'

Appalled at their unpatriotic stance, Kikuko ignored their pleas. She and the other girls underwent a complex series of changes during the battle for Okinawa. They stopped being teenage daughters – indeed their menstrual cycles stopped – and they became almost soldier-like, inuring themselves to gruesome hardships, dedicated, even fanatical: 'Looking back, I think we had become something other than human in those three months. And I believe it was because of this, that we were able to survive those three months.' In some ways, theirs was a paradigm of the changes that the Japanese at war would have to pass through before becoming daughters and sons again.

Barely trained to tie a bandage, Kikuko was immediately confronted with appalling battle injuries. One of the girls' regular duties was to dispose of body parts after amputations:

An adult man's leg is big, and since they are too heavy for one to carry alone, two of us had to take them outside. We dodged, terrified, through the rain of shells flying around us, and threw them into bomb craters. Although at first the students were revolted, and very reluctant to do this, after a while they were carrying arms and legs around just as if they were everyday objects.

They lived and worked, not in hospitals, but in the caves with which Okinawa is honeycombed. Surrounded by pain, dirt and death, they leaned on one another for support, and never doubted that Japan would win. The local propaganda department cooked up fictitious newspaper reports of American ships sunk, and great

Japanese victories, which boosted their morale. Then, after several weeks, Kikuko was told their hospital cave was to be abandoned. As with Hisashi Hiraoka's patients (see Chapter 10), all the wounded who could not walk were given poison. Kikuko Miyagi had left before this happened and never believed rumours about their fate, until a survivor told her his story:

> Among the patients who were given the milk mixed with cyanide was a man determined not to die, and he regurgitated the milk by sticking his fingers down his throat. He then threw himself off the bed... and crawled away from the hospital through the mud until he was rescued by the Americans... He had seen the rest of the patients rolling about on the floor in agony, tearing at their throats and suffocating... I didn't believe the story was true, until he told me. I could not bring myself to think that Japanese had killed other Japanese who were too weak to move.

The girls fled to the cliffs at the south of the island with their teachers, who carried hand grenades to end their lives when capture seemed inevitable. They had all been conditioned to believe the Americans would rape them, and implored their teachers to pull the pins. Kikuko was no exception: 'I also begged the teacher to pull the pin from the grenade. It was while we were all imploring the teachers that Keiko Itabashi, sitting next to me, suddenly shouted out in a flood of tears: "I want to be with my mother just one more time!" After this incident, we all became girls again. I screamed, again and again, out to sea: "Mother, Mother!"'

Yet Kikuko did not suddenly lose her fanaticism. When a Japanese soldier tried to surrender near her, she shouted, 'You coward!' at him. Before he could reach the American lines, another Japanese shot him. Nor did her distrust of the Americans diminish, and with some justification. Native Okinawan civilians moving about at night, which many did to look for relatives or fresh hiding-places, took their lives in their hands. George Peto saw the consequences:

> If they ran into a roadblock and didn't have the password they would automatically be shot, and the guard or the sentry had no

way of knowing whether they were civilians or whether they were soldiers. Well, on one of these occasions when I was checking the lines in the morning I found this pile of bodies there, and there was several babies, women carrying babies that had been shot, but it was through no fault of anybody's, it's just one of the misfortunes of war.

It could not be argued that rape was nobody's fault, and that happened at the hands of both Americans and Japanese. There is American archive film of dead Okinawan women, stripped almost naked. George Peto encountered one girl whose response at seeing a group of US soldiers left little doubt as to what she expected: 'That girl just looked like she was going to die right there, but the first thing she did was reached up and took her dress, opened it up and dropped it, and here is three guys that hadn't, I hadn't seen a woman in two years, and it was a shock to me. It was worse on me than it was her, I believe, but anyway I told her to get her clothes back on and we just went on.'

When asked if there were cases of rape, George Peto is unhesitant: 'Oh, sure. If it was convenient, sure there was, but with us, there were always too many of us together. I mean if, you know, I'm in charge of this patrol, if anybody was to do anything wrong I would have to do something about it.'

Two hundred and three of Kikuko's fellow-students and sixteen teachers died in the battle for Okinawa. She was herself caught by the Americans with her fingers round the pin of a grenade. 'When I looked up, they all had demonic faces just like we'd been told. They were heavily tanned and naked to the waist. They were huge.' She refused their offers of water, believing it to be poisoned, and then watched horrified and puzzled as they bandaged and tended her wounded classmates. One of them was at death's door, but an American soldier doggedly set to with a hypodermic to find a vein in her stiffening arm. He finally succeeded and the colour came back to her cheeks; Kikuko was amazed at her enemies' response:

When Sonoko opened her eyes, all the American soldiers leapt with joy and cheered her on... This confused me even more and I struggled to understand, 'Why? Why are they acting like this?'... It is immensely difficult to unlock yourself from the thoughts and ideals which have been educated and implanted in you over many decades, especially when the whole nation has been educated in this way.

NO BRIEF ACCOUNT OF THE Pacific War's non-military victims is complete without the *maruta* of Unit 731. *Maruta* is the Japanese for log, a code word used by Japan's germ warfare researchers. When the scientists wanted more bodies for a test, they ordered 'logs' from the army – what they received was certainly organic, but anything but inanimate. Until the Russian invasion of Manchuria in August 1945, thousands of Chinese prisoners and some Russian POWs, men and women, were systematically used for intensely painful and fatal experiments.

Japan's biological and germ warfare experimentation began in Manchuria a couple of years after her invasion in 1931. Too dangerous and politically sensitive for the homeland, China offered a perfect testing ground for these weapons. Under the control of General Shiro Ishii, the corps expanded rapidly. The most famous of these was known as Unit 731, or the 'Kwantung Army Epidemic Prevention and Water Supply Unit'. It moved into specially constructed headquarters between 1938 and 1939, housing some 3,000 employees behind high-voltage fences. Their work focused primarily on the production of plague, cholera, typhoid and gas gangrene, and they conducted experiments into frostbite. Other research out-stations were dotted around the Asia–Pacific region.

Although Japan is known to have used biological weapons in China and against the Russians prior to the outbreak of war in 1941, the worst abuses relating to Japan's germ warfare project occurred within the production process. Yoshio Shinozuka worked at the headquarters of Unit 731: 'The role of this unit was to mass-produce bacteria when ordered. So, for this purpose we needed to test the toxicity of what we had produced. The easiest way to test the bacteria was on Chinese people, in which process they were killed... the fact that we called them *marutas* shows that we treated them as materials... I don't think we regarded them as people.'

The victims were injected with the plague and then, while they were still alive, Yoshio Shinokuza would take part in the operation to harvest germs from their gut:

I was ordered to wash the body with a brush for cleaning the floor. I had difficulty bringing myself to brush someone's body as if it was a piece of floor, especially when I was told to brush the face as well. However, I obeyed. I was shivering though. Then one person listened to the heartbeat and the other stood there with a dissecting scalpel... As far as I know, no anaesthetic was used... At the beginning, I kept looking away. I was ordered to scrape the culture medium against the dissected gut. This was the first time I was involved. We did the same with the second and by the time we got to the third person, I was no longer shivering. I think this was how I, as a member of Unit 731, was turned into a murderer.

The subjects of the experiments did not submit easily at first, while they still had their strength: 'It wasn't so much that they were frightened; they tried initially to resist. So, there was a special officer wearing a white coat, a hat and long boots holding a gun, with which he threatened the men. I heard that these officers were allowed to shoot any prisoner who resisted... Some of the prisoners were women. One was blonde – I heard she was Russian. Also, there were Chinese women.'

The prisoners were kept naked in cages barely four feet long, as they slowly succumbed, under observation, to various terminal diseases. In Nanking, at one of numerous branch units run by General Ishii, Hiroshi Matsumoto was involved with the production of bacteria using live Chinese as disease 'incubators': 'What was injected were live pathogens like cholera, bubonic plague, cancerous plague, lung plague, typhus, typhoid, tetanus, and others. Where I was, we had prisoners with cholera, typhus, typhoid, and the plague. After five to six months, these people produced the bacteria within their bodies so we were after their blood.'

The blood was removed by an incision in the groin vein. Every last drop was collected, with the person still – just – alive: 'The accompanying soldier, or the civilian war worker, stood on the chest and pressed down on the ribs, or jumped with all his weight, rather. He repeated it several times. The ribs were probably broken. I could hear them break. This way, the very last drop of blood was collected. This is what actually happened.'

Forbidden to speak about his work even with his colleagues, Hiroshi Matsumoto had recurring nightmares. So why did he continue with it? 'We had to do it as "work", as part of the daily cycle. Otherwise, you were sent to the army court and punished. I wanted to avoid that. I also had to do what I did for the sake of the people in my village who saw me off saying, "Do your best for the country".'

In fact his village might well have been appalled to learn what he had been doing, if his mother's reaction at the end of the war is any guide: 'My mother told me to sit down and asked me what I had done. So, I told her that they injected bacteria into Chinese people and let them die in a hospital and that my job was to watch this. My mother was livid at me... She thundered, "You are no human!"... I realized that I had done wrong and needed to be castigated by my mother – and to change my life.'

This was a key moment in Hiroshi Matsumoto's life, like the progression that Kikuko Miyagi had to go through on Okinawa, in which humanitarian values reasserted themselves after a period in which the individual seemed almost to become another person. It was an opportunity for rebirth not granted to the women and children who jumped off Marpi Point in Saipan, or Dionisia Carlos's family in Manila, or the *maruta* of Unit 731.

12

BEARING THE UNBEARABLE

'Help me! Give me some water! Mummy!' Every voice was calling for their mother.
SUZUKO NUMATA, Hiroshima survivor

When you have to deal with a beast you have to treat him as a beast. It is most regrettable but nevertheless true.
PRESIDENT HARRY TRUMAN, to the US Federal Council of Churches of Christ, a few days after the nuclear bomb was dropped on Nagasaki

LOOKING BACK NOW AT THE nuclear bombing of Hiroshima and Nagasaki, the view is dominated by the unparalleled human suffering. Radiation has continued to hurt and kill the survivors for well over half a century. It is difficult for many born after the war to reach past the images and experiences of the victims to understand the circumstances that led to the decision to drop the two bombs. The temptation is to condemn it as sheer callousness, to proclaim the Japanese on the point of surrender, to ignore the scale of loss and suffering that a land invasion of Japan would have entailed, to forget the momentum of world events. It is also almost impossible to imagine how intense public hatred of Japan was during the Pacific War; the Americans had largely stopped regarding the enemy as human. In January 1944 Britain's ambassador to Washington had noted a 'universal "exterminationist" anti-Japanese feeling'. It was a feeling that only increased as the war dragged on.

Some atom scientists working on the bomb, such as Niels Bohr and James Franck, did have strong reservations, not all humanitarian, while some social scientists who knew the Japanese argued that they should be treated as people, not vermin. These were very much minority opinions; defending the human rights of the people of Hiroshima and Nagasaki was low on the US national agenda. American public opinion was growing impatient. By this stage, a good many simply wanted the Japanese people dead. Nancy Potter remembers this mood: 'There was a great groundswell and a great anger that the war was taking so long, and that made us even more enthusiastic about getting it over rapidly and bringing the [boys] back home again.'

The closer Allied forces got to Japan, the fiercer the Japanese fought. Their defensive tactics were both stubborn and highly skilled, as the Americans had learned in the campaign for Okinawa. Their capacity for sacrifice seemed limitless. Huge bombing raids over Japan were not leading to the waving of white flags. The prevailing attitude of America's military leaders and planners was that a way must be found to end the war without a land invasion. There was no doubt about eventual victory; the problem was its price. Okinawa had been a debilitating battle of attrition; intelligence reports were now saying that the Japanese had concentrated huge forces in Kyushu – the very place US forces planned to land. Estimates of projected US casualties were revised up to around one million. This would be unacceptable to the American public.

There was another worrying factor, which several highly patriotic and decorated veterans have remarked on, and which may have had an effect on US military thinking: cracks in morale. Combat fatigue levels were running very high; corpsman Stan Dabrowski says of Iwo Jima that: 'Of the 18,000 people that went out of action due to wounds and such, maybe 4,000 of those may have been combat fatigue cases.' On Okinawa, Eugene Sledge's company runner had to take a group of fresh soldiers up to the front line: 'They passed dead Japs and shell holes and all kinds of debris and the odour was terrible... and he said six or eight of them out of the thirty just totally broke down right there. They just said, "I can't stand it, I just can't stand this, I can't go up there."' The runner's instinct, as a veteran of three campaigns, was to force them but, as an officer said, '"If they're in that kind of a shape, they won't be any good," so he just tagged them and sent them to the rear.' Also on Okinawa, George Peto realized men were deserting positions:

> *We only had about five foxholes strung along that little ridge, and so the lieutenant, he rounds up some stragglers and brings them up there, and I posted them on the line... I checked the holes every hour, and when I came back they were gone. I mean the morale had been pretty well shattered. That would have been unthinkable before Peleliu... I would hate to have ever been involved in a landing on the mainland of Japan. I doubt if we could have pulled it off. I'm speaking from experience. We didn't have the personnel.*

CATAPULTED OUT OF THE SEMI-OBSCURITY of his vice-presidential duties and sworn into office on 12 April 1945, the day Franklin D. Roosevelt died, President Harry Truman faced a series of daunting tasks: defeat Germany; defeat Japan; counter the communist threat; bring the boys back home; steer the economy towards civilian production; and win the next election. In the outskirts of ruined Berlin in mid July 1945, with only the first task completed, Truman had his baptism in international diplomacy. At the Yalta Conference in February, Roosevelt had agreed with Stalin that within ninety days of the end of the war in Europe, the Soviet Union would declare war on Japan. By Potsdam, three-quarters of the time was up. The idea appalled Truman; the pressure was on to end the war before Stalin's troops were swarming over Japan.

The day Truman arrived in Berlin, the world's first nuclear bomb was detonated at Alamogordo in the New Mexico desert, prompting Dr J. Robert Oppenheimer, who headed the team of scientists, to quote the Hindu god Vishnu from the Bhagavad-Gita: 'I am become death, the destroyer of worlds.' Another scientist said: 'I am sure that at the end of the world – in the last millisecond of the earth's existence – the last man will see what we saw.' News of the successful detonation was immediately wired to the President: 'Baby satisfactorily born.' Churchill, about to lose the British elections to Clement Attlee, immediately realized that here was the means to end the Pacific War. 'After all our toils and perils,' he later wrote, 'a miracle of deliverance.'

Only on the last day of discussions did Truman mention a 'very powerful new explosive' to Stalin, who casually replied, 'Good, I hope the United States will use it.' Stalin's poker face left Truman unsure if he had been correctly understood. Stalin understood only too well. The KGB had several spies operating deep inside the Manhattan Project, as the atom-bomb programme was known. The working relationship that had been built up between world leaders in their common struggle against Nazi Germany was already crumbling, to be replaced by the suspicion and hostility that would dominate forty-five years of super-power confrontation.

On 26 July 1945, the United States, Great Britain and China issued the Potsdam Declaration, calling on Japan to avoid the utter devastation of her homeland by proclaiming the 'unconditional surrender of all Japanese armed forces'. Neither the atomic bomb nor the Soviets' imminent entry into the war were mentioned.

Tokyo flatly rejected the declaration. A leading daily, the *Asahi Shimbun*, dismissed it with the headline 'LAUGHABLE MATTER'. Japan's third wartime Prime Minister, Admiral Kantaro Suzuki, more formally declared he would 'ignore' the statement, using the term *mokusatsu*, which carries the meaning of 'treating with contempt'. He told the director of the Cabinet Information Bureau that there was no need to stop the war, because the declaration clearly revealed weakness on the American side: 'For the enemy to say something like that means circumstances have arisen that force them to end the war. That is why they are talking about unconditional surrender. This is precisely the sort of moment when, if we hold firm, they will yield before we do.'

Most of the Japanese leadership, with the notable exception of the Foreign Minister Shigenori Togo, badly misread the Potsdam Declaration. It had demanded an immediate response to its uncompromising terms, yet the Navy Minister's judgement was that: 'Churchill has fallen, America is beginning to be isolated. The government will therefore ignore it. There is no need to rush.'

The Japanese leadership defies simplistic analysis during those apocalyptic weeks. There were the military diehards, who believed in some combination of eventual victory and glorious death; realists who knew defeat was inevitable and sought to mitigate its effects; theorists abstrusely debating the future of the divine imperial system; machinating politicians joining cliques and plotting the downfall of others. There were those who feared that Japan's social fabric was on the point of collapse – or communism – and that the people were about to round on the Emperor and the ruling elites. There were some who subscribed to more than one of these postures. And there was the Emperor himself.

Warnings that public confidence might deteriorate to crisis level were given to Emperor Hirohito from February 1945 onwards. His anxiety over the future of the *kokutai* or national polity – the question of whether the emperor system would survive the war – would become his primary concern. There is no positive evidence of his views about the Potsdam Declaration, nor is there any indication that he disapproved of its dismissal by Suzuki. He is known to have had two particular concerns during the weeks prior to the bombing of Hiroshima. First, the Emperor wanted to send a special envoy to open negotiations with the Soviet Union with the aim of somehow safeguarding his imperial position, but without agreeing to an unconditional surrender. This mission was, as his able and far-sighted Moscow ambassador Naotake Sato had warned it would be, refused by the Soviet Union, which realized that the envoy had no concrete proposals. The Soviets anyway wanted to acquire Japanese possessions; they knew they would get more as her enemy than as her peace broker.

Secondly, Hirohito twice gave orders for the three sacred emblems of his imperial rule to be brought into the safest protection possible. His authority and his legitimacy were embodied in a mirror, a sword and a curved jewel. His concerns for them are in accord with the brief of his envoy's aborted mission to Moscow: to preserve his own position and that of his line. There is no evidence during this period that the Emperor was at all distressed by his people's suffering, let alone that he wanted it to end. Nor is there any sign that he or his military and political leaders were ready to compromise their determination to secure a peace deal on as favourable terms as possible, if victory proved unachievable.

Some have argued that Japan was on the brink of collapse and that the atomic bombs were needless cruelty. Historian Richard Frank has studied the intelligence decrypts of both military and diplomatic Japanese communications traffic during this period.

He has concluded that there is no evidence prior to the dropping of the atom bombs that Japan's leadership was prepared to accept unconditional surrender even with the Emperor's position safeguarded. Ambassador Sato in Moscow expressly discussed this option with Foreign Minister Togo, but Togo ruled it out. Frank's verdict is:

> *Nothing approaching unconditional surrender was acceptable even within the limited circle that was contemplating peace negotiations... [Intelligence intercepts] showed without exception Japan's armed forces girding for Armageddon... [US] naval intelligence expressly identified the fundamental obstacle to peace as the Imperial Army's belief that it could achieve success against an invasion.*

Certainly the oral historical evidence supports the idea that despite some dissent and the belief by some that defeat was inevitable, the people of Japan would have fought on to the end. Kikuko Miyagi, as we saw in the last chapter, was a sixteen-year-old schoolgirl who had fought in the battle for Okinawa: 'I am certain that if the mainland had been attacked, the scale of things would have been much vaster and more serious since the population was far greater there than in Okinawa. Therefore I am just glad that the war ended without the people in the mainland having to suffer the things we went through in Okinawa.'

Another Japanese schoolgirl and war worker, Kikuyo Iida, never doubted the people's commitment: 'If it was for Japan's peace, people were happy to die. For Japan, people would sacrifice themselves. That was our attitude... we never thought of losing.'

Suzuko Numata worked in an office in the centre of the city of Hiroshima: 'We never imagined that Japan might lose. We worked hard to defend the home front for the country... I don't think we would have given up. We'd have fought to the end. I was absolutely determined to devote myself to the war no matter what happened.'

Devotion to the war could not be thought of independently of devotion to the Emperor. Ironically, while he was worrying about how much longer he might see his imperial reflection in the sacred mirror, senior Americans were facing the probability that they would need his authority to get the Japanese to stop fighting, and help effect the transition into a peaceful nation. This was not a late thought; throughout the conflict the Imperial Palace had never been deliberately targeted. Pilots were told 'the Emperor of Japan is not at present a liability and may later become an asset'. At Potsdam, General George C. Marshall, chairman of the US Joint Chiefs of Staff, stated: 'From a purely military point of view the attitude of the Joint Chiefs of Staff should be that nothing should be done prior to the termination of hostilities that would indicate the removal of the Emperor of Japan, since his continuation in office might influence the cessation of hostilities in areas outside Japan proper.'

The fear was that the military might achieve victory in Japan, leaving Japanese forces across Asia and the Pacific fighting to the death in the name of a deposed or manacled Emperor. He was needed in place, at least for the foreseeable future, for reasons that outweighed the call for retribution for war responsibility.

The immediate problem was that the Japanese leadership showed no clear signs of being about to give up. The more intelligence intercepts indicated how far Japan was from unconditional surrender, the greater the pressure to use the atomic bomb. The President's Interim Committee, including Dr J. Robert Oppenheimer, had considered giving the Japanese a demonstration of the bomb rather than dropping one directly on them, but discounted it: 'We can see no acceptable alternative to its direct military use... we can propose no technical demonstration likely to bring an end to the war.' They advised using the bomb 'against the enemy as soon as it could be done'. The new weapon seemed to offer the answer to three questions: how to bring Japan to her knees, while saving as many American lives as possible; how to shake a big stick at Stalin at the dawn of the Cold War; and how to find out what this hugely expensive, cutting-edge science could actually do.

THE PILOT WHO WOULD FLY the first atomic bombing mission had to combine superb technical precision with calm, unquestioning dedication. The man chosen was Colonel Paul Tibbets, who named the B-29 *Enola Gay* after his mother. He never lost sight of the experimental nature of what he had to do. A number of targets had been selected, including Kokura, Nagasaki and Hiroshima. Orders had gone out that as far as possible these cities should not be subject to conventional air raids, so that the scientists could subsequently measure the damage knowing it had been caused by the new bomb. As Paul Tibbets says: 'They wanted a target that was basically virgin, had not been struck by other explosives, because they wanted to get a study on what that bomb did to different material, different things and types of construction. So, they were almost as clean as you can get. They were being saved for us, that's for sure.'

Suzuko Numata had no explanation for her hometown's apparent lucky break: 'As the war became more and more intense, other prefectures started to be bombed. I heard it on the news. But Hiroshima was not being bombed. There was an army base, three arms factories and a naval port there, but we didn't have any bombing. I thought it was very strange.'

She went to work early on the morning of 6 August 1945. It promised to be a lovely day: 'The sky was deep blue and there was no trace of cloud. I still remember the colour vividly.' They had already had an air-raid alarm that day, but it was soon cancelled. The beauty of the weather sealed Hiroshima's fate. It was always the primary target, but Paul Tibbets had been told to bomb only with clear visibility, both to verify it was the correct city and for aiming accuracy. He sent a plane out over each of the three potential cities to check the weather, and they were already in the air towards Japan when the reports came in: 'I remember the radio operator said, "Clear and unlimited," and I said, "That's fine, we're going to go to Hiroshima"... and away we went.' It was the weather plane that had triggered the sirens Suzuko Numata heard that morning.

She went up on the roof where some of her co-workers were doing exercises. They chatted for a while, and then she went down to clean the office. In the air, Paul Tibbets had already informed the twelve crewmen that they were carrying a particularly powerful bomb – security was too tight to tell them it was nuclear, but one of them guessed: 'My tail-gunner, who was a little bit more discerning than the rest of them, he looked at me, he said: "Colonel, we wouldn't be playing with atoms, would we?" I said:

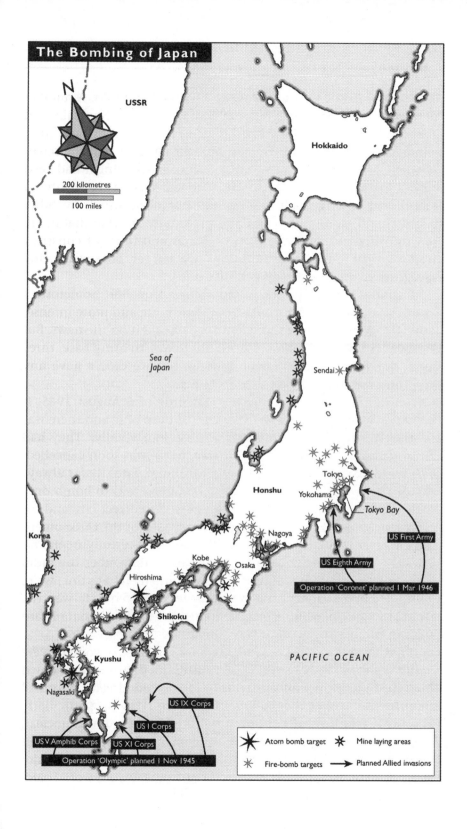

The Bombing of Japan

N

USSR

200 kilometres

100 miles

Hokkaido

Sea of
Japan

Sendai

Honshu

Tokyo

Yokohama

Tokyo Bay

US First Army

Nagoya

US Eighth Army

Korea

Kobe

Osaka

Operation 'Coronet' planned 1 Mar 1946

Hiroshima

Shikoku

Kyushu

PACIFIC OCEAN

Nagasaki

US IX Corps

US I Corps

US V Amphib Corps

US XI Corps

Operation 'Olympic' planned 1 Nov 1945

Atom bomb target

Mine laying areas

Fire-bomb targets

Planned Allied invasions

"Yes, Bob" – his name was Bob Caron – I said: "You're right, Bob, that's what it is." He said: "I thought so all along."'

Bombardier Tom Ferebee lined the *Enola Gay* up on the aiming point, which was not Hiroshima's military bases but a distinctive T-shaped bridge in the city centre itself, just 1,000 yards from Suzuko Numata's office block: 'He only had to make one correction all the way in, made a slight wind correction, and then he turned round to me, he said: "I can't do anything else with it." He's smoking and chewing on his cigar. And he said: "I can't do anything with it, it's going right down the track." And I said: "Fair enough. If it ain't broke you can't fix it."'

At quarter past eight the atomic bomb itself was released. It would take the bomb forty-three seconds to fall to 1,890 feet above the ground where the scientists had calculated it would do the most damage. A second plane simultaneously dropped three small radio-linked instrument packages for measuring shock waves and radioactivity, turning Hiroshima into a giant laboratory with 350,000 live test subjects. While the atom bomb was dropping, Suzuko Numata went down to empty her bucket: 'I took a bucket in my left hand and ran downstairs to the fourth floor. The washroom was just next to the staircase on the fourth floor. It must have taken less than a minute for me to go to the hallway outside the washroom. I suddenly saw a beautiful colour. It was like a mixture of red, yellow, blue, green and orange.'

Six miles above her, Paul Tibbets threw his B-29 into a tight turn, to get as far from the blast as he could. He saw a flash of purple and blue light, and suddenly got a taste of lead in his mouth: the effect of electrolysis on the lead fillings in his teeth. The skin of the plane was rippled by three shock waves which sent Suzuko Numata flying: 'A blast of wind blew me across the fourth floor. The interior of the building was destroyed and I was buried under it. My left foot was cut off at the ankle and I fell unconscious.'

The bomb exploded over a city starting its day – streets full of children off to school and workers to factories and offices. At the epicentre of the blast the temperature rose to 100,000,000 degrees Fahrenheit and the light shone ten times brighter than the sun. All that remained of some people were shadows – burnt into the few walls that survived the thunderous shock wave which instantly flattened the city centre. After the initial blast, cold air rushed inwards as hot air raced up, producing the atom bomb's hallmark mushroom cloud. Colonel Tibbets watched the billowing cloud surge upwards – till it towered three miles above him: 'I had seen the city clearly on the way in, but I couldn't see anything but a black boiling mass down there... like when I was a child and they used to pave the streets with tar – always over the barrel, there was a layer of steam, moisture and air... And that's the way I saw Hiroshima.'

Caught inside that black boiling mass was Suzuko Numata. Around her, a firestorm raged, turning eight square miles of buildings and people to cinders. She was pulled from the rubble as the sky darkened and black, radioactive rain started to fall. She was taken to a temporary hospital, which could not cope with the terrible burns and had no remedy for the world's newest ailment – radiation sickness:

I can never forget the sight of those people. They were burnt so badly that they didn't look human. Half of their ears were gone and their eyes were crushed. They didn't look like human beings. A person next to me said in a strained voice, 'Help me! Give me water!' The next moment, he was dead. Many people lost their hair, bled from their gums, got a rash on their bodies and discharged blood from their bowels... I was in a living, unimaginable, hell.

Four days after the blast Suzuko Numata's leg was amputated – without anaesthetic – to stop the spread of infection. She was lucky to live. Thousands who survived the initial blast succumbed to radiation sickness in the next few weeks. One of Suzuko Numata's colleagues came with his pregnant wife to the makeshift hospital in search of their three missing children:

Soon afterwards the wife went into labour... When the baby boy was born, there was a wisp of happiness in the horrendous atmosphere at the temporary hospital. Then I heard he had a rash of small, purple blotches all over his body. He died three days later, and his mother went mad and died... Her husband's face didn't look human. Nor did his body. He was red all over his body from burns. Finally, on 25 August, he collapsed near me with a strained scream and died. So the whole family perished.

Upwards of 80,000 people died immediately; by the end of the year, radiation sickness would push the death toll to around 140,000. Since then, 60,000 more may have subsequently died as a direct result of the bomb. Many more have lived in pain, grief and anxiety. Suzuko Numata speaks for many of the remaining survivors: 'We don't know how much radiation we received, but it is certain that it damaged our bodies. We've been living with this worry. That atomic bomb was actually tested out on human beings. We feel very angry about it.'

The co-pilot Robert Lewis wrote two words in the *Enola Gay's* log after seeing the pall of smoke and fire blanketing Hiroshima: 'My God!' A wire sound recording was made of what was said in the plane during the bomb run, but it has never come to light. Paul Tibbets expresses no doubts about his mission:

I was never the type that sat around and mulled anything over about something like that, the morality of it... There's no morality in warfare as far as I'm concerned... I had a job to do, put a bomb on a target, and I knew I could do it, and that's what I was going to do... I'm sorry for the people that had to have it happen to 'em. But I didn't cause that. They caused it. Their side did that. No, I can't carry any guilt. I hated to see it happen, you know. I've heard stories told, people were melted, babies and everything else. I'm sure they were. But at least they didn't suffer. Now the ones that got too much radiation did suffer, that was a different deal... I don't apologize to anybody. I don't feel a bit bad. I feel good... There's many different ways to look at it. But I've never lost a night's sleep and I never will.

It took a while for the Japanese to understand what had actually happened in Hiroshima. On the evening the atom bomb was dropped, a Japanese news bulletin announced: 'A few B-29s hit Hiroshima city... and fled after dropping incendiaries and bombs. The extent of the damage is now under survey.' In a brief statement issued the next day, the military stated a 'bomb of a new type' had been used. It would take a further two days before Japan's leading physicist, Yoshio Nishina, himself researching atomic weapons, arrived in Hiroshima to confirm what the Americans were now declaring to the world.

'The force from which the sun draws its power,' read the White House statement, 'has been loosed against those who brought war to the Far East.' The Japanese were warned to expect 'a rain of ruin from the air' if they did not accept surrender terms. The Japanese did not reply, and on 9 August 1945 a second nuclear device – this time a plutonium bomb – was winched into a B-29 bomber. The primary target was the city of Kokura, but dense cloud forced a switch to Nagasaki, where the weather was also poor. Patches of clear sky enabled the city to be positively identified but the bombing run itself was made on radar, and the target was missed by a mile and a half. The bomb nevertheless killed around 35,000 people; the toll would double by the end of the year.

Adding to Japan's problems was the Soviet declaration of war on 8 August 1945. Within hours, Russian forces crossed the long frontier shared between the USSR (and its dominion state of Outer Mongolia) and the northern part of China controlled by Japan's Kwantung Army. Prime Minister Suzuki responded to the news with the comment: 'The game is up.' Over a million and a half men were deployed by the USSR, although the Japanese grossly underestimated the scale of the assault. Ultimately the war ended before the planned invasion of Hokkaido (the northern island of Japan), but Manchuria, northern Korea, Sakhalin and the Kurile Islands were all swiftly occupied. The speed of the invasion, and the panic it created, was such that while many Japanese fought bravely, many others simply turned and fled. Soviet troops, battle-hardened in the crucible of the European war and unhindered by the vast distances of the Pacific Ocean, advanced closer to Tokyo in less than a month than the Americans managed in more than three and a half years of fighting.

Yet incredibly, the twin blows of the USA's atomic bombs and the USSR's massive assault did not immediately convince Japan's leadership that unconditional surrender would best serve the country's interests. The 'big six' ruling Japan through the Supreme Council for the Direction of the War comprised the Prime Minister, Foreign Minister, Army Minister, Navy Minister, Chief of the Army General Staff and Chief of the Naval General Staff. These men governed by consensus, although it was based on fear rather than on trust or empathy. Any radical break from the declared policy of the militarists risked triggering a split, with the concurrent danger that hard-liners might resort to assassination or a *coup d'état*.

Amid the deadlock some did urge surrender but others – such as Army Minister General Korechika Anami – remained radically opposed. He told his colleagues (in a gross overestimate of US capabilities) that America might have as many as 100 atomic bombs which they could start dropping at a rate of three a day, yet he still recommended the war be continued: 'We cannot pretend to claim that victory is certain, but it is far too early to say the war is lost. That we will inflict severe losses on the enemy where he invades is certain, and it is by no means impossible that we may be able to reverse the situation in our favour, pulling victory out of defeat.'

Into the impasse stepped the Emperor. There are long-standing academic arguments about his role in the war. The traditional view has been that he was a figurehead, whose imperial seal was affixed to commands without his knowledge, who played no active role in the war's direction or conduct. Sanitized post-war accounts from the palace distanced him from the running of the war, in accord with the American decision not to prosecute him as a war criminal but to retain him as Emperor. Recently, the work of historians such as Akira Yamada and Herbert Bix has brought new evidence to light – from participants' notes of meetings and personal memoirs – which forces revision of him as a mere puppet, remote in his palace.

On 31 December 1942 Hirohito told an imperial conference convened to discuss the situation in Guadalcanal that he was prepared to sanction the withdrawal of forces from the island, but stated: 'We must launch offensives elsewhere.' 'Torpedoes aren't enough,' he told Navy Chief of Staff Nagano after one skirmish. 'Can't you get closer to the enemy ships and fire cannons directly at them?' Persistent Allied advances across the south-west Pacific led him to demand of the Army Chief of Staff on 5 August 1943: 'When and where on earth are you [people] ever going to put up a good fight? And when are you going to fight a decisive battle?' On 17 June 1944, two days after the American landing on Saipan, he told the Naval Vice-Chief of Staff: 'Rise to the challenge; make a tremendous effort; achieve a splendid victory.' When the Battle of Leyte (in the Philippines) ended in disaster, he stated in January

1945: 'Now a decisive battle will have to be fought on Luzon as Leyte has been lost... We will have to conceal this from the people.' In April 1945, concerned about the tactics of the Okinawa garrison commander, Hirohito asked: 'Why doesn't the local army fight back? If there aren't enough men, I propose reinforcements should be sent to land on Okinawa.'

Now, with Hiroshima and Nagasaki in radioactive ruin, and Soviet troops advancing, Emperor Hirohito intervened for the last time in a war he realized only he or the Allies could end. If it were left to the Allies, it would not matter how safely the mirror, curved jewel and sword had been hidden. There would be no one and nothing left to be Emperor of. A message was sent to the Americans agreeing to the terms of the Potsdam Declaration, with just one condition: 'The understanding that the said declaration does not comprise any demand which prejudices the prerogatives of His Majesty as a Sovereign ruler.' Historian Saburo Ienaga is scathing in contempt: 'Japan's leaders showed a supreme indifference to the suffering and despair of the populace to the very end. That callous determination was unshaken by two atomic bombings. The "national polity" took precedence over the people.'

In Washington, the Cabinet now had to decide whether to retain the Emperor, and whether to allow the surrender to become conditional – the Allies were haunted by the disastrously inconclusive ending of the First World War. Their solution was elegant. The surrender did not have to be defined as conditional, as keeping the Emperor was already part of their thinking. Secretary of State Henry Stimson summed it up:

> *Even if the question hadn't been raised by the Japanese, we would have to continue the Emperor ourselves under our command and supervision in order to get into surrender the many scattered armies of the Japanese... Something like this use of the Emperor must be made in order to save us from a score of bloody Iwo Jimas and Okinawas all over China and the New Netherlands [Indonesia].*

The Americans were careful not to be seen to be accepting Japan's condition. Truman wanted the war over before Stalin could demand a role in post-war Japan, but he had to avoid a response that could be interpreted as a concession, for fear of being 'crucified' by US public opinion. The reply was ambiguous: the Emperor's place in Japan's future was not guaranteed, but nor was it rejected. Military historian Richard Frank has commented: 'The message implied much but firmly promised nothing.' In Tokyo the man behind the *kamikaze* effort, Admiral Takijiro Onishi, spoke for those who wanted to pursue the war, declaring: 'If we are prepared to sacrifice 20 million Japanese lives in a special attack [*kamikaze*] effort, victory will be ours!' While Japan dithered, America rushed a third nuclear weapon to the Pacific, and Soviet troops advanced.

The final spur to Japan's surrender came from an unexpected quarter. American propaganda leaflets dropped over Japan on 13 August 1945 detailed the full text of the government's conditional surrender offer and the Allies' reply. Hirohito felt obliged to act decisively. The public could now see for themselves the extent to which negotiations to preserve the Emperor were prolonging an already lost war. On 14 August Hirohito secretly recorded a short speech announcing Japan's surrender. That night, a group of rebel officers launched a coup aimed at preventing the Emperor from surrendering, but by morning it had collapsed. At the same time he reined in the hard-line members of the 'big six'.

The Emperor's declaration was broadcast at noon the next day. Millions of Japanese across the home islands and Asia listened in awe. It was the first time they had ever heard his high-pitched voice. Using archaic and euphemistic language, Hirohito declared:

...the war situation has developed not necessarily to Japan's advantage, while the general trends of the world have all turned against her interest. Moreover, the enemy has begun to employ a new and most cruel bomb, the power of which to do damage is, indeed, incalculable, taking the toll of many innocent lives... We have resolved to pave the way for a grand peace for all the generations to come by enduring the unendurable and suffering what is insufferable.

Miho Yoshioka bowed prostrate before the radio: 'I heard the Emperor's voice for the first time. I thought, "So, this is what he sounds like." And then, I wished he had surrendered earlier.

Everyone cried. And yes, I cried. But my tears were in hope that my husband would come back.' In fact, her husband had already been killed on Okinawa.

A small gathering collected outside the Imperial Palace. Some had come to apologize to the Emperor for failing his expectations but others cheered and rejoiced that the war was, at long last, over. Across Asia his armies prepared to lay down their weapons. So smooth was this process that several royal princes, specially selected to carry the imperial edict to commanders in the field, were not despatched. Some time later General William Slim, the victorious British general in Burma, was criticized by his Japanese experts for causing the Japanese to lose face by insisting on them giving up their samurai swords; it might encourage them to kill themselves. His reply was that 'Any Japanese officer wishing to commit suicide would be given every facility.' In fact, only a few hundred officers did commit ritual suicide – no more than the number of Nazis who killed themselves following Germany's defeat.

What, in effect, had saved the Emperor was the abstract sense of blind obedience and devotion his people showed him. The war ended before anyone had to find out if, in fact, the Japanese people would have fought to the finish. Navy Minister Admiral Mitsumasa Yonai put his finger on the feeling of relief that the ending of the war had been forced on Japan by strength from outside, rather than weakness from within. Shortly before Japan's surrender he told the Emperor: 'I think the term inappropriate, but the atomic bombs and the Soviet entry into the war are, in a sense, gifts from the gods. This way we don't have to say we quit the war because of domestic circumstances.'

Many Allied prisoners and combatants, like Sy Kahn, also have no doubt that the nuclear weapons represented salvation:

I have not yet met a soldier who served in the South Pacific who has an iota of regret about the atomic bomb. I think it saved our lives, and I think that's what Truman thought when he ordered it to be dropped, that it would save a lot of lives, and I think it did. I have no sympathy with the people who were not there who talk about the brutality of it and so on. The brutality was already behind us, the brutality was already experienced.

Australian Tom Morris looks back on the bomb in terms of its benefits to the Japanese as well as everyone else: 'It was a dreadful weapon, I think it was used possibly at the right time because not only did it save my miserable life and the few internees and POWs, but it saved hundreds of thousands if not millions of Japanese: Japanese women, Japanese children, Japanese soldiers, and American and any other Allied servicemen.'

Suzuko Numata finds it impossible to see the bombs, which killed so many in her city of Hiroshima and in Nagasaki, as savers of other Japanese lives who never had to face a flame-throwing tank with a sharpened bamboo pole: 'I don't think we Japanese ever thought that it was good that the war ended because of the atomic bomb. Rather, our anger and sadness were stronger now that the war had come to an end.'

Two weeks after the cessation of hostilities, Japan formally surrendered to the Allies aboard the USS *Missouri* in Tokyo Bay. Toshikazu Kase, the young diplomat who had drafted Japan's declaration of war, now accompanied Foreign Minister Mamoru Shigemitsu to the event that ended it. He was a reluctant witness: 'In my position, I had to be involved; I couldn't get out of it. I prepared myself for it, and I went. But I didn't want to.'

It was a ceremony infused with symbolism. Generals Percival and Wainwright, who had surrendered Singapore and Corregidor respectively, had been liberated by Soviet troops and flown in to see the tables turned after more than three years. The flag at the battleship's main masthead was the one that had fluttered over the White House on the day Pearl Harbor was attacked. Admiral Halsey had ordered a precious relic to be sent from the Naval Academy Museum at Annapolis: the Stars and Stripes flown by Commodore Matthew Perry's flagship when he entered Tokyo Bay ninety-two years before, to open up Japan to the world. It was now displayed on the surrender deck, presiding over the event that would end nearly a century of subsequent Japanese expansion. Gunner's mate Cy Topol watched the proceedings from a nearby gun turret:

My heart was beating and my adrenaline was flowing, and I knew that I was in on something big, really big... Here they were, the greatest force in their minds when they knocked out Pearl Harbor, they must have celebrated, thought that they had us really on our hands and knees, and here they're signing away the surrender... It was electrifying: history in the making... This was the end of a world war bigger than ever before, and it meant going home, which was to me wonderful.

After the surrender documents were signed, General MacArthur declared the proceedings closed, and Toshikazu Kase left with Foreign Minister Shigemitsu to report to the Emperor: 'His view was, I think, that there was no alternative because we had lost. We had to accept defeat manfully and the question then was, how to recover from it.'

13

I'VE SERVED MY TIME IN HELL

My home was like an overturned anthill. Many people had come to my house to see me... I was not sure how I was going to be accepted because of having been a POW... Then an old friend from school, said, 'What are you talking about, Masaru? We are all prisoners in Japan now. You don't have to shoulder the responsibility on your own. You got wounded as a result of all your efforts as a soldier. Don't be so humble. You can hold your head high. What do you think, everyone?' They all applauded him. They all told me how happy they were that I was back.

MASARU MORIKI, Japanese prisoner of war

When I came home it was as though I lived among aliens because nobody understood... there is an old Marine poem... it says: 'When I get to heaven, To St Peter I will tell, Another Marine reporting sir, I've served my time in hell.'

EUGENE SLEDGE, US Marine veteran of Peleliu and Okinawa

GOING HOME CAN BE THE most difficult journey a soldier ever makes. He – or she, for there were many military nurses (and female POWs) in the Pacific – has long thought about it, in foxhole or tent or prison-camp, dreamed about it, worried it would never happen, imagined how it would be if it did. What will it be like to see family again? To wear dry, clean clothes? To have a fresh, cooked meal? To sleep in sheets? To have a bath? To go to a lavatory? To get drunk? To have sex? To see children play? To have no one bossing me around? Not to live in the midst of death or to fear it every day? Will home have changed? Will there be work? What will become of me? Will loved ones have been faithful? What can I tell them? Will anyone understand?

Then, with that journey made, they have to face the reality: a world that has not stood still and that cannot really imagine what the returned soldier has been through. Going home closes a big gap, but can leave a small one gaping.

The Emperor's radio broadcast, on 15 August 1945, ended many wars. It brought the Second World War to a close. It drew a line under Japan's fifteen-year conflict in Manchuria, and her eight-year war with China. For many young Japanese it was the first taste of peace in their lives. It also concluded a host of smaller-scale but intense struggles: for survival in prison camps, to keep going through air raids and bereavement, to retain one's sanity. Indeed, the conflict ended almost uncannily smoothly – exposing the lie that 'all Japanese prefer death to surrender' – but the torrent of violence and hatred that had flooded the region could not be turned off like a tap. The Imperial Army executed eight captured airmen in the last hours of the war and the US Air Force sneaked a massive thousand-plane bombing raid in – after the Emperor's declaration but before Truman had time to order a ceasefire.

A handful of Japanese fought on; famously never realizing the war had ended till they were enticed out from their island hideaways. Some freed prisoners and Allied troops guarding the defeated enemy extracted, where possible, personal revenge. Slowly the war's combatants filtered home, many never quite fitting back into the world they had known before. But if few had predicted such a sudden end to hostilities, even fewer guessed at the strategic alliance America and Japan would go on to forge.

News of peace triggered a wave of emotions: relief, anger, joy and confusion washed over the survivors. Because the Japanese fought so tenaciously, and nobody knew about the atomic bomb, there was no reason to believe the war could possibly end without invading Japan proper. Eugene Sledge's response was surprise: 'When we were told the war was over I just couldn't believe it... I felt they would turn us right around and go back through the islands and wipe out every Japanese on every island because we had no idea that they would quit when the Emperor said quit.' Sy Kahn had never thought he would survive the war, and had built up defence mechanisms which did not disappear the minute he heard the news:

I couldn't celebrate, what I needed to do was decompress, and I felt like I had to wait till all of the protective ice sheaths that I had layered on for two and a half years began to melt and crack and let me out of that expectation of death and that expectation of the endlessness of this war. And that finally here was a crack of light, maybe it was true and maybe I would live and maybe I would get home again.

Allied prisoners of the Japanese had known that their armies were winning the war. Precious secret radios, the sight of short-range fighter aircraft flying overhead and even censored news reports from the Japanese all indicated major Allied advances. But would the prisoners live to see Japan's defeat? It was not just a question of fighting off hunger and disease a little longer. Historian Gavan Daws has found a number of cases where POWs were liquidated when invasion seemed imminent: on Wake island almost a hundred POWs were machine-gunned to death; on Ballale island (in the south-western Pacific) some ninety prisoners were bayoneted to death; and on Palawan (in the Philippines) over a hundred men were killed.

Daws also quotes an entry in a headquarters journal in Taihoku on Formosa describing 'extreme measures' to be implemented in 'urgent situations'. It is rare documentary evidence showing Japanese plans to kill all Allied POWs in the event of an invasion: 'Whether they are destroyed individually or in groups, or however it is done, with mass bombing, poisonous smoke, poisons, drowning, decapitation, or what, dispose of the prisoners as the situation dictates. In any case it is the aim not to allow the escape of a single one, to annihilate them all, and not to leave any traces.'

Many former POWs got the distinct impression that, just before the war ended, the Japanese were preparing to kill them. Fred Seiker was sent with other prisoners outside their small maintenance camp along the Burma–Thailand Railway and ordered to start digging: 'They made us dig a trench. Oh, a deep trench about three yards deep... and very wide and very long, and what are we doing this for? and then somebody said, do you know what this is, this is a bloody mass grave, this is for us.'

When the Japanese disappeared overnight he was doubly relieved: 'I remember thinking it's over three and a half years ago that these bastards made me into nothing. I now, just like that, as quickly, in seconds, I am free, I am free! You know, you have to realize what that means after all these years, after all these years to be free.'

For others, it was quite difficult to define the moment when they were, actually, free. A week after witnessing a strange mushroom cloud blossom over the city of Nagasaki some thirty-two miles away, the men in Lester Tenney's forced labour camp were fairly certain the war was over. Three of the indicators they had long since worked out had materialized: they were not being made to work that day, they had been given as much rice to eat as they wanted and Red Cross parcels had been distributed for the first time. Tenney, by now a passable Japanese speaker, was chosen to apply the fourth test:

> My buddies... said, 'Go ahead out and say hello [to] the guard without bowing to him, see what happens.' So, I went out, again, with the philosophy if I take another beating, what the hell's another beating? Anyhow, I went outside, and I looked at the guard, and I said, 'Hi, how are you this afternoon?' And he looked at me, stood at attention and bowed, and said, 'I'm fine, Sir.' We knew the war was over.

One of their first acts of liberty were acts of vengeance: 'There must have been eight or ten different groups of eight, ten, twelve men, and they went out looking for guards or looking for civilians in the [coal] mine. And when they found anybody that they knew or they recognized, they beat him, and they killed him.'

Former prisoners were not the only men to assert victor's justice. Allan Clifton, a translator in the Australian Imperial Force, begins his sympathetic description of post-war Japan, *The Time of Fallen Blossoms*, with an eyewitness account of the vengeance inflicted by Australian troops upon surrendered Japanese in Sandakan, on the island of Borneo. Of the 2,500 Australian and British prisoners in the camp in Sandakan, only six survived the war. Disease, malnutrition, torture and two forced 'death marches' killed the rest.

> *By Christ we'd got even. We'd beaten up the unarmed Nip working parties lined up on the Sandakan Wharf after the surrender. Rolled quarter-ton drums of petrol over them as they lay there too... That was the way to find criminals. Some of them had done nothing, of course, but what did that matter? A Jap's a Jap.*
>
> *And the embarkation of the sick and wounded, about 2,000 of them... When they couldn't climb the ladders we hauled 'em up the LSTs' [Landing Ship Tanks] side with a rope. The lads with the lifeboat paddles were waiting for 'em on deck. Sounded good, the crack of wood on their skulls. Bloody hard skulls some of them were too; broke some of the paddles. Those that fell were kicked in the face; if they couldn't get up, overboard they went... They died like flies on the trip back... We tied weights to 'em and cheered as we slid 'em overboard...*
>
> *...And then the fellow we made dig his own grave. He'd been given a hell of a belting, but he still said he knew nothing about the Sandakan march, wasn't even there. But you know you can't take a Nip's word for anything... When he had finished [digging] they knelt him down on the edge of the hole and stood over him with an axe. He was screaming his innocence and begging for time to pray when I turned it in. I told them I couldn't stand for any more. They went and got another interpreter...*

Ted Tsukiyama, the Japanese American from Hawaii suspended from military duties after Pearl Harbor (see Chapter 5), recalled his desire for vengeance after being allowed later to rejoin America's war effort. He was sent to Burma in 1944, where he worked behind the lines in signals intelligence, never actually seeing the enemy till after their surrender:

> *Well, as far as I was concerned the Japanese were my enemy, and I go back to the Pearl Harbor day attack... I vowed at that time that the first Japanese soldier I see, I'm going to knock him down and kick him in the balls and just crush him for all the suffering that I know we are going to have to endure because of what that country has done, and I carried that feeling throughout the war.*

And the sequel to that is finally in Burma, three years later, I have a chance to visit this Japanese POW camp...

So we went into this compound with a very belligerent feeling, and then somebody yelled a command and all these ragged prisoners jump up and they bow, and you look at them and they're just kids, young kids, they look like fifteen, sixteen, maybe farmers' boys have been drafted, shoved into the army and made to fight a war that they probably didn't believe in. And what we saw was not this proud arrogant great fighting machine that we had been told to expect. These were just beaten dogs and we could see that we hadn't been really told the truth, if that's what the enemy was and looked like, and you know all this anger and resentment just sort of faded out when you looked at them.

In the end it was the very inaccuracy of both sides' propaganda that made the rapprochement between the Allies and Japanese so smooth. Most victorious American, British and Australian troops were no more demonic, vicious killers than the majority of vanquished Japanese were rabid beasts, desperate to fight to the death. Popular imagery was forced to adapt. It did so, and revealed itself to be remarkably flexible. As a case in point, Ted Tsukiyama's fear of a rabid enemy, whom he was expecting to find in the POW camp, turned out not to be. Yet he still employs a canine analogy: the 'beaten dogs' that he had till recently hated are now pitiful and possibly repentant. It is even possible to imagine these 'dogs', if trained, becoming loyal and lovable friends.

Perhaps the most startling example of a new application for an old image appeared on the September 1945 cover of the marine magazine *Leatherneck*. Celebrating Japan's capitulation, the cover shows a small, cuddly and slightly peeved chimp, dressed in a Japanese army uniform, sitting in the arms of a bulky, joyful marine. Historian John Dower notes: 'The cover... reveals the malleability of wartime stereotypes, as the simian caricature was almost immediately transformed into an irritated but already domesticated and even charming pet.'

THE POWS HAVE VIVID MEMORIES of the moment when the first Allied representatives appeared at their camps. Fred Seiker cannot talk about it after fifty-five years without his eyes filling with tears:

'I remember there was a British medic and he took me... [He sighs]. He held my head in his arms and he said, "Are you all right, mate?" and that's a moment I can never forget, never, ever. You know, that voice, "Are you all right, mate?" – to be among your own, it's a terrific feeling. And that was freedom. Marvellous.'

Pat Darling remembers the sharp contrast between the emaciated, sick nurses and the team fresh from Australia sent to collect them: 'They were dressed in these incredible pants and safari jackets and gaiters and all the rest of it, and of course only twenty-four of us surfaced. And the look on her face when she said, "But where are the rest of you?" and none of us could say anything, and then I don't know whose voice it was, it was from the back, said, "They're all dead."'

American military nurse Madeline Ullom was a POW in the Philippines in Santo Tomas, a camp with families and children. When the American liberation forces arrived, the children wanted to get their own back on the Japanese guards, to whom they had had to make frequent deep bows of respect: 'The little children kept yelling to Captain Burrows "make them bow, make them bow, MAKE THEM BOW!" And of course they didn't; our troops didn't know about the bowing procedure, and they thought the little children were kind of barmy, so they said, one of the troopers said to one of the little boys, "How would you like a nice ice-cream cone?" and the little fella said, "What's that?"'

Some died of disease and wounds on the way home. Tom Morris remembers a man who did not survive the boat trip for another reason: 'He fell overboard and we assumed he committed suicide because he had learned at Perth that his marriage had disintegrated. And we circled for an hour or so, and his body was never recovered.' Lester Tenney had got through desperate years in prison camp by his determination to get home to his wife:

She was a lovely girl, she was very nice to me, always wonderful, and I lived really because of her. And I found out that she was notified that I was missing in action, presumed dead. And she waited... about two and a half years and then finally, she remarried... And I sort of was very flamboyant about it, you know, I was 'Oh yeah, well I can understand that', you know. But emotionally, it really hit me, really hit me hard... for the next thirty days, I

became a drunkard, and I hit the bottle every single night. Took me
about thirty days until I finally said, you know, this is ridiculous,
I've got to get on with my life.

The US Army was racially segregated; Nelson Peery remembers
the 850 men of his outfit standing on the deck of the ship carrying
them home, singing 'Lift every voice and sing till earth and
heaven ring with the harmony of liberty'. Having won their battle
honours and proved themselves the equal of white men, many
black troops were determined not to be treated any longer as
second-class citizens in the country whose freedom they had been
defending. Nelson Peery knew 'that when I touched that dock I
was going into a new battle, this time a battle to impose on
America what we imposed on Germany and Japan'. The freedom
movement that eventually broke the back of segregation in
America drew much of its strength and drive from the experiences, aspirations and bravery of Nelson Peery's generation of
black soldiers.

They would need great bravery. In Tokyo Bay, on the deck of
the USS *Missouri*, General MacArthur had proclaimed the hope
that, out of the war's carnage, a better world would emerge
'dedicated to the dignity of man and the fulfilment of his most
cherished wish for freedom, tolerance and justice'. As Nelson
Peery recalls, they were values in short supply in the United States:

A black soldier on his way home, a guy by the name of Isaac
Woodward... he got to Alabama and they told him he had to go
to the back of the bus. He said, 'Mister, I just got off the front line
so I'm not going to the back,' and so the police came and beat him
half to death and gouged his eyes out. 'Nigger, if you can't see that
Whites Only sign we're going to fix you so you don't see anything,'
and so they gouged his eyes out.

Not all the stories are scarred by tragedy. Many returned home
to outstretched arms and pats on the back. Australian Bill Spencer
had fought in the Middle East and across the Pacific:

A wonderful feeling to know that you were going home, a
wonderful feeling to know that you had a lot of mates that were

going home with you, and then of course the feeling of getting home, well that's something out of this world. There are no other pleasures in life that match coming home to loved ones. A lot didn't have that pleasure, but we made up for it.

British 14th Army veteran Bhim Singh recalls his return to his village in India:

The villagers – when a man returns, they feel our man is back after a long time. They say, 'Brother, it took you a long time.' So when you meet your family, your eyes fill with tears – because you're home. No fear of anything here... So that day there was great celebration – my family distributed sweets and so on – to say our man is home and he's alive.

Several veterans reported a strange reluctance at the last moment to face actually going home. Marine George Peto ducked into a bar 'and it was a week later when I finally surfaced. I was out in Cicero somewhere, and I was broke, and I decided it was time to go home.' Sailor and POW Otto Schwarz got within a couple of miles of his home in New Jersey, but delayed making that last journey for hours: 'For some reason or other I kept holding back. Strange.' Soldier and POW Dick Gordon remembers the deep unease he felt when his hospital train finally pulled into Pennsylvania Station in New York City. His younger brother came aboard to look for him:

He came in that car, he says, 'Does anyone know Gordon?' and I turned my face away and looked in a different direction, I could not bring myself to say here I am, and I had the greatest urge to say turn this train around and take me back to prison camp, where I felt a little secure. It was the strangest feeling, I never thought I would experience that but I did... I was frightened of coming home, but I didn't realize it until that moment when my brother got in that car looking for me.

Almost two million Japanese soldiers and sailors died as a consequence of the war. But three and a half million troops, based outside the home islands, survived. Together with some three million civilians (living in occupied territories) they were slowly repatriated. Many returned to find their homes and livelihoods destroyed, their families and loved ones dead. Those who had been taken prisoner were particularly unsure of how they would be received. Takeo Yamauchi had surrendered on Saipan, but his family in Japan had believed he was killed in action. The town held a funeral service for him at which his father made a formal speech of thanks to all who attended. Then, a year later, Takeo returned:

> My brothers and sisters came to pick me up at Kyoto station and we saw each other, we all broke down in tears and they truly expressed their happiness in seeing me again. After that I went home and saw my parents. My mother was crying with joy but my father had a somewhat complicated look on his face. Inevitably, he could not hide his glee at seeing his very own son returning alive.

Some soldiers clung on in Pacific islands for years after the war. There were those who knew the war was over, but would not give up without orders to do so. Others did not know, or had vague suspicions but no easy way of either finding out for sure or giving up safely. On Peleliu, in the central Pacific, thirty-four men hid and survived for nearly two and a half years. The US had fully secured the island before the end of 1944 but the group was mostly confident that the Japanese army and navy would one day return in triumph. The men foraged for food from the American occupation forces, which included some women; one of the Japanese stragglers recalls the feeling of puzzled shock when he found a lipstick-stained cigarette butt on the side of a road through the jungle. The Americans knew the men were there, and left notes scattered over the island stating the war was long over, but they meant nothing to Ei Yamaguchi and his men: 'I guess, if only we could have read English, the situation might have been different but in any case, no one thought we would lose, and neither did anyone think about surrendering.'

Eventually one of the group, Kiyokazu Tsuchida, grew suspicious that the war was over, and decided to find out exactly what the situation was: 'When I first made my escape, I was more afraid of the other thirty-three... than the Americans. I was an escaped soldier. Runaway soldiers were unheard-of in the Japanese military.' After learning the truth, it took a while to work out what would convince his colleagues that Japan had indeed lost. Eventually he organized letters to be sent from their families back in Japan stating the truth; he and a senior Japanese officer took them and other corroborative materials to the cave where Ei Yamaguchi and the others were hiding:

When I examined the content of the letters, I felt it wasn't neces-sarily all made up... I asked Sumikawa [the commander] to come into the cave we were hiding in. He did so and talked to us. Tsuchida [who had loyally returned] was too scared to come – he thought we might harbour hostile feelings towards him. After seeing the various bits of evidence such as books and articles, and hearing an explanation of the situation on the mainland since the end of the war, we decided to believe them – that Japan had lost... We were taken straight to the HQ where we performed a surrender ceremony... I turned in my military sword and the Japanese flag...

How did I feel? I had mixed feelings – both sad and happy. I couldn't feel entirely happy because so many people had died. But since we had lost the war and the Emperor himself had surren-dered, I didn't feel so ashamed of having surrendered, especially since we had tried so hard.

SCARCELY TWO WEEKS AFTER JAPAN'S SURRENDER, the first American troops arrived in Japan. They met no opposition, only stares from a bemused populace. Homer Bigart, a Pulitzer Prize-winning correspondent, visited Hiroshima a month after the nuclear attack; he found the lack of hostility puzzling: 'There was hatred in some glances but generally more curiosity than hatred. We were representatives of an enemy power that had employed a weapon far more terrible and deadly than poison gas, yet in the four hours we spent in Hiroshima none so much as spat at us, nor threw a stone.'

Sy Kahn was in the occupation force, and saw a little of its ugly side:

There was some insulting of the Japanese by troops that were perhaps more raucous and more vengeful and cruder in the kinds of things they asked the recent enemy to do... they stopped men on the street and made them bow endlessly to them, things of that sort, or they ridiculed them, they mocked them and they cheated them... and they would occasionally cause stripping, young women to strip...

Some Allied forces did much worse. The first recorded rape occurred barely forty-eight hours after the first occupying troops began to arrive in Japan on 28 August 1945. Two US Marines had been in the country scarcely four hours before they raped a mother and daughter at gunpoint. Allan Clifton saw the result of an act of mass rape by his fellow Australians: 'I stood beside a bed in a hospital. On it lay a girl, unconscious... A doctor and two nurses were working to revive her. An hour before she had been raped by twenty soldiers. We found her where they had left her, on a piece of wasteland.' According to historian Yuki Tanaka, there were cases of young girls raped in front of their parents and pregnant women assaulted in maternity wards. 'Over a period of ten days (August 30–September 10) there were 1,336 reported cases of rape of Japanese women by US soldiers in Kanagawa prefecture... alone.' Tanaka records that only 247 US soldiers were prosecuted for rape in the second half of 1945 – and that covers occupied Europe as well as Japan.

The Japanese leadership had predicted the problem, putting in place pre-emptive measures that were meant to offer a remedy. With the country's surrender barely agreed upon, the men behind Japan's so-called 'comfort stations' redeployed their skills, contacts and organizational abilities to 'protect' the purity of Japanese women. They appealed to all – but recruited mostly from the poor – for women who might perform 'the difficult task of comforting the occupation army'. The public's equation of virtue and self-sacrifice, so ruthless exploited during the war, had not vanished altogether. Over a thousand women in the Tokyo region alone signed up. In a ceremony performed the day the first Americans arrived, hundreds of volunteers, many of them virgins, gathered outside the Imperial Palace to pronounce an oath that, by its historical comparisons and sacrificial content, shows just how easily the language of total defence could be moulded and redirected:

... we unite and go forward to where our beliefs lead us, and through the sacrifice of several thousands of 'Okichis of our era' [Okichi was a nineteenth-century consort who served America's first consul] build a breakwater to hold back the raging waves and defend and nurture the purity of our race... we are but offering ourselves for the defence of the national polity...

The Asian 'comfort women' of the war had been forced into sexual slavery; the Japanese women volunteered. Yet in an echo of their fate, some were expected to service as many as sixty Allied soldiers in a day. Inevitably, many women came to regret their naivety; some deserted and a few committed suicide. Nor did the brothels of the Recreation and Amusement Association end rape, any more than the 'comfort stations' of the war had done, either outside the 'official' brothels or within. In 1946 General Douglas MacArthur clamped down on the practice of 'public' prostitution.

MacArthur was now Supreme Commander, Allied Powers in Japan; he was often referred to as the 'new emperor' because of his power and autonomy as head of the Allied occupation force. On 1 January 1946 the Emperor renounced his divinity, and was recast by MacArthur as a symbol of Japan's nascent anti-militaristic democracy, thereby ensuring popular acceptance of the redrafted Japanese constitution. It was based on what historian Saburo Ienaga calls 'the three great principles of popular sovereignty, guaranteed human rights, and peace...' Ienaga writes of a 'shameful stigma on the Japanese people that liberation came from foreigners and not by their hands'. One of those foreigners was Beate Sirota. As we saw in Chapter 5, she had been brought up in Japan. Now she returned and joined the US team drafting the civil rights section of the new constitution. She played a significant role in the writing of the women's rights section, but still regrets it did not go far enough:

There were three people, two men and I. And, they looked at me, and they said, 'Well, you're a woman, so why don't you write the women's rights?' Of course, I was delighted, and since I was only twenty-two years old, I guess I must have been quite cheeky... I wanted very much to really give all the freedoms that I knew that the Japanese women didn't have into this section in the civil rights... I looked at all the different constitutions of various countries that I could find in the libraries... I wanted to give Japanese women, not only fundamental rights, but all sorts of social welfare rights... I included everything. And then, when it was presented to the steering committee of the government section, which decided on what was to go into the constitution or not... they felt that social welfare rights did not belong in a constitution, that they should be in the civil code... And so now, fifty-four years later, the Japanese women still don't have those rights.

Yet the lives of most Japanese women were improved: they were finally granted the rights to vote, to enter parliament, to hold property and a right to higher education. Adultery was decriminalized and contract marriages outlawed. For people such as Beate Sirota who loved Japan and her people, these were exciting times: 'When we wrote the new constitution of Japan, we were exhilarated by the feeling that this was fertile ground for a democracy; that we had [been] given this unusual opportunity to actually write a constitution which would be the foundation of a democratic Japan.'

THE UNITED NATIONS WAR CRIMES Commission tried over 7,600 Japanese for a variety of crimes and executed around 900, mostly for atrocities against POWs. Many cruel camp guards escaped capture because the witnesses to their crimes – the prisoners – simply did not know their names. Dick Gordon was instrumental in the conviction of one guard because he did know his real name – thereby linking man and prison camp nickname: '[POWs] were asked, "Well, who are you talking about? Big Glass Eye, Little Glass Eye, Mickey Mouse, Donald Duck, who is that?" and I'm sure some of them got off because they were never properly identified. In the case of Little Glass Eye, I testified against him, and I knew his last name, and that's one of the reasons he was convicted and got ten years.'

The most famous of the tribunals began work in Tokyo on 3 May 1946 and lasted over two years. The twenty-eight men accused of the most serious war crimes (known as 'A class' crimes or 'crimes against peace') were in the dock, of whom seven were condemned to death, two died before the trial ended, and one was declared insane. All but two of the rest were given life sentences. The war responsibility of Hitler and Emperor Hirohito cannot be compared, yet at both Nuremberg and Tokyo there was an unfilled seat. Hitler had cheated justice by taking his life in the bunker; the Emperor was never summonsed.

The vacuum caused by the Emperor's total absence from the proceedings was felt on both sides. The Japanese defendants diligently tried to exclude the Emperor from the scenario of decision-making they depicted, which was difficult given that all orders were given 'in the name of the Emperor'. This put them in a terrible bind: they could legitimately claim that they were simply part of a chain of responsibility, but did not want to implicate the Emperor by affirming his position at the top of that chain. Occasionally the façade slipped, as on the occasion when the Allies' bogeyman General Hideki Tojo claimed he was simply the Emperor's most senior servant, and had to be reminded to stick to the script.

MacArthur strongly advised against prosecuting the Emperor. He cabled the US Army Chief of Staff in January 1946:

[Hirohito's] connection with affairs of state up to the time of the end of the war was... automatically responsive to the advice of his councillors... His indictment will unquestionably cause a tremendous convulsion among the Japanese people, the repercussions of which cannot be overestimated. He is a symbol which unites all Japanese. Destroy him and the nation will disintegrate... It is quite possible that a million troops would be required which would have to be maintained for an indefinite number of years.

The chief prosecutor toed MacArthur's line, arguing in court that 'The Emperor had been in the power of "gangsters".' Incredibly the prosecution never bothered to meet Hirohito, nor troubled him with any written questions. As historian John Dower has noted: 'With the full support of MacArthur's headquarters, the prosecution functioned, in effect, as a defence team for the Emperor.' The Australian president of the tribunal, Chief Justice Webb, made no secret of his frustration that the Emperor had escaped prosecution. He went so far as to argue that the twenty-five men found guilty of 'crimes against peace' should be treated leniently, given the Emperor's absence:

The authority of the Emperor was proved beyond doubt when he ended the war. The outstanding part played by him in starting as well as ending it was the subject of evidence led by the pro-secution... It is, of course, for the prosecution to say who will be indicted; but a British Court in passing sentence would, I believe, take into account, if it could, that the leader in the crime, though available for trial, had been granted immunity.

The justice administered in the Tokyo Trial was haphazard and, some argue, grossly manipulated: a case of the victors blaming the losers, applying punishments to crimes not embodied in existing laws, and ignoring their own responsibilities for the war. One of the eleven judges, Justice Radhabinod Pal of India, stated in his dissenting minority opinion that the best example of orders to commit 'indiscriminate murder' may well have been 'the decision coming from the Allied powers to use the atom bomb'. The failure to deal with Japan's war crimes in an open and apolitical manner at the trials went in tandem with a reluctance to make Japanese society face up to its wartime record, perhaps because America needed a strong, grateful Japan as an ally against communism.

As Saburo Ienaga says: 'The basic issue – war responsibility – was obscured in legalistic charges of "victor's justice" and was never resolved.' More than fifty years later, it remains a major obstacle in Japan's relations with neighbouring Asian countries, and a source of bitterness for many surviving victims. Lester Tenney remains livid that Tokyo has dodged its responsibility to provide a sincere apology:

You get on a train in Japan, and the conductor goes through, and the first thing he does is bows and tells everybody he's sorry to have to interrupt their good time, but he's got to collect the tickets. He apologizes to collect the tickets. They're a nation that always apologizes, why aren't they willing to do this? This would be so simple. Because they would not be able to save face, that's the whole reason.

Jiang Xiu Ying, a Chinese woman raped by the Japanese army on their way into Nanking has, after years of silence, decided to speak openly about her ordeal in a desperate attempt to exorcize her hatred and confront those who deny the massacre of 1937 ever occurred: 'Of course I didn't dare tell my son, I was afraid I'd lose face... [But] when I went to Japan, I vented my anger. I revealed the facts in full. They don't admit it!... When I'm reminded of the Japanese, I feel a hatred in my very marrow! They don't admit it! They don't admit it! Everyone from Nanking feels hatred in their bones when the Japanese are mentioned.'

While some of the war's victims fight for apology and compensation, or argue for forgiveness and reconciliation, ex-POW Fred Seiker feels his duty lies with those who have no voice:

Who the hell am I to forgive when I've got thirty-six of my mates been murdered, and they were murdered. [They] have no say in what I'm going to say on their behalf, they haven't a voice to utter their opinion, it's not my right, I will never do that, I cannot forgive. It would be treacherous to the people I loved, and they would agree with me, I know that, because they would do the same... Reconciliation, for what? Forgiveness? No. No way.

Singaporean Elizabeth Choy takes a different view. A victim of Japanese torture, she argued after the war that her tormentors should not be executed:

I said, 'It's the war that is so wicked. If it hadn't been war, if they were in their own homes, they would be just like you and me. They have got their families, they have got their father, they have got their mother and they have got their wives and they've got their children, and they've got their jobs, so they are ordinary people. Because of the war they are forced to be so cruel and brutal.' So I say I forgive them.

Not all crimes were examined by the courts. General Ishii and his co-workers in Unit 731 escaped prosecution for their systematic germ warfare experiments on live humans by giving the US and Britain full access to their research results. Their immunity was maintained even when former POWs insisted they had suffered experimentation (despite assurances from General Ishii that this had not happened) and although the Soviet Union prosecuted twelve former members of Ishii's team in 1949. But some Japanese veterans, such as Yoshio Shinozuka who worked in Unit 731, are anxious to acknowledge their crimes:

> I believe peace can only be achieved by sharing the truth about the war. Reconciliation is not possible without Japan admitting what it has done. The victims will never forget what was done to them. I believe we must tell the truth about the ruthless things the Japanese army did in order for us to be completely reconciled with the world and there to be peace... I feel hatred against myself. I cannot forgive myself for the fact that I performed such ruthless acts. Even if I had opposed the order and had been killed for it, I think I would have still preferred that.

Some survivors have spent decades trying to bring the two sides in the Pacific War closer together. Suzuko Numata talks to people of many nationalities about Hiroshima – but imposes a bridge-building condition on the conversation:

> Before I talk about my own experience of the atomic bomb, I think I should understand the horrible treatment which local people received from the Japanese army. So I say to them first, 'I came here to learn from you things which I don't know'... they start telling me terrible stories, one after another. When I listen to them, I can't even look them in the eye, so I listen to them face down. And I weep. Then they ask me, 'What happened to your leg?' I tell them that I lost my leg from the atomic bomb. Wherever I go, in China or the Philippines, people tell me that we are both – we are all – victims of the war.

SINCE MAKING THAT DIFFICULT JOURNEY home, the veterans, like those of every war, have had to learn how to live with the experience. Many opt for silence, except with others who know what they are talking about. Some have drunk too much, or had breakdowns. Others have had happy, well-adjusted lives, without ever forgetting the comrades of those years. Memorials and reunions provide vital public, social recognition of the debt owed to the dead by the living, as ex-POW Richard Gordon explains: 'If we can keep their memories alive they really didn't die. It's when you forget someone they die.' He is perhaps looking ahead to the time when his generation will no longer be around to keep faith with old comrades. The Bataan memorial he helped organize in the Philippines is there for the future – he needs no help remembering those who perished on the death march and at Camp O'Donnell.

As another veteran, Bill Spencer puts it, the loss of mates 'stops with you for ever'. Nor are they only a source of sorrow. Eugene Sledge sums it up: 'I have many friends and I enjoy them thoroughly, but in a sense I live in my mind with my old buddies.'

CHRONOLOGY OF EVENTS

Date	Pacific	World
1931		
18 Sep	Japan invades Manchuria.	
1932		
1 Mar	Japan declares Manchukuo (renamed province of Manchuria) a sovereign state.	
8 Nov		Roosevelt elected President of USA.
1933		
30 Jan		Hitler becomes German Chancellor.
21 Feb	Japan walks out of League of Nations.	
14 Oct		Germany quits League of Nations.
1936		
7 Mar		German troops enter Rhineland.
9 May		Mussolini's Italian forces take Ethiopia.
18 Jul		Spanish Civil War begins.
1937		
7 Jul	Marco Polo bridge incident, triggering Japan's large-scale invasion of China.	

Date	Pacific	World
13 Dec	Japanese forces enter Nanking – Rape of Nanking begins.	

1938

12–13 Mar		German 'Anschluss' or union with Austria.
30 Sep		British Prime Minister Chamberlain appeases Hitler at Munich.

1939

15 Mar		German troops enter Prague; Czechoslovakia dismembered.
28 Mar		Spanish Civil War ends.
Aug	Major Japanese defeat during border clashes with Soviet Union.	
23 Aug		Nazi–Soviet Pact signed.
1 Sep		German invasion of Poland.
3 Sep		Britain, France, Australia, New Zealand declare war on Germany.

1940

10 May		Germany invades France, Belgium, Luxembourg, Netherlands. Churchill becomes British Prime Minister.
27 May		Evacuation from Dunkirk begins.
10 Jun		Italy declares war on Britain and France.
14 Jun		Fall of Paris.
10 Jul		Battle of Britain begins.
7 Sep		Start of London Blitz.
22 Sep	Japanese troops occupy northern part of French Indo-China.	
27 Sep	Japan signs Tripartite Pact. Formation of Rome–Berlin–Tokyo Axis.	

Date	Pacific	World
11 Nov		British planes attack Italian fleet at Taranto from aircraft carriers in first ever attack of its kind. Japanese planners study the raid.
14–15 Nov		German bombing raid on Coventry.

1941

12 Feb		Rommel arrives in Tripoli.
11 Mar		Roosevelt signs Lend-lease Act.
13 Apr	Japan and Soviet Union sign neutrality pact.	
22 Jun		German invasion of Soviet Union – Operation Barbarossa.
26 Jul	US freezes all Japanese assets.	
28 Jul	Japanese troops occupy southern part of French Indo-China.	
1 Aug	US, Britain and Dutch East Indies announce oil embargo against Japan.	
15 Sep		Siege of Leningrad begins.
17 Oct	Tojo becomes Japanese Prime Minister.	
5 Dec		Moscow offensive abandoned for winter.
7 Dec	Pearl Harbor attack. (occurs at same time as other attacks of 8 Dec, Hawaii being on other side of international date line).	
8 Dec	Japanese landings in Malaya and Thailand. Japanese bombing raids on US bases in Philippines. Japanese invasion of Hong Kong. Japanese bomb Singapore.	US and Britain declare war on Japan.

Date	Pacific	World
8 Dec (continued)	HMS *Prince of Wales* and HMS *Repulse* depart Singapore. Japanese shell or bomb US bases on Wake, Guam and Midway Islands.	
9 Dec	China declares war on Japan and Germany.	
10 Dec	Japanese capture Guam. Japanese sink HMS *Prince of Wales* and HMS *Repulse*.	
11 Dec	Japanese forces attack Burma.	Germany and Italy declare war on US.
14 Dec		Germans forced to retreat on outskirts of Moscow.
23 Dec	Japanese capture Wake Island.	
25 Dec	Japanese capture Hong Kong.	

1942

Date	Pacific	World
2 Jan	Japanese secure Manila.	
3 Jan	Japanese landings on Borneo.	
7 Jan	Siege of Bataan in Philippines begins.	
11 Jan	Japanese invasion of Dutch East Indies begins.	
15 Jan	Japanese move into Burma.	
23 Jan	Japanese landings on New Guinea and Solomon Islands.	
30 Jan	Japanese landings on Ambon Islands in Dutch East Indies.	
1 Feb	Causeway between Singapore and Malaya blown.	
8 Feb	Japanese capture Rangoon.	
14 Feb	Japanese invade Sumatra in Dutch East Indies.	
15 Feb	Singapore surrenders. Japanese landings on Bangka Island.	
19 Feb	Japanese bomb Darwin in Australia.	
27–29 Feb	Battle of Java Sea.	

Date	Pacific	World
1 Mar	Japanese sink USS *Houston*. Japanese land on Java.	
2 Mar	Japanese capture Batavia (Jakarta).	
7 Mar	Last British defenders leave Rangoon; Japanese enter city outskirts.	
8 Mar	Allied force on Java surrenders.	
11 Mar	MacArthur leaves Philippines for Australia.	
Apr		Japanese Americans ordered to relocation centres.
5 Apr	Japanese carrier raids on the port of Colombo, Ceylon (now Sri Lanka).	
9 Apr	American and Filipino troops on Bataan in Philippines are surrendered.	
18 Apr	Doolittle bombing raid over Tokyo.	
1 May	Japanese capture Mandalay in northern Burma.	
3 May	Battle of Coral Sea begins	
7 May	Corregidor in Philippines surrenders.	
20 May	Japanese conquest of Burma complete.	
4–7 Jun	Battle of Midway.	
6 Jun	Japan invades Kiska and Attu in Aleutian Islands.	
9 Jun		Nazis liquidate Czech village of Lidice, in reprisal for Heydrich's assassination.
21 Jun		Tobruk falls to Rommel.
7 Aug	First US landings on Guadalcanal.	
25 Aug	Japanese land at Milne Bay.	
7 Sep	Japanese forces defeated by Australian troops at Milne Bay.	
13 Sep		Battle of Stalingrad begins.

Date	Pacific	World
17 Sep	Japanese advance on Port Moresby halted.	
21 Sep	Arakan campaign begins in Burma.	
23 Oct		Battle of El Alamein begins.
8 Nov		Operation Torch begins – US landings in North Africa.
10 Dec	Japanese base at Gona in New Guinea captured.	
17 Dec	Indian troops advance into Arakan.	

1943

2 Jan	Japanese base at Buna, New Guinea, captured.	
2 Feb		German surrender at Stalingrad.
7–9 Feb	Japanese troops evacuate Guadalcanal.	
8 Feb	Wingate's Chindits' first expedition into Burma.	Soviets retake Kursk.
18 Apr	Admiral Tsoroku Yamamoto shot down.	
11 May	US landings on Attu (Aleutian Islands).	
12 May	Arakan campaign ends in stalemate.	End of fighting in Africa – Axis forces surrender in Tunisia.
30 May	Japanese resistance on Attu ends.	
29 Jun	US landings in New Guinea.	
9, 10 Jul		Allies invade Sicily.
24 Jul		Allied air raid on Hamburg – firestorm.
25 Jul		Mussolini falls.
15 Aug	US unopposed landings on Kiska in Aleutians.	
8 Sep		Italy surrenders.
13 Oct		Italy declares war on Germany.
1 Nov	US Marines land on Bougainville.	

Date	Pacific	World
20 Nov	US Marines land on Tarawa.	
23 Nov	Japanese resistance on Tarawa ends.	
28 Nov		Start of Big Three Conference, Tehran.
15 Dec	US landings on New Britain.	

1944

Date	Pacific	World
22 Jan		Allies land at Anzio, Italy.
27 Jan		Leningrad liberated.
31 Jan	US troops land on Kwajalein in Marshall Islands.	
4 Feb	Kwajalein Atoll secured.	
17 Feb	US landings on Eniwetok.	
21 Feb	Eniwetok secured.	
29 Feb	US landings on Admiralty Islands.	
5 Mar	Second Chindit operation begins.	
8 Mar	Japanese offensive from Burma into India begins.	
24 Mar	Wingate killed in air crash.	
29 Mar	Imphal (in India) siege begins.	
6 Apr	Kohima (in India) siege begins.	
18 Apr	Kohima relieved.	
22 Apr	US landings at Hollandia, New Guinea.	
18 May	US operations in Admiralty Islands end.	
27 May	US landings at Biak, New Guinea.	
2 Jun	Allied counter offensive at Kohima.	
4 Jun		Rome (held by German troops) falls to Allies.
6 Jun		D-Day – Allied landings in Normandy.
14 Jun		First V-1 'flying bomb' hits London.
15 Jun	Saipan landings. First US bombers hit Japan since Doolittle raid.	
19 Jun	Battle of the Philippine Sea.	
22 Jun	Siege of Imphal ends.	

Date	Pacific	World
3 Jul		Soviets take Minsk.
4 Jul	Japanese defeated at Imphal.	
9 Jul	Saipan secured.	
18 Jul	Tojo resigns as Prime Minister; succeeded by Koiso.	
21 Jul	US landings on Guam.	
24 Jul	US landings on Tinian.	
1 Aug	Tinian resistance ends.	
10 Aug	Guam organized resistance ends.	
25 Aug		Liberation of Paris.
3 Sep		Allies enter Brussels.
8 Sep		First V-2 'flying bomb' hits London.
15 Sep	US landings on Peleliu.	
17 Sep		Arnhem operation to seize a bridge over the Rhine begins.
20 Oct	US landings at Leyte, Philippines.	
23–26 Oct	Battle of Leyte Gulf.	
16 Dec		Battle of the Bulge.

1945

Date	Pacific	World
9 Jan	US troops land on Lingayen Gulf, Luzon.	
15 Jan	1st convoy along the new Ledo road reaches Myitkyina (start of the Burma Road).	
17 Jan		Soviets liberate Warsaw.
22 Jan	Burma Road reopened. Japanese land blockade of China lifted.	
27 Jan		Auschwitz liberated.
3 Feb	US forces enter Manila; Battle of Manila begins.	
4 Feb		Start of Yalta conference.
13 Feb		Allied bombing of Dresden.
19 Feb	US landings on Iwo Jima.	
26 Feb	US troops recapture Corregidor in Philippines.	
3 Mar	Battle for Manila ends.	
4 Mar	Indian/British troops take Meiktila in Burma.	

Date	Pacific	World
7 Mar		US troops cross Rhine at Remagen.
9 Mar	Allied troops reach outskirts of Mandalay in Burma.	
9–10 Mar	Massive fire-bombing raid on Tokyo – start of the USAF blitz.	
21 Mar	Mandalay secured.	
26 Mar	Iwo Jima fighting ends.	
Apr	Japanese Prime Minister Koiso replaced by Suzuki.	
1 Apr	US landings on Okinawa.	
6 Apr	Large-scale *kamikaze* attacks on Okinawa invasion fleet.	
7 Apr	Japanese battleship *Yamato* sunk.	
12 Apr	Roosevelt dies; Truman becomes US President.	
16 Apr		Final Soviet attack on Berlin.
28 Apr	Arakan secured (in Burma).	
30 Apr		Hitler commits suicide.
2 May		Berlin falls to Soviet troops.
3 May	Allies recapture Rangoon.	
7 May		Formal surrender of all German forces.
8 May		Victory in Europe (VE) Day.
11 May	Australians take Wewak, New Guinea.	
10 Jun	Australians begin landings on Borneo.	
22 Jun	Okinawa resistance ends.	
30 Jun	Luzon campaign in Philippines officially ends.	
13 Jul		Italy declares war on Japan.
16 Jul		First A-bomb test, New Mexico.
17 Jul		Potsdam Conference begins.
26 Jul	Potsdam Declaration demands Japanese surrender.	Attlee replaces Churchill as British Prime Minister.
28 Jul	Japan rejects Potsdam Declaration.	

Date	Pacific	World
6 Aug	Atom bomb dropped on Hiroshima.	
8 Aug	Soviet Union declares war on Japan; launches massive invasion on Manchuria.	
9 Aug	Atom bomb dropped on Nagasaki. Japanese offer Allies conditional surrender.	
10 Aug	Japanese agree to unconditional surrender.	
14 Aug	Soviet troops continue advances into Sakhalin and Kurile Islands.	
15 Aug	Emperor's radio announcement.	Victory over Japan (VJ) Day.
29 Aug	Mountbatten and Slim accept surrender of Japanese forces in Singapore.	
2 Sep	MacArthur accepts formal surrender in Tokyo Bay.	
13 Sep	Japanese surrender in Burma signed.	
Nov		Nuremberg trials begin.

1946

3 May	Tokyo war crimes tribunal begins.	
3 Nov	New Japanese constitution promulgated.	

1949

1 Oct	China becomes communist. Nationalist forces under Chiang Kai-Shek flee to Formosa (now Taiwan).	

1950

25 Jun	Korean War begins.	

1951

8 Sep	San Francisco Peace Treaty – American-led occupation of Japan ends.	

BIBLIOGRAPHY

The complete transcripts of all interviews are lodged with the archives of the Imperial War Museum, London.

Aida, Yuji, *Prisoner of the British: A Japanese Soldier's Experiences in Burma*, trans Hide Ishiguro and Louis Allen, London, Cresse Press, 1966

Aldrich, Richard J., *Intelligence and the War Against Japan: Britain, America and the Politics of Secret Service*, Cambridge, New York, Cambridge University Press, 2000

Alexander, Joseph H., *Utmost Savagery: The Three Days of Tarawa*, New York, Ballantine Books, 1995

Allan, James, *Under the Dragon Flag: My Experiences in the Chino–Japanese War*, London, Heinemann, 1898

Allen, Louis, *The End of the War in Asia*, London, Hart-Davis MacGibbon, 1976

Allen, Louis, *Singapore, 1941–42*, London, Davis-Poynter, 1977

Allen, Louis, *Burma: The Longest War 1941–45*, London, Dent, 1984

Aluit, Alfonso J., *By Sword and Fire: The Destruction of Manila in World War II, 3 February–3 March 1945*, Manila, Lucky Press, 1994

Ba Maw, *Breakthrough in Burma: Memoirs of a Revolution, 1939–1946*, London, Yale University Press, 1968

Bacque, James, *Other Losses, on investigation into the mass deaths of German prisoners at the hands of the French and Americans after World War II*, Toronto, Stoddart, 1989

Beasley, W. G., *Japanese Imperialism 1894–1945*, Oxford, Clarendon Press, 1987

Beaumont, Joan, *Gull Force, Survival and Leadership in Captivity, 1941–1945*, Sydney, Allen & Unwin, 1988

Beaumont, Joan (ed), *Australia's War, 1914–18*, NSW, Allen & Unwin, 1995

Beaumont, Joan (ed), *Australia's War 1939–45*, NSW, Allen & Unwin, 1996

Behr, Edward, *Hirohito: The Man Behind the Myth*, London, Hamish Hamilton, 1989

Benda, Harry J., *The Crescent and the Rising Sun: Indonesian Islam under the Japanese Occupation, 1942–1945*, The Hague, W. van Hoeve, 1958

Benedict, Ruth, *The Chrysanthemum and the Sword: Patterns of Japanese Culture*, London, Secker & Warburg, 1947

Best, Antony, *Britain, Japan and Pearl Harbor: Avoiding War in East Asia, 1936–41*, London, Routledge, 1995

Bidwell, Shelford, *Gunners at War: A Tactical Study of the Royal Artillery in the Twentieth Century*, London, Arms & Armour Press, 1970

Bigart, Homer W., in *New York Herald Tribune*, 5 September 1945

Bischof, Gunter, and Stephen E. Ambrose (eds), *Eisenhower and the German POWs: Facts Against Falsehood*, Louisiana State University Press, 1992

Bix, Herbert P., *Hirohito and the Making of Modern Japan*, New York, HarperCollins, 2000

Boon, Goh Chor, *Living Hell: Story of a WWII Survivor at the Death Railway*, Singapore, Asiapac Books, 1999

Bowden, Tim, *Changi Photographer: George Aspinall's Record of Captivity*, Sydney, ABC Enterprises, 1985

Brown, Cecil, *Suez to Singapore*, New York, Random House, 1943

Butow, Robert J. C., *Japan's Decision to Surrender*, Stanford, Stanford University Press, 1954

Calvocoressi, Peter, Guy Wint and John Pritchard, *Total War: The Causes and Courses of the Second World War*, vol II, *The Greater East Asia and Pacific Conflict* (rev 2nd edn), London, Penguin, 1989

Chand, Tara, *History of Freedom Movement in India*, vol IV, New Delhi, Government of India, 1972

Chang, Iris, *The Rape of Nanking: The Forgotten Holocaust of World War II*, New York, BasicBooks, 1997

Checkland, Olive, *Humanitarianism and the Emperor's Japan, 1877–1977*, New York, Macmillan, 1994

Chennault, Claire Lee, *Way of a Fighter: The Memoirs of Claire Lee Chennault*, ed Robert Hotz, New York, G. P. Putnam & Sons, 1949

Churchill, Winston S., *The Second World War*, London, Cassell, 1952

Clayton, James D., *The Years of MacArthur: Triumph and Disaster, 1945–64*, Boston, Houghton Mifflin, 1985

Clifton, Allan S., *Time of Fallen Blossoms*, London, Cassell & Co., 1950

Cohen, Stan, *Destination Tokyo: A Pictorial History of Doolittle's Tokyo Raid, April 18, 1942*, Missoula, Montana Pictorial Histories Publishing Company, 1983

Colvin, John, *Not Ordinary Men: The Story of the Battle of Kohima*, London, Leo Cooper, 1994

Connaughton, Richard, John Pimlott and Duncan Anderson, *The Battle for Manila*, London, Bloomsbury, 1995

Cook, Haruko Taya, 'The Myth of the Saipan Suicides', *Military History Quarterly*, 7.3 (Spring 1995): 12–19

Coomaraswamy, R., UN Commission on Human Rights, *Report of the Special Rapporteur on violence against Women, its causes and consequences, UN Report on the mission to the Democratic People's Republic of Korea, and Japan on the issue of military sexual slavery in wartime*, 4 January 1996

Costello, John, *The Pacific War*, London, Collins, 1981

Craig, William, *The Fall of Japan*, New York, The Dial Press, 1967

Creelman, James, *On the Great Highway: The Wanderings and Adventures of a Special Correspondent*, London, Charles H. Kelly, 1901

Daniels, Roger, *Concentration Camps USA: Japanese Americans and World War II*, London, Holt, Rinehart and Winston, 1971

Davidson, Edward, and Dale Manning, *Chronology of the Second World War*, London, Cassell, 1999

Daws, Gavan, *Prisoners of the Japanese: POWs of World War II in the Pacific – The Powerful Untold Story*, London, Robson, 1995

Dorwart, Jeffery M., *The Pigtail War: American Involvement in the Sino-Japanese War of 1894–1895*, Amherst, University of Massachusetts Press, 1975

Dower, John W., *War Without Mercy, Race and Power in the Pacific War*, New York, Pantheon, 1986

Dower, John W., *Japan in War and Peace: Essays on History, Culture and Race*, London, HarperCollins, 1995

Dower, John W., *Embracing Defeat: Japan in the Aftermath of World War II*, London, Allen Lane, 1999

Drea, Edward, J., *In Service of the Emperor: Essays on the Imperial Japanese Army*, Lincoln, University of Nebraska Press, 1998

Edoin, Hoito, *The Night Tokyo Burned*, New York, St Martin's Press, 1987

Ellis, John, *The Sharp End: The Fighting Man in World War II* (rev edn), London, Pimlico, 1993

Elphick, Peter, *Singapore, the Pregnable Fortress: A Study in Deception, Discord and Desertion*, London, Hodder and Stoughton, 1995

Foss, Joe, with Donna Wild Foss, *A Proud American: The Autobiography of Joe Foss*, New York, Pocket Star Books, 1992

Frank, Richard B., *Guadalcanal: The Definitive Account of the Landmark Battle*, New York, Random House, 1990

Frank, Richard B., *Downfall: The End of the Imperial Japanese Empire*, New York, Random House, 1999

Friend, Theodore, *The Blue-Eyed Enemy: Japan Against the West in Java and Luzon, 1942–1945*, Princeton, NJ, Princeton University Press, 1988

Gailey, Harry A., *The War in the Pacific: From Pearl Harbor to Tokyo Bay*, California, Novato, 1995

Gallagher, O'Dowd, *Retreat in the East*, London, Harrap & Co, 1942

Gibney, Frank (ed), Beth Cary (trans), *Senso: The Japanese Remember the Pacific War, Letters to the Editor of 'Asahi Shimbun'*, London, M. E. Sharpe, 1995

Girdner, Audrie, *The Great Betrayal: The Evacuation of the Japanese Americans during World War II*, London, Macmillan, 1969

Glines, Carroll V., *Four Came Home*, New York, London, Van Nostrand Reinhold, 1966

Goldstein, Donald M., and Katherine V. Dillon (eds), *The Pearl Harbor Papers: Inside the Japanese Plans*, Washington, London, Brassey's (US), 1993

Gonzalez, Andrew, and Alejandro T. Reyes, *Our Martyrs*, a reprint of *These Hallowed Halls*, Manila, De La Salle University Press, 1999

Goodman, Grant K. (ed), *Japanese Cultural Policies in Southeast Asia during World War 2*, London, Macmillan, 1991

Gordon, Beate Sirota, *The Only Woman in the Room*, Kodansha International, 1997

Gordon, Harry, *Voyage from Shame: The Cowra Breakout and Afterwards*, St Lucia, Queensland, University of Queensland Press, 1994

Gordon, Richard M., *Horyo: Memoirs of an American POW*, St Paul Minnesota, Paragon House, 1999

Goto, Kenichi, chapter in Peter Duus, Ramon H. Myers and Mark R. Peattie (eds), *The Japanese Wartime Empire, 1931–1945*, Princeton, NJ, Princeton University Press, 1996

Hardie, Robert, *The Secret Diary of Robert Hardie*, Imperial War Museum, London

Harris, Sheldon, *Factories of Death: Japanese Biological Warfare 1932–45 and the American Cover-up*, London, Routledge, 1994

Harrison, Kenneth, *Road to Hiroshima* (previously published as *The Brave Japanese*), rev edn, Adelaide, London, Rigby, 1983

Heidhues, Mary F. Somers, *Southeast Asia: A Concise History*, London, Thames & Hudson, 2000

Hinode, November 1944

Hiroiwa, Chikahiro, *Suzuko Numata: Hiroshima, Witness for Peace*, Tokyo, 1993

Hiroyuki, Agawa, *The Reluctant Admiral: Yamamoto and the Imperial Navy*, Tokyo, Kodansh International, 1982

Hoffman, Carl C., *Saipan: The Beginning of the End*, Washington, USA, Departments of State and Public Institutions. Marine Corps Division of Public Information, Historical Section

Hohenberg, John (ed), *The Pulitzer Prize Story: News Stories, Editorials, Cartoons, and Pictures from the Pulitzer Prize Collection at Columbia University*, New York, Columbia University Press, 1959

Hough, Richard, *The Hunting of Force Z*, London, Fontana, 1978

HRH Prince Philip, Interview, Buckingham Palace Press Office, Friday 18 August 1995

Huffman James L. (ed), *Modern Japan: An Encyclopedia of History, Culture and Nationalism*, New York & London, Garland Publishing Inc, 1998

Ienaga, Saburo, *The Pacific War: Japan's last war, World War II and the Japanese, 1931–1945*, trans Frank Baldwin, Oxford, Blackwell, 1979

Ike, Nobutaka (trans, ed), *Japan's Decision For War: Records of the 1941 Policy Conferences*, Stanford, California, Stanford University Press, 1967

Iriye, Akira, *Power and Culture, the Japanese–American War, 1941–1945*, Cambridge, Mass., London, Harvard University Press, 1981

Irokawa, Daikichi, *The Age of Hirohito: In Search of Modern Japan*, New York, Free Press, 1995

Isaacs, Jeremy, and Taylor Downing, *Cold War*, London, Transworld Publishers, 1998

Jackson, Tabitha, *The Boer War*, London, Channel 4 Books, 1999

Jose, Ricardo T., and Lydia N. Yu-Jose, *The Japanese Occupation of the Philippines: A Pictorial History*, Manila, Ayala Foundation Inc, 1997

Kahn, Sy M., *Between Tedium and Terror: A Soldier's World War II Diary, 1943–45*, University of Illinois Press, 1993

Kaminski, Theresa, *Prisoners in Paradise: American Women in Wartime South Pacific*, University Press of Kansas, 2000

Keegan, John, *The Second World War*, London, Pimlico, 1997

Keegan, John (ed), *Routledge Who's Who in World War II*, London, Routledge, 1995

Kirby, Stanley Woodburn, *The War Against Japan*, 5 vols, London, HMSO, 1957–69

Kirby, Stanley Woodburn, *Singapore: The Chain of Disaster*, London, Cassell, 1971

Knox, Donald, *Death March: The Survivors of Bataan*, Harcourt Brace Jovanovich, 1981

Knox, Ralph M., *The Emperor's Angry Guest: A World War II Prisoner of the Japanese Speaks Out*, Connecticut, Southfarm Press, 1999

Krebs, Gerhard and Christian Oberlander (eds), *1945 in Europe and Asia: Reconsidering the end of World War II and the change of the world order*, Munich, Ludicium, 1997

LaFeber, Walter, *The Clash: A History of US–Japanese Relations*, New York, London, W. W. Norton, 1997

Lamont-Brown, Raymond, *Kamikaze: Japan's Suicide Samurai*, London, Arms and Armour, 1997

Lane, Kerry, *Marine Pioneers: The Unsung Heroes of World War II*, Schiffer Military/Aviation History, 1997

Lebra-Chapman, Joyce, *The Rhani of Jhansi: A Study in Female Heroism in India*, Honolulu, University of Hawaii Press, 1986

Lee, Lee Kip, *Amber Sands*, Singapore, Federal Publications, 1995

Leighton, Alexander, *Human Relations in a Changing World: Observations on the use of the social sciences*, New York, E. P. Dutton, 1949

Lindbergh, Charles A., *The Wartime Journals of Charles A. Lindbergh*, New York, Harcourt Brace Jovanovich, 1970

Linderman, Gerald F., *The World within War: America's Combat Experience in World War II*, Cambridge (Massachusetts), London, Harvard University Press, 1999

Lone, Stewart, and Gavan McCormack, *Korea since 1850*, Melbourne, Longman Cheshire, 1993

Lord, Walter, *Incredible Victory*, London, Hamish Hamilton, 1968

Lyall Grant, Ian, *Burma, the Turning Point: The seven battles on the Tiddim Road which turned the tide of the Burma War*, Chichester, Zampi Press, 1993

Lyall Grant, Ian, and Kazou Tamayama, *Burma 1942, the Japanese Invasion: Both Sides tell the Story of a Savage Jungle War*, Chichester, Zampi Press, 1999

Lynn, Vera, *Vocal Refrain: An Autobiography*, London, W. H. Allen, 1975

Manchester, William, *Goodbye, Darkness: A Memoir of the Pacific War*, London, Joseph, 1981

Mayo, Lida, *Bloody Buna: The Campaign that halted the Japanese invasion of Australia*, London, New English Library, 1977

McDonald, Neil and Peter Brune, *200 Shots: Damien Parer, George Silk and the Australians at War in New Guinea*, NSW, Allen & Unwin, 1999

Menezes, S. L., *Fidelity and Honour: The Indian Army from the Seventeenth to the Twenty-First Century*, New Delhi, Oxford, Oxford University Press, 1999

Michiko, Nakahara, 'Labour Recruitment in Malaya under the Japanese Occupation: The Case of the Burma–Siam Railway'

Middlebrook, Martin, *Battleship: The Loss of the 'Prince of Wales' and the 'Repulse'*, London, Allen Lane, 1977

Miller, Stuart Creighton, *'Benevolent Assimilation': The American Conquest of the Philippines, 1899–1903*, London, Yale University Press, 1982

Minear, Richard Hoffman, *Victor's Justice: The Tokyo War Crimes Trial*, Princeton, Princeton University Press, 1971

Moffatt, Jonathan, and Audrey Holmes McCormick, *Moon Over Malaya*, Stroud, Gloucestershire, Tempus Publishing Ltd, 2001

Moore, B., and K. Fedorowich (eds), *Prisoners of War and Their Captors in World War II*, Oxford, Berg., 1996

Mueller, Joseph N., *Guadalcanal 1942: The marines strike back*, campaign series 18, London, Osprey, 1992

Nagatsuka, Ryuji, *I Was a Kamikaze: The Knights of the Divine Wind*, trans Nina Rootes, London, Abelard-Schuman, 1973

Nakamura, Masanori, *The Japanese Monarchy, Ambassador Joseph Grew and the making of the 'Symbol Emperor System' 1931–1991*, trans Herbert Bix, Jonathan Baker-Bates and Derek Brown, London, M. E. Sharpe, 1992

National Archives of Singapore, *The Japanese Occupation, 1942–1945: A Pictorial Record of Singapore During the War*, Singapore, Times Editions, 1996

Nelson, Hank, 'A Map to Paradise Road: A Guide for Historians', *Journal of the Australian War Memorial*, issue 32, March 1999

Nelson, Hank, and Gavan McCormack (eds), *The Burma–Thailand Railway*, Chiang Mai, Thailand, Silkworm Books, 1993

Newell, William H. (ed), *Japan in Asia, 1942–45*, Singapore, Singapore University Press, 1981

Nish, Ian, *Japanese Foreign Policy, 1869–1942: Kasumigaeki to Miyakezaka*, London, Routledge and Kegan Paul, 1977

Nitobe, Inazo, *Bushido: The Soul of Japan*, Tokyo, Simpkin, Marshall, 1901

Norman, Elizabeth M., *We Band of Angels: The untold story of American nurses trapped on Bataan by the Japanese*, New York, Pocket Books, Simon and Schuster Inc, 1999

Nunneley, John, *Tales from the King's African Rifles: A Last Flourish of Empire*, Petersham, Askari Books, 1998

Partridge, Jeff, *Alexandra Hospital: From British Military to Civilian Institution 1938–1998*, Singapore, Alexandra Hospital and Singapore Polytechnic, 1988

Peery, Nelson, *Black Fire: The Making of an American Revolutionary*, Edinburgh, Payback Press, 1995

Pluvier, Jan M., *Southeast Asia from Colonialism to Independence*, London, Oxford University Press, 1974

Prange, Gordon W., *At Dawn We Slept: The Untold Story of Pearl Harbor*, London, Michael Joseph, 1982

Pyle, Ernie, *Last Chapter*, New York, Henry Holt, 1945

Ray, John, T*he Second World War: A Narrative History*, London, Cassell, 1999

Reid, Anthony, 'Indonesia: From Briefcase to Samurai Sword', in Alfred W. McCoy (ed), *Southeast Asia under Japanese Rule*, Yale University Southeast Asia Studies, Monograph Series no. 22, 1980

Reid, Anthony, and Oki Akira (eds), *The Japanese Experience in Indonesia: Selected Memoirs of 1942–45*, Ohio, Ohio University Center for Southeast Asian Studies, 1986

Rhodes, Anthony, *Propaganda, the Art of Persuasion: World War II*, London, Angus & Robertson, 1976

Robertson, John, *Australia Goes to War, 1939–1945*, Sydney, Doubleday, 1984

Rodriggs, Lawrence R., *We Remember Pearl Harbor*, Newark, CA, Communications Concepts, 1991

Roeder, George, *The Censored War: American Visual Experience During World War Two*, New Haven, London, Yale University Press, 1993

Rooney, David, *Burma Victory: Imphal, Kohima and the Chindit Issue, March 1944 to May 1945*, Arms and Armour Press, 1992

Russell, E. F. L., *The Knights of Bushido: A Short History of Japanese War Crimes*, London, Cassell, 1958

Rutledge, Tillman J., *My Japanese POW Diary Story*, Vantage Press, New York, 1997

Sakurai, Tadayoshi, *Human Bullets: A Soldier's Story of Port Arthur*, trans Masujiro Honda, London, Archibald Constable and Co., 1907

Sancho, Nelia (ed), *War Crimes on Asian Women: Military Sexual Slavery by Japan During World War II, The case of the Filipino Comfort Women*, Manila, Asian Women Human Rights Council India Regional Secretariat and Manila Secretariat, 1998

Sato, Shigeru, *War Nationalism and Peasants, Java under the Japanese 1942–1945*, ASAA Southeast Asia Publications Series No. 26, NSW, Allen & Unwin, 1994

Schmidt, D.A., *Ianfu: The Comfort Women of the Japanese Imperial Army of the Pacific War, Broken Silence*, Lewiston, Lempeter, Edwin Mellen Press, 2000

Sigal, Leon V., *Fighting to a Finish: The Politics of War Termination in the United States and Japan, 1945*, New York, London, Cornell University Press, 1988

Sledge, Eugene B., *With the Old Breed at Peleliu and Okinawa*, Oxford, Oxford University Press, 1981

Slim, William, *Defeat into Victory*, London, Macmillan, 1986

Spector, Ronald H., *Eagle against the Sun: The American War with Japan*, Harmondsworth, Viking, 1985

Stouffer, Samuel A., *The American Soldier*, vols I–II, Princeton, Princeton University Press, 1949

Tanaka, Yuki, *Hidden Horrors: Japanese War Crimes in World War II*, Oxford, Westview, 1996

Tenney, Lester L., *My Hitch in Hell: The Bataan Death March*, Washington, London, Brassey's, 1995

Terkel, Studs, *'The Good War': An Oral History of World War Two*, Harmondsworth, Penguin, 1986

Thorne, Christopher, *Allies of a Kind: The United States, Britain and the War Against Japan, 1941–1945*, London, Hamilton, 1978

Tibbets, Paul W., *Return of the 'Enola Gay'*, Columbus, Ohio, Mid Coast Marketing, 1998

Time, 'The Enemy, Perhaps He Is Human', 5 July 1943

Toland, John, *The Rising Sun: The decline and fall of the Japanese Empire, 1936–45*, London, Cassell, 1971

Tregaskis, Richard William, *Guadalcanal Diary*, Redhill, Wells Gardner, 1943

Tsuji, Masanobu, *Singapore: The Japanese Version*, trans Margaret E. Lake, ed H. V. Howe, Sidney, 1960

Udall, Stewart L., *The Myths of August: A Personal Exploration of Our Tragic Cold War Affair With the Atom*, New York, Pantheon, 1994

Wallace, David, and Peter Williams, *Unit 731: The Japanese Army's Secret of Secrets*, London, Hodder & Stoughton, 1989

Warner, Denis, and Peggy Warner, *The Sacred Warriors: Japan's Suicide Legions*, Avon, 1982

Wheal, Elizabeth-Anne, and Stephen Pope, *The Macmillan Dictionary of the Second World War*, London, Macmillan, 1989

Wright, Derrick, *The Battle of Iwo Jima 1945*, Stroud, Sutton Publishing, 1999

Wygle, Peter R., *Surviving a Japanese POW Camp: Father and Son Endure Internment in Manila during World War II*, Pathfinder Publishers of California, 1991

Yank, The Army Weekly, 20 April 1945, 'Massacre at Palawan'

Yarrington, Gary A. (catalog ed), *World War II, personal accounts – Pearl Harbor to V-J Day*, A travelling exhibition by the National Archives and Records Administration, Austin, Texas, Lyndon Baines Johnson Foundation, 1992

Yew, Lee Kuan, *The Singapore Story: Memoirs of Lee Kuan Yew*, Singapore, London, Prentice Hall, 1998.

Yong, Yap Siang, Romen Bose and Angeline Pang, *Fortress Singapore: The Battlefield Guide*, Singapore, Times Books International, 1992

Young, Shi, and James Yin, *The Rape of Nanking: An Undeniable History in Photographs*, Chicago, Innovative Publishing Group, 1997

INDEX

Page numbers in *italics* refer to maps.

LIST OF MAPS

PICTURE CREDITS

First set of plates:

Page 1: Top: National Archives, Washington DC (80-G-638942); middle: Zenji Abe; bottom: National Archives, Washington DC (80-G-30551).

Page 2 – Top: National Archives, Washington DC (80-G-324199); bottom left: Chase Nielsen; bottom right: National Archives, Washington DC (80-G-41191).

Page 3 – Top: National Archives, Washington DC (127-GR-111-114541); bottom left: Australian War Memorial (negative number 0101099); bottom right: Dick Gordon.

Page 4 – Top left: Ralph Crane/TimePix/Rex Features; top right: Pat Darling; bottom: National Archives, Washington DC (111-SC-230147).

Page 5 – Top: National Archives, Washington DC (208-AA-80B-1); bottom: National Archives, Washington DC (127-GW-320-110599).

Page 6 – Top: National Archives, Washington DC (127-GW-899-50963); bottom: National Archives, Washington DC (127-GW-906-74085).

Page 7 – Australian War Memorial (negative number 014028).

Page 8 – Top: Australian War Memorial (negative number 026821); bottom: National Archives, Washington DC (127-GW-918-53444).

Second set of plates

Page 1 – Top left: *Punch*; top right: Ben Steele's personal collection; bottom left: taken from *War without Mercy: Race and Power in the Pacific War* by John W Dower (Pantheon Books, New York, 1986); bottom right: Courtesy of *Leatherneck*, magazine of the US Marines. Artist: Second World War Marine and former *Leatherneck* staff member, Fred Lasswell.

Page 2 – Top left: Australian War Memorial (negative number 044170); top right: National Archives, Washington DC (319-CE-10-SC-271823); bottom: Duncan Ferguson.

Page 3 – Top: Dick Lee; middle: Fred Seiker; bottom: Ei Yamaguchi.

Page 4 – Top left: Suzuko Numata; top right: Dionisia Carlos; bottom: Kikuko Miyagi.

Page 5 – Top left: Elizabeth Choy; top right: Hiroshi Yamagami; bottom left: Kanji Suzuki; bottom right: Bert Ward.

Page 6 – Top: Stan Dabrowski; middle: Hulton Archives (JE4581); bottom: National Archives, Washington DC (127-GW-294-110109).

Page 7 – Top: Hulton Archives (HJ3602); bottom: Hulton Archives (JE0860).

Page 8 – Top: Hulton Archives (KEY 496305); middle: Hulton Archives (KEY566286); bottom: Hulton Archives (KEY4/510415).